FOR THE LAND
AND THE LORD

FOR THE LAND AND THE LORD:
Jewish Fundamentalism in Israel

Ian S. Lustick

Council on Foreign Relations
New York

COUNCIL ON FOREIGN RELATIONS BOOKS

Library of Congress Cataloging-in-Publication Data
Lustick, Ian, 1949–
    For the land and the Lord: Jewish fundamentalism in Israel / by Ian S. Lustick.
      p.   cm.
    Includes index.
    ISBN 0-87609-037-4: $19.95. ISBN 0-87609-036-6 (pbk.): 11.95
    1. Gush emunim (Israel) 2. Israel—Politics and government.
3. Religious Zionism—Israel. 4. Jewish–Arab relations—1973–
I. Title. II. Title: Jewish fundamentalism in Israel.
JQ1825.P373G8754 1988
322.4′4′ 095694—dc19
                                  88-10838
                                      CIP

To Terri and Hilary

Contents

Preface

Following the sentencing of Jonathan Jay Pollard, an American Jew convicted of spying for Israel while employed by the United States Navy, Americans were shocked to hear that some Israelis viewed Pollard as a prisoner of war and his incarceration in an American jail as akin to the predicament of an Israeli pilot shot down behind enemy lines. How could the United States, a country whose generosity toward Israel is virtually unprecedented in international relations or American politics, possibly be seen in Israel as an enemy?

A partial answer to this question lies in the radical change that Jewish fundamentalism has effected in the climate of Israeli political life. Jewish fundamentalism is a movement that arose in Israel in the wake of the 1967 and 1973 wars, and that subsequently developed into a major political and cultural force on the Israeli scene. Despite its importance, Americans share with many Israelis a dangerous ignorance of the beliefs that animate it. The time has come to take these beliefs seriously enough to understand them. If Americans do not appreciate just how radically different is the fundamentalist worldview from their conception of what Israel and Israelis are all about, they will continue to be shocked, surprised, and sometimes exploited by Israeli actions and policies that materialize within a political context heavily influenced by it.

In the long run such ignorance could lead to the view that most or all Israelis embrace Jewish fundamentalism's radical and hostile conception of Israel's relationship to the rest of the world. It is therefore important for Jewish fundamentalist beliefs to be clearly understood and distinguished from the conventional interpretations of Jewishness and Zionism that still command the loyalty of most Israeli Jews. As a practical matter, if American policy-makers, or even Israeli politicians, do not understand fundamentalist ideology, they will miss important opportunities to divide, isolate, and defeat those seeking to implement it.

My primary purpose in this study is to add substance to the debate over Israel's future by explaining what Jewish fundamentalists want, how they believe they will get what they want, what they fear, and what they disagree about among themselves. While their aspirations suggest how much is riding on the intense political competition now under way within Israel, their fears and doubts may help provide a basis for shaping its outcome. A secondary purpose is to encourage others to ask systematic questions about the short- and long-term impact of Jewish fundamentalism on Israeli society. Necessarily, I will give some attention to this topic. But my main focus will be on the ideological and political dynamics of the fundamentalist movement itself, particularly its largest and most important component—Gush Emunim (the Bloc of the Faithful).

This book originated in a research paper written under contract for the Defense Academic Research Support Program of the United States Department of Defense. I wish to thank Robert Slater, director of the program, and his staff for their encouragement and support. It is important, however, to stress that no constraints of any kind regarding the conception, preparation, conclusions, or publication of the original manuscript, or of this book, were imposed as a result of that contract. Nor, of course, do the argument and conclusions presented here reflect the views of the Department of Defense or the United States government.

With the advice of a group assembled by the Council on Foreign Relations, the original paper, broadened in scope and deepened in analysis, developed into this book. The members of the group—Myron Aronoff, Peter Grose, Rita Hauser, Arthur Hertzberg, J.C. Hurewitz, Paul Jabber, Paul Kreisberg, David Lowenfeld, and Yoram Peri—gave generously of their time and critical attention. I also benefited greatly from comments made on earlier drafts of this book by David Biale, Jerrold Green, Don Peretz, Gershon Shafir, and Israel Yungher. I am appreciative as well of the guidance and editorial assistance provided by William Gleysteen, vice president for studies at the Council on Foreign Relations, and David Kellogg, director of the Council's publishing program. Dore Hollander's insightful copyediting made the manuscript flow much more smoothly and Jeremy Brenner, managing editor of the Council's publishing program, brought all the pieces together. At Dartmouth College, I was fortunate to have the opportunity to explore key conceptual issues in a course on comparative fundamentalism funded by the Andrew Mellon Foundation that I co-taught with Professors Gene Garthwaite, Rob Oden, and Charles Stinson. Also at Dartmouth, Lawrence Levine and Professor David G. Becker were more than generous in the assistance they gave me in the production of the manuscript.

In acknowledging the assistance I received from so many, I help explain whatever merits this book may have. No one but myself is responsible for the flaws it contains and the conclusions it reaches.

Finally, I want to thank my wife, Terri, for her love, her patience, and her steadfast support of my work on this project over several years.

I
Introduction

Amos Elon's classic portrait of Israel, *The Israelis: Founders and Sons,* begins with a description of the national mood on Independence Day, 1968:

So moving was the scene in Jerusalem on May 2, 1968, that some people in the vast crowd wept. Many more felt their blood quicken in a mood of rare exultation. Israelis were commemorating the twentieth anniversary of their independent state; they were also celebrating their year-old victory in the Six Day War of 1967. There was dancing in the streets and old-timers wandered starry-eyed through the teeming squares. According to newspaper reports the next morning, the remarks most often heard were: "It's wonderful! It's almost unbelievable!" Other people were more circumspect and said: "Let us hope it lasts."[1]

Nineteen years later, Elon's description of Israel's thirty-ninth Independence Day suggests how great a change had occurred in the interim.

Veteran observers this year could not remember a more subdued Independence Day or one highlighted by so much political divisiveness. In former years, the celebrations were marked by displays of national unity in the face of outside threats. . . . This year, there was not even a semblance of unity: doves and hawks, and secular and religious groups, were at each others throats as never before in the country's short history. The consensus on making war or making peace was broken.[2]

1

Ironically, the transformation of Israel from a country distinctive for its national pride, dedication, intimacy, and élan to a nation bitterly divided over basic assumptions about its collective life can be traced to the consequences of Israel's military triumph in 1967, especially the occupation of the West Bank and Gaza Strip. Simply put, in the Six Day War, Israel inflicted a quick but tremendous military defeat on the Arab world, and the beginning of a prolonged political and cultural crisis upon itself. Expressive of that crisis has been a polarization of sentiment and opinion on the most profound questions facing Israeli society. The religious and emotional fervor surrounding the renewal of contact between Jews and the historic heartland of ancient Judea, the appearance of real opportunities for an accommodation with the Arab world based on territorial compromise, and the sustained challenge of Palestinian nationalism have opened and reopened fundamental questions to which common answers simply do not exist. Indeed, for many Israelis it has become impossible even to find a common language in which to discuss these questions.

This is a study of one movement in Israel that possesses unequivocal answers to these questions—answers that it claims are the only authentic Jewish and Zionist response to Israel's current predicament, that are based on an unappealable authority, that promise a glorious future, but that demand total devotion to the movement. I will refer to this movement as Jewish fundamentalism, a term to be defined later in this chapter.

As explained in chapter 2, the reemergence of the fundamentalist impulse in Jewish national life occurred in the mid-1970s. After more than eighteen centuries of dormancy, the distinctive blend of messianic expectation, militant political action, intense parochialism, devotion to the Land of Israel, and self-sacrifice that characterized the Jewish Zealots of Roman times caught the imagination of tens of thousands of young religious Israeli Jews and disillusioned but idealistic secular Zionists. Through their intensive, sometimes illegal settlement of the West Bank and Gaza Strip, effective lobbying efforts, ideological and cultural influence on wide sectors of Israeli society, and readiness to challenge the very legitimacy of any Israeli government working toward withdrawal from "parts of the Land of Israel," Jewish fundamentalists have assumed an importance in Israeli politics and in the constellation of Arab–Israeli affairs that belies their relatively small numbers. Despite divisions on the Arab side, and the intransigence of many Palestinians, it is the Jewish fundamentalist movement that has emerged as the greatest obstacle to meaningful negotiations toward a comprehensive Arab–Israeli peace settlement.

Though its political fortunes shift from year to year, the movement's basic vitality is nurtured by the very conditions of occupation, distrust, and mutual hostility that its actions help to perpetuate. Its objectives are to ensure Jewish rule over the "whole Land of Israel," substitute its radical and apocalyptic vision of Jewish destiny for the pragmatic Zionism that Israel's founders had made the "common sense" of the society they created, and advance the world-historic process of redemption in which the Jewish people and the State of Israel play central roles. While the fundamentalist minority is far from realizing its ultimate aspirations, it has moved toward them by becoming a powerful force within Israeli politics and by helping to destroy the national consensus on the meaning of Jewish nationalism and the territorial shape of the State of Israel that had crystallized in the first two decades of independence.

Indeed, Jewish fundamentalism has helped plunge the Jewish state into a true Kulturkampf, in the context of which the country's social democratic tradition is facing unprecedented challenges. The ideological and philosophical chasm separating fundamentalists, and their annexationist political allies, from social democratic and liberal-dovish opponents is broad as well as deep. To date it has manifested itself most vividly in regard to policies toward Arabs. The new intensity of this intra-Jewish struggle is understandable only against a backdrop of a rapidly growing, militant, and sophisticated Palestinian Arab population living within the area ruled by Israel. Violent clashes with this large and embittered community aside, Israeli Jews are increasingly aware of, and increasingly frightened by, the prospect that within only fifteen years Arabs within Israeli jurisdiction are likely to outnumber Jews. The fear and uncertainty that this demographic shift is generating within the Jewish population as a whole make more attractive fundamentalist appeals to use Joshua's destruction and subjugation of the Canaanites as a model for solving the contemporary "Arab problem."

From an international perspective, the importance of the Jewish fundamentalist movement as an energetic and radical force in Middle Eastern affairs derives from the peculiar explosiveness of the Arab-Israeli relationship within which it is embedded. Israel and its neighbors have fought six major wars in the last forty years. Associated with these wars has been a series of direct political and military confrontations between the superpowers. Nowhere else in the world do adversaries armed with nuclear and chemical weapons, and conventional forces as well endowed and as sophisticated in many respects as the armies of NATO and the Warsaw Pact, face each other over issues involving the vital interests of each. Add to this the economic and strategic importance of the Middle East, the intimacy of Israel's relationship with the United States, the proximity of the protagonists in this conflict to the Soviet Union, and the political and social turbulence associated with resurgent Islam, and one can appreciate how delicate is the structure of international security in the eastern Mediterranean, and how attentive the rest of the world must be to developments within Israel or the Arab states that challenge what chances for a stable peace do exist.

In this context the power and purpose of Jewish fundamentalism cannot be ignored. The minimum requirements it sets for the satisfaction of Jewish ambitions are explicitly incompatible with the most generous offers credible Arab leaders could make. Within the belief system that animates the movement there exist ideological imperatives capable of justifying violent measures—against the local Arab population, the surrounding Arab states, or targets of opportunity, such as Muslim holy places in Jerusalem—as a means of advancing, or of preventing retreat, in what is seen as a cosmically ordained process of redemption.

Definitions and Terminology: Fundamentalist vs. Ultra-Orthodox

Fundamentalism is a term much more commonly used than defined. It is employed here not to refer to hyper-religiosity, nor to evoke images of fanaticism or simplistic styles of thinking, but to focus attention on a certain kind of politics. A clear and consistently applied definition of the term is necessary.

The word *fundamentalist* first appeared in early twentieth-century America as a self-description of those Protestant Christians who accepted what were known as the five fundamentals of their faith.[3] Subsequently it has often been used in strictly religious terms, referring to undeviating belief in a precisely rendered catechism or a religious tradition dedicated to the literal interpretation of scriptures. But most claims made about the impact of fundamentalism concern its implications for politics.

For purposes of political analysis, the etymologically based use of *fundamentalist* is unsatisfactory. It would apply as well to monastic sects and traditionalist religions whose rigid enforcement of elaborate rules entails complete withdrawal from society as to crusades designed to reorder the world according to the dictates of the Holy Writ. It would, on the other hand, exclude chiliastic movements that imbue their followers with a passionate commitment to sacrifice everything to achieve transcendental ends, if the ideologies governing those movements were not purely theological, or if the voice of God or his Prophet, unmediated by holy scriptures, were the direct authority defining legitimate behavior.

A more useful approach is offered by the authors of a major comparative study of ten fundamentalist movements, who understand fundamentalism as implying "a view of the universe and a discourse about the nature of truth . . . [that] encompasses and transcends the religious domain. For that reason, every movement or cause is potentially fundamentalist."[4] Thus, whether applied to Evangelical Protestants in America, Khomeinist Muslims in Iran, revolutionary Sunni Muslim groups in Egypt, redemptionist-oriented Jews in Israel, Sikhs in the Punjab, Maoists in China, or Pan-Turanists in Turkey, fundamentalism is conceived as a style of political participation characterized by unusually close and direct links between one's fundamental beliefs and political behavior designed to effect radical change.

Most active participants in politics tend toward pragmatism. That is, they usually allow a host of intermediate values to intervene between their ultimate beliefs about what is right and wrong and what they insist must be changed about the society here and now. What distinguishes fundamentalists is their relative unwillingness to compromise with reality in seeking to implement sweeping changes in society ordained by whatever transcendental source of ultimate value they acknowledge. Their commitments are political, but they are uncompromising, dogmatically based, and comprehensive. Accordingly, for the purposes of this study, a belief system is defined as fundamentalist *insofar as its adherents regard its tenets as uncompromisable and direct transcendental imperatives to political action oriented toward the rapid and comprehensive reconstruction of society.*

This concept encourages thinking about fundamentalism not in either/or terms, but as a phenomenon with several dimensions. Individuals, organizations, or movements may be regarded as fundamentalist to the extent that they (1) base their activities on uncompromisable injunctions; (2) consider their behavior to be guided by direct contact with the source of transcendental authority; and (3) are actively engaged in political attempts to bring about rapid and comprehensive change. Inclusion of political commitments to achieve direct and radical change in the shape of society within the definition excludes pietistic or monastic movements. But by leaving open the question of the substantive character of the source of ultimate value and the medium through which it is transmitted, hypotheses about different kinds of fundamentalist movements (purely religious, partly religious, nonreligious, scripture-based, charismatically based, and so on) can be framed and tested.

In the Jewish context, this notion of fundamentalism helps avoid including 2,000 years of rigorously observant, but politically cautious, rabbinic Judaism within its compass. In contemporary Israel it is helpful in distinguishing between the energetically political, redemptionist nationalism of Gush Emunim (the Bloc of the Faithful)—the most important organized expression of Jewish fundamentalism—and pietistic ultra-Orthodox groups, whose extreme traditionalism reflects their orientation toward prayer and personal observance, and whose communal requirements lead to their isolation from the social and political mainstream. Although sometimes considered fundamentalist, ultra-Orthodox Jews, referred to in Hebrew as the Haredim (literally, the fearful or God-fearing ones), do not engage actively in politics in order to achieve rapid and comprehensive change in Israeli society. Their lives revolve around the careful fulfillment of thousands of rules contained within the *halacha* (code of Jewish law), as interpreted by their rabbis. Their distinctive seventeenth-century garb, their self-segregated neighborhoods, obsessive ritualism, and indifference or opposition to Zionism reflect commitments to isolate their way of life from the State of Israel, not to impose, through politics, their way of life upon it. The behavior of ultra-Orthodox Jews, bizarre to the eyes of Western journalists, often attracts a good deal of sensationalist press attention. Indeed, outbursts among the Haredim, often violent, have increased in recent years. Their growing numbers, their desire to establish homogeneity in the new neighborhoods into which they have expanded, and their competitive desire to display militancy to financial supporters of their institutions in the United States have led to dramatic protests against the operating hours of theaters, the location of public swimming pools, and the sexual content of advertisements. But although Haredi representatives may wield substantial bargaining power on issues of direct religious concern, they tend not to regard macropolitical issues, including territorial questions, as matters of great consequence. Because they are non-Zionist, or even anti-Zionist, the Haredim have, effectively, opted out of key political struggles over the course that Israeli society will take. Accordingly, despite Haredi beliefs that they, or their rabbis, are in relatively direct contact with the sources of transcendental authority, and despite their refusal to compromise on questions of ritual and religious law, they cannot be considered fundamentalist according to the definition employed here.

In Israel, fundamentalism finds its most powerful and oft-commented upon expression in the politicized messianism of Jews who grew up within the neo-Orthodox, "national religious" wing of the Zionist movement.[5] In contrast to the Haredim, the national religious, or Mizrahi, movement has sought to integrate relatively strict observance of the halacha with full participation in a modern, Zionist society. Its state-supported school system educates 25–30 percent of Israeli Jewish children. As a result of its traditional control of the Ministries of Interior and Religious Affairs, the Mizrahi movement's political arm, the National Religious Party, has exerted predominant influence over the enforcement of the religious status quo. For reasons discussed in chapter 3, the Six Day War gave impetus to radical changes within this movement. Incubated within its schools, youth movement, and seminaries, and within the National Religious Party, was the Young Guard, which expressed disgust with the machine-style, status quo politics of the older generation. Instead, the *tzeirim* (youth) advanced a political program focusing on establishment of Jewish sovereignty over the whole Land of Israel as a decisive step toward hastening a divinely ordained process of redemption, which they believed had already begun. This leadership cadre, and the national religious subcultural cohort it represented, formed the basis of Israel's Jewish fundamentalist movement—dedicated to the uncompromising implementation of transcendental imperatives through political action.

As explained in more detail below, this movement welcomed the participation of nonreligious Jews in moving Israeli society along the road to redemption. Indeed, the beliefs and political behavior of secular ultra-nationalist Jews, drawn from activist elements of the Labor Zionist and Revisionist (right-wing Zionist), movements, require that they also be included within contemporary Jewish fundamentalism. As we shall see, their absolute commitment to the fulfillment of biblical promises to the Jewish people, and to the achievement of maximalist Zionist ambitions, reflects their sense of political action as directly determined by uncompromisable, transcendentally valid imperatives.[6]

Gush Emunim: The Organized Focus of Jewish Fundamentalism

Although within Israel a wide variety of organizations, political parties, prominent individuals, vigilante groups, institutes, and personal networks make up what is referred to here as Jewish fundamentalism, the clearest and strongest expression of fundamentalist tendencies in Israeli society has been concentrated in Gush Emunim—an umbrella organization of 10,000–20,000 activists. Its slogan is "The Land of Israel, for the People of Israel, According to the Torah [Bible] of Israel." By any measure, it has been the most successful extraparliamentary movement to arise in Israel since the state's establishment in 1948.

A large measure of its success has been due to the symbiotic relationship it forged with the Likud, Israel's major right-wing political party. Apart from populist slogans, vigorous assertions of Jewish national rights, and associated irredentist claims, Likud politicians and activists lacked a systematic ideological doctrine capable of justifying sacrifices or coordinating sustained implementation of their annexationist objectives. Insofar as this ideological vacuum was filled, it was filled by the ultranationalism and active messianism of Gush Emunim. Fundamentalist thinking also provided a systematic and evocative symbol system for rising Likud politicians, such as Ariel Sharon, to endow their ambitions with an aura of Jewish authenticity and Zionist idealism. Finally, neither Herut [Freedom] nor the Liberal party, the Likud's two major components, had a strong settlement movement of its own. Thus, the practical expertise and pioneering zeal of thousands of enthusiastic fundamentalist settlers provided the Likud governments of 1977 and 1981 with an indispensable resource.[7]

However, as I shall illustrate in chapters 2 and 3, if the Likud used the fundamentalist movement, particularly Gush Emunim, so have the fundamentalists exploited their relationship with the Likud. The friendly ties that fundamentalist leaders enjoyed with the highest echelons of government, and the public sympathy and even admiration that Likud ministers and other officials displayed toward Gush Emunim settlers, greatly helped to legitimize fundamentalist ideas in the national debate over the future of the territories and their Arab inhabitants. Moreover, the enormous financial resources that both Likud governments put at the disposal of Gush Emunim and Gush supported settlement projects in the West Bank and Gaza Strip were of crucial importance in sustaining the movement's activism and enhancing its credibility.[8]

Nor should the importance of the devotion displayed by members of the fundamentalist movement be underestimated as a factor accounting for its success. The men and women of Gush Emunim have made it their life's work to ensure that the occupied West Bank and Gaza Strip are permanently incorporated into the State of Israel. The level and intensity of their commitment, flowing from the fundamental, even cosmic, issues they perceive to be directly at stake, had largely disappeared from Israeli politics. Their operational objective is to accelerate the pace at which the Jewish people fulfills its destiny. This includes, for most of these activists, establishment of Jewish sovereignty over the entire, biblically described, Land of Israel, substitution of "authentically Jewish" forms of governance for Western-style liberal democracy, and rebuilding the Temple in Jerusalem, thereby implementing the divinely ordained, albeit long-delayed, messianic redemption. They insist that direct political action is the means to accomplish the rapid transformation of Israeli society according to uncompromisable, authentically Jewish, cosmically ordained imperatives.

The core of Gush Emunim is in the more than 130 settlements established in the West Bank, the Gaza Strip, and the Golan Heights since 1967. But, as is discussed in chapter 3, the recruitment pools for the movement within Israeli society are much wider. These include the religious youth movement Bnei Akiva (Sons of Akiva), a network of paramilitary field seminaries (Yeshivot Hesder), the religious educational system, and many middle-class Israelis with strong political commitments to expansive versions of Labor Zionism or to Revisionist Zionism. Though officially nonpartisan, Gush Emunim is actively supported in the national political arena by several leading cabinet ministers. A half-dozen members of Knesset are known personally as Gush Emunim leaders. A parliamentary coalition known as the Lobby, formed in the spring of 1985 to exert pressure on behalf of Gush Emunim settlement objectives, was made up of members from five different political parties. Initially it included 23 members of Knesset, but within four months that number had grown to 38, or 32 percent of the entire parliament.[9] The Lobby reportedly operates with dependable support from a total of fifty ministers and members of Knesset.[10]

Gush Emunim itself has never had a formal membership list or an elected leadership. Nevertheless, it maintains an organizational network that spans the "green line," the 1949 armistice line dividing Israel from the territories occupied in 1967. It also has its own settlement building and sustaining organization—Amana (Covenant). Its settlements are organized within Yesha (Salvation), the Association of Local Councils in Judea, Samaria, and the Gaza District. Moetzet Yesha (the Yesha Council) gives Gush Emunim a semiofficial governing body, substantial administrative and economic resources, and direct involvement in the implementation of government policies in the occupied territories. The movement has also spawned overlapping groups and corporations dedicated to specific objectives, including propaganda, land acquisition, economic investment, construction, immigration, political outreach, security, research, publishing, and artistic development.

Made up primarily of well-educated, Ashkenazic (Jews of European or American extraction), middle-class Israelis, Gush activists have close and often personal ties with Israel's traditional ruling groups. Major Gush marches and demonstrations have drawn from 10,000 to 150,000 participants. In 1984, parties running on explicitly fundamentalist platforms (Tehiya, the National Circle, Kach, and Morasha) received 150,000 votes, electing eight (of 120) members of parliament. But strong and crucial support for the movement also comes from the Likud and the National Religious Party, which together received 37 percent of the vote in 1984 (45 seats in the parliament). Although Israel's Oriental Jews, (those who immigrated from, or whose parents immigrated from, Asian and African countries, and who are a large majority of the Jewish working class) are not prominent in the fundamentalist movement itself, the bulk of their votes go to the political parties that support its territorial demands.

The continuing strength of the movement is readily apparent. Four polls taken from July 1986 to June 1987 showed, on average, that Tehiya itself had enough support to gain between seven and eight seats in new Knesset elections.[11] In the fall of 1986, the fundamentalist movement launched a national campaign on behalf of amnesty for Jewish terrorists, affiliated with Gush Emunim, who were convicted and imprisoned in 1984. By the spring of 1987 approximately 300,000 signatures had been gathered. The petition appears to have had a substantial effect. Forty members of the Knesset, including Prime Minister Yitzhak Shamir, Industry and Trade Minister Ariel Sharon, and Minister of Transportation Haim Corfu, voted for a bill, formally opposed by the cabinet, to grant a blanket amnesty to the *machteret* (underground) prisoners. Likud ministers Moshe Arens, David Levy, Yitzhak Modai, Moshe Nisim, and Moshe Katzav showed their sympathy for the measure by pointedly absenting themselves from the vote.[12] President Chaim Herzog himself seems to have reversed his earlier opposition to clemency. Of the twenty-seven men convicted in 1984, twenty were free by September 1986, eight as a result of presidential pardons. In April 1987, President Herzog permitted most of the remaining prisoners to enjoy a holiday leave from jail and reduced the sentences of the three who had been given life terms to a maximum of 24 years, thereby making them eligible for parole.[13]

On the other hand, Gush Emunim is not now riding a crest of popularity and prestige. Nor will the broader movement that it represents make Israel a Jewish fundamentalist state in the near future. As we shall see, Gush Emunim is currently coming to terms with its own institutionalization and with the need to introduce regular procedures for choosing, criticizing, and replacing its own leaders. In the summer and fall of 1987 it was still adjusting to a leadership shake-up designed to resolve a prolonged and intense, though not altogether unprecedented, internal crisis.

Assessing the Influence of Jewish Fundamentalism

It is difficult to determine how deep and wide fundamentalism's influence on Israel's Jewish population as a whole has been or might be. Spokesmen for Gush Emunim are, of course, expansive in their assessments. Gush Emunim, they say, represents the minority presently "making Jewish history." In this respect, they see Gush's contemporary role as identical to that of the Zionist movement in the late nineteenth and early twentieth centuries, which attracted only a tiny proportion of world Jewry to Palestine.

> After the pogroms in Russia *two million* Jews emigrated to the United States. Only *one percent* of this number: twenty thousand, came to the Land of Israel. But we are speaking here of quality Judaism: Jewish, nationalist, and Zionist. To be sure, these are shameful and dreadful facts. But in the final analysis, who determined the course of Jewish history in our age, the two million that created a new Exile or the twenty thousand that built the foundation of Israel's independence?[14]

Consistent with this view, fundamentalist ideologues are also fond of comparing Gush Emunim, as an influential, highly energized minority emphasizing pioneering values and a grand vision of the meaning of Zionism, to the kibbutz movement of the prestate era. The comparison is not without merit. At its height, in 1947, the kibbutz movement included no more than 7 percent of Israel's population. Nonetheless, the kibbutz movement, kibbutz members, and the socialist Zionist leadership associated with the kibbutzim provided the Yishuv (the Jewish population living in Palestine/the Land of Israel) with its most salient models for Jewish patriotism, Zionist commitment, civic duty, and spiritual guidance. In the 1950s and 1960s the kibbutz movement lost much of its élan.[15] Since 1967 Gush Emunim, its "pioneering settlers" in the West Bank and Gaza, and the charismatic and rabbinic leaders it has raised to prominence have been the most salient such models available to the present generation of Israelis. As did the kibbutzim of an earlier period, say fundamentalist theoreticians, Gush Emunim has helped shape the political and ideological ethos of a generation.[16]

The results of a survey conducted in the spring of 1987 support this view. The Hebrew weekly *Hadashot* asked a panel of twenty-two leading Israelis, from all parts of the political spectrum, to name the "person of the generation, the man or woman who has had the greatest effect on Israeli society in the last twenty years." First place in this poll was shared by Menachem Begin and Rabbi Moshe Levinger. Levinger, who established the first Jewish settlement in Hebron, in 1968, has been closely associated with the rise of Jewish fundamentalism and was identified by Gush Emunim in May 1987 as its overall ideological guide. Boaz Epplebaum, an adviser to Shimon Peres, explained why he cited Levinger as the person of the generation. "Prime Ministers have come and gone," he said, "but Levinger is still riding high. All of us have adapted ourselves to his dimensions and his scale."[17]

Associated with the growth of Jewish fundamentalism has been an impressive body of scholarly research, focusing mainly on the origins, composition, and political influence of Gush Emunim. The conclusions drawn by these researchers support the choice of Levinger as symbolic of the transformation Israel has undergone since 1967. Ehud Sprinzak has portrayed what he calls Zionist fundamentalism as "the most dynamic social and cultural force in Israel today."[18] Still other students of the fundamentalist movement have emphasized the need to look beyond its relationship to right-wing political parties and its political clout with respect to settlement of the occupied territories and related issues. Gideon Aran, Myron Aronoff, Leon Wieseltier, David Schnall, and Ofira Seliktar have drawn attention to the broad cultural, psychological, and religious impact of Gush Emunim. Schnall has commented as follows:

> There can be no doubt that Gush Emunim has had a profound influence upon the Israeli political system, to limit the analysis purely to the specifics of government policy would be to miss a significant part of its impact. The group has fundamentally influenced the fabric of Israeli society in ways that transcend the political market place and relate to the heart of Israeli society.[19]

Even those who have argued that Gush's influence may have passed its peak, such as Eliezer Don-Yehiya, acknowledge the great impact the movement it represents has had, as well as its potential for further growth.[20]

The most important and widely cited consequence of Gush Emunim's influence is the establishment of Jewish settlements in sensitive, heavily populated areas of the West Bank—settlements that discredit, if they do not negate, traditional Israeli willingness to trade territory for peace. Indeed, writers assessing Jewish fundamentalism's overall importance are virtually unanimous in their anticipation that efforts to negotiate and implement a territorial compromise with Jordan, if ever attempted, would precipitate serious political violence and unprecedented threats to the integrity of parliamentary rule. The interruption of normal legal and political processes, which most of these authors expect would occur in such circumstances, will result from Gush Emunim's categorical opposition to peace agreements based on territorial compromise and the presence of the nearly 70,000 Jews its indefatigable efforts have helped bring to the West Bank.[21]

It seems clear that Gush Emunim's central role in the implementation of the Likud's annexationist policies—and its pioneering image, vivid ideas, and inspiring self-confidence—resulted in the transmission of fundamentalist perspectives to wide strata of Israeli society, both religious and nonreligious. Public opinion polls, which have been a growth industry in Israel over the last two decades, are notorious for their variability, but they do show two points of interest. First, they support the thrust of what the literature on Gush Emunim's impact has concluded—namely, that the movement it represents can no longer be considered an extremist fringe group in Israeli society or politics. Despite the compre-

hensiveness of Gush Emunim's challenge to the ideas that have
governed Israeli and Zionist political thinking for decades, one
1983 poll showed, for example, that more Israeli Jews were ready
to outlaw the moderate, liberal, conventionally Labor Zionist
Peace Now movement than favored declaring Gush Emunim illegal (22 vs. 27 percent).[22] Second, analysis of large numbers of
polls shows a fairly stable pattern in responses to certain categories
of questions. The clustering of these responses can be seen as
convincing evidence of significant support for Gush Emunim
thinking among Israeli Jews, an even wider readiness to grant
approval to the implementation of key elements in the fundamentalist program, and the presence of sentiments and concepts that
could, under the proper circumstances, greatly facilitate Gush
efforts to convert wider segments of the population to its ideology.

More specifically, fairly radical fundamentalist beliefs, attitudes,
and political programs that were regarded as crackpot extremism
by the vast majority of Israelis in the late 1960s (for example,
destroying Muslim shrines in Jerusalem, rebuilding the Temple
before the Messiah comes, or forming Jewish terrorist groups to
strike at local Arabs) appear to be embraced by approximately 20
percent of the Israeli Jewish population.[23] About 30–35 percent
of Israeli Jews are now willing to associate themselves with closely
related policies and beliefs (such as agreement with policies of
subjugation and expulsion for Arabs, support of the 1980 attacks
on the Arab mayors, opposition to any freeze on the establishment
of new settlements, and willingness to sharply reduce standards of
living to lessen Israeli dependence on America).[24] In a poll taken in
April 1987, some 62 percent of Israeli Jews interviewed indicated
they were "against the evacuation of settlements in Judea and
Samaria, even in exchange for a peace agreement." Most significantly, however, 45–50 percent expressed support for the key
Gush Emunim demand that the West Bank and Gaza Strip be
permanently and unconditionally ruled by Israel. This level of
support for territorial maximalism appears to be very solid and has
been confirmed by scores of polls during the last several years. It
represents an increase of 30–50 percent over levels of support for
permanent incorporation of the territories that prevailed in the
mid-1970s.[25]

In the picture that emerges from the polling data and the
research available on the influence of the fundamentalist move-

ment, Gush Emunim and related groups neither command nor are likely soon to command the loyalty of a majority of Israeli Jews. Nonetheless, the fundamentalist movement has become, and will unquestionably remain, a major player in the elemental struggle now under way to determine the shape and purpose of Israeli society—a struggle necessitated and largely defined by the fundamentalists' own settlement activities in the West Bank and Gaza Strip. Despite the intense opposition to de facto annexation that exists in Israel, the Jewish state has moved very far toward permanent incorporation of the territories. This is itself a boon to the Jewish fundamentalist movement, since associated with it, and the international isolation it has caused, have been significant shifts in the minds of many Israelis toward self-images and images of the outside world that are conducive to the fundamentalists' long-term objective—to make their vision of the Jews' "lonely destiny" the only one available to Israelis.

The next chapter places Jewish fundamentalism's contemporary emergence in Jewish historical perspective and locates the key factors responsible for the timing and coloration of the movement. In chapter 3 I provide a brief analysis of the the social basis of the movement and describe the specific political and organizational evolution of Gush Emunim and associated groups. In chapter 4 I present the worldview of fundamentalist activists, including their basic beliefs and the assumptions about national and international politics that flow from those beliefs. The character of shared perceptions, commitments, and beliefs within the movement having been established, I analyze in chapter 5 the substantial range of disagreement among fundamentalists on six basic issues. In chapter 6 I discuss prospects for the continued growth and influence of the fundamentalist movement in light of the leadership crisis within Gush Emunim, the changing composition of the Israeli population in the occupied territories, the campaign to change the status quo on the Temple Mount (Hur Ha Bayit—known by Muslims as Haram el-Sharif (the Noble Sanctuary), and the rivalry and potential for cooperation that exist between Gush Emunim and the Haredim. In the concluding chapter, I consider some broader theoretical and policy-relevant implications of my analysis.

II

The Emergence of Jewish Fundamentalism in Historical Perspective

---

The most important political resource for any state or regime is a pervasive and deeply felt belief among the people it governs that its authority over their lives is legitimate. Lacking this, governments must either purchase or coerce compliance with their decisions, though neither approach can be sustained on a long-term basis. Fundamentalist movements seek radical transformation based on beliefs that substantially contradict the myths under which prevailing political institutions legitimize their power. Such movements are likely to enjoy success to the extent that their own comparative advantage over political competitors becomes important—that is, to the extent that they are able to present a dramatic, inspiring, authenticated alternative to the legitimizing ethos of their society.

To explain the rise of Jewish fundamentalism in contemporary Israel, we must identify the general conditions likely to be propitious for any fundamentalist movement and then show that they were present in Israel. First, behavior of a regime or of dominant elites or groups must be able to be convincingly portrayed as contradicting *their own* legitimizing myths. Second, discrepancies between the distinctive myths preserved by the fundamentalist elite and those associated with the prevailing political and social order must be dramatized. Third, mobilizable sectors of the population must be available and be led to interpret events as existential threats to their perceptions of the worthiness of their society, their own self-worth, and the capacity of the society to provide for their basic human needs. Under such conditions the particular comparative advantage that religious elites enjoy *vis-à-vis* others becomes politically important. That advantage is their authoritative access to symbols bearing on transcendental or cosmic concerns—reassuring symbols of ultimate purpose and meaning that resonate with an undeniable authenticity for the community, symbols that must ultimately be used to justify the exercise of state power.

To take advantage of available opportunities, a politically astute fundamentalist elite must exist. This elite must be capable of presenting itself not only as the legitimate expression of authentic and overarching symbols and values, but also as untainted by, and a credible substitute for, the old, dominant elite. One should not underestimate the difficulty faced by a fundamentalist elite in translating its particular kind of abstract and invisible resource into real political power. Only by exploiting carefully cultivated, well understood, and powerful beliefs that large numbers of people share—beliefs capable of justifying heavy sacrifices for virtually unrealizable ends—can this elite overcome the obstacles that usually confront political movements not capable of furnishing direct material incentives to their followers. The skill of the movement's leaders as political entrepreneurs seeking to capitalize on their particular comparative advantage will be crucial in determining its degree of success. They will have to identify those dimensions of their society's mythic repertoire to which they have special access and that cannot be explicitly rejected by the regime or dominant elites. They can then emphasize these dimensions and use them to design and protect militant actions—actions that implicitly or explicitly contradict prevailing doctrines or policies. These actions must have a dramatic aspect that cannot be ignored by the regime and that can be effectively cast as expressive of consensually accepted sacred, or "authentic," values.

In this chapter and the next, I will attempt to explain how previously obscure elites successfully used the historic success of Zionism and the consequences of both the Six Day War and the Yom Kippur War to revitalize ancient Jewish myths, thereby advancing their own political fortunes and shifting the agenda of Israeli politics from pragmatism toward redemption.[1]

Jewish Fundamentalism and Zionism: A Historical Perspective

The reestablishment of Jewish sovereignty in the Land of Israel is a true revolution in the structure of Jewish life. As with any revolu-

tion, Zionism has had consequences that its architects never anticipated—indeed, that they would have shuddered to contemplate.
The crystallization of a deeply rooted and effective Jewish fundamentalist movement is one such consequence. The immediate
catalyst for the contemporary emergence of Jewish fundamentalism was the Six Day War in 1967. The initial stage of the movement's development ended seven years later, in the wake of the
Yom Kippur War, with the establishment of Gush Emunim. Before considering the relationship of the wars to the specific ideas
and political processes that produced Gush Emunim, it is necessary to understand the historical implications of Zionism for creating conditions under which activist messianism, long suppressed
by rabbinic Judaism, could reemerge as a powerful expression of
Jewish peoplehood.

Long before the Romans brought an end to Jewish independence in Palestine and banished or killed most of the Palestinian
Jewish population, a majority of Jews lived outside the Land of
Israel. Ancient Jewish communities, located in Persia, Egypt, and
Turkey, could usually find some way to accommodate themselves
to prevailing cultures and political systems. Generally, these communities were able to do so without giving up their faith or their
cultural, religious, and economic ties to the Land of Israel, the
Yishuv itself, the Temple in Jerusalem, and the priests who maintained the Temple cult. But inside the Land of Israel, Jews apparently found it much more difficult to reconcile their beliefs with
the absence of what we would now call national sovereignty.

In the framework of the power and myth upon which political
authority in ancient Israel was based, certain biblical motifs were
central. These specified the Jews as God's chosen and holy people,
charged with and ultimately destined to play the central role in a
divinely orchestrated redemptive drama. The organization of the
community and its performance of rituals according to God's law,
including regular pilgrimages to Jerusalem and elaborate sacrifices
at the Temple, were necessary if the people of Israel were to inherit
all the land they had been promised and to draw sustenance from
it. Rule over the land was, in turn, important evidence that the
authority wielded over the Jewish people, in their land, was legitimate.

Had the God of the Jews been as tolerant of other gods as were those worshiped by other ancient peoples, it might have been possible for Jews to accept the severe limitations powerful empires imposed on the structure of their life in the Land of Israel. But the Jewish God was extremely jealous. The God of Israel was not only also the Lord of the Universe, he was the only god. God's injunction to his chosen people was to enforce his Law as interpreted by the anointed King and the priestly caste, and thereby to maintain their special holy status, preserve their rights to the land, and contribute to their redemption and that of mankind.

From the time of the early prophets, in the eighth century B.C.E., to the destruction of the last vestiges of Jewish political autonomy in Persia and Palestine, in the fifth century C.E., beliefs in and struggles to achieve God's redemption of his people formed the mythic core of Jewish political life.[2] The redemption itself, whether brought about solely by spiritual repentance and ritual observance or in combination with political and military activity, would be signaled by the return of Jews from Exile to the Land of Israel, the establishment of Jewish sovereignty over it, territorial expansion, reconstruction of the Temple, and economic prosperity. Particularly in times of crisis or oppression, factions or classes eager to wield political power were required to characterize their values and preferences as appropriate, if not imperative, for the advancement of the redemptive process. In other words, especially for Jews living in the Land of Israel, the content of Jewish political mythology systematically advantaged those aspirants to power who could evoke images of an imminent redemption and credibly exploit divine imperatives to enforce exclusive Jewish rule according to Jewish law over the whole land. It was thus very difficult for Jewish politicians to adopt elements of the conqueror's "civilized" culture or to accept the occasional introduction of idolatrous practices, and still be counted as legitimate candidates for political leadership within the Yishuv.

An excellent example of the dynamic that grew out of this kind of political environment is the Maccabee (Hasmonean) defeat of the hellenized Jewish aristocracy in 165 B.C.E. Declaring themselves motivated by a pure and authentic faith in the God of Israel and his commandments, rough-hewn Jews from the hill country, in league with lower class urban dwellers, took up arms in 166

B.C.E. against rule of the country by the Syrian–Greek (Seleucid) Empire. Despite the apparently overwhelming superior strength of the Syrian–Greeks and their hellenized Jewish allies, the Maccabees were victorious. The war culminated in the formal rededication of the Temple, the inauguration of 200 years of Jewish sovereignty, and unprecedented territorial expansion. The Hasmoneans were not descendants of the house of David and therefore restrained themselves from declaring their own kingdom as messianic. Nonetheless, they were, they said, preparing the way for the Messiah and would deliver the kingdom to him when he appeared.[3]

In Roman-ruled Judea during the first century C.E., the Zealots advocated immediate rebellion against Rome on behalf of a reconstituted Davidic kingdom that would herald the advent of the redemption. For contemporary Jews, exposed to both the cosmopolitan influences of a world empire and the sudden, but repeated, imposition of religious restrictions and various repellent forms of emperor worship, it was difficult to resist their appeals. In hindsight, the arguments of those who warned against challenging the Roman Empire, which was at the height of its power, may seem utterly persuasive.[4] But this perception ignores the implications of the heavily apocalyptic Jewish political culture and the evocative memories of the stunning success of the last such fundamentalist upsurge, two and a half centuries earlier.

Within the space of seventy-five years, two major revolts against Rome erupted in Judea, the Great Revolt (66–73 C.E.) and the Bar Kochba Rebellion (132–135 C.E.).[5] Each was based on fundamentalist appeals that God's direct commandments to his people regarding Jewish independence in the Land of Israel and the integrity of the Temple cult made compromise impossible. The first revolt, which resulted in the destruction of Jerusalem and of the Temple, is estimated to have reduced the Jewish population of Judea by 25 percent. The second was led by Simon Bar Kochba and endorsed by the leading rabbi of the period, Akiva, who is reputed to have declared Bar Kochba the Messiah, announcing that the redemption had begun. The Bar Kochba Rebellion ended in the death of more than a half-million Jews, the mass enslavement of survivors, and the elimination of a Jewish majority in the Land of Israel.[6]

According to most students of Judaism and Jewish history, the rabbinic reaction to these events was decisive in the subsequent survival of Jews as a people, a faith, and a political community. After the destruction of the Temple in 70 C.E., Rabbi Yohanan Ben-Zakkai, who had opposed the Great Revolt, received Roman permission to found an academy in Yavneh, a small city on the coastal plain. He taught his disciples that in the Diaspora and in the absence of the Temple, Judaism could survive only if prayer and righteous behavior were substituted for Temple sacrifice; if study of the Law were emphasized instead of its observance in spheres where events had made such observance impossible; and if active messianic redemptionism were replaced by a doctrine requiring Jews effectively to withdraw from history, to wait passively for God to bring redemption, and meanwhile to accept the sufferings of his people. Not only redemptively oriented actions ("pushing the end"), but even attempts to "calculate the end," were eventually proscribed. To protect Jews from the terrible consequences of fundamentalist politics, messianic/redemptive ideas had to be removed from the center of Jewish consciousness. "If you have a sapling in your hand," taught Rabbi Yohanan, "and it is said to you, 'Behold, there is the Messiah'—go on with your planting, and afterward go out and receive him."[7]

But despite Rabbi Yohanan's Ben-Zakkai's enormous prestige and the influence of his teachings, his most revered student, Akiva, found it impossible to resist the fundamentalist impulse. As noted, sixty-five years after the Jews' defeat in the Great Revolt, he declared Simon Bar Kochba the Messiah and led the Jewish people to a second catastrophe.

However, in the aftermath of this defeat, with the destruction of organized Jewish life in most of the Land of Israel and the gradual shift of Judaism's center of gravity to the Diaspora, the rabbinic rejection of Jewish political messianism took root. The Jewish people, taught the rabbis, had been administered formal oaths not to calculate the end of days, seek to advance its arrival, or organize a mass and forcible return to the Land of Israel. Apocalyptic elements in holy writings and in the oral tradition were systematically deemphasized or censored. Bar Kochba himself was rarely mentioned, and when discussed was characterized as a sinful, if heroic, false Messiah.[8] He typically was referred to not as Bar

Kochba (Son of a Star) but as Bar Koziba (Son of a Lie).[9] The sages even used legends ascribing extraordinary powers to Bar Kochba to prove the utter futility of military and political action to hasten the redemption.[10] The early rabbis thus used all the exegetical skills at their disposal to accomplish what Nahum Glatzer has characterized as a transformation in Jewish messianism "from activist and militant into passivist and peaceful; from an urgent expectation of change into a distant, quiet hope; from a history-centered doctrine into a meta-historical one."[11]

But despite sustained rabbinic opposition to apocalyptic, messianic, and redemptionist themes, exilic Judaism was never purged of operational expectations of the "dawn of Redemption."[12] Jewish mysticism dealt heavily in eschatological speculation and honored virtuoso attempts to hasten the redemption through direct communion with God. The Jewish calendar contained fast days and other ritualized remembrances of the Temple and Jewish life in the Land of Israel. The structure of daily liturgy was based on the Temple service and contained detailed accounts of sacrificial worship. Inextricably linked to all Jewish contemplation of the redemption was belief in the eventual end of the Exile and the rebuilding of the Temple. The return to Zion was, in fact, "the cornerstone of the Jewish Messianic ideal."[13]

For the rabbis, the most worrisome aspect of Jewish redemptionism was the tendency during times of severe persecution for false Messiahs to arise. Deeply troubled times might always signify "the birthpangs of the Messianic age." Jewish communities down through the centuries, in Yemen, Persia, Poland, and elsewhere, produced in such times charismatic figures whose followers were willing to forsake their homes, their livelihood, and even the halacha itself to join in the long-awaited return to the Land of Israel. Such episodes usually involved challenges to rabbinic authority and ended in despair, economic dislocation, or antinomian excesses. "The Rabbis," Gershom Scholem wrote, "were well aware of the "anarchic element in the very nature of Messianic utopianism; the dissolution of old ties which lose their meaning in the new context of Messianic freedom."[14]

No rabbinic authority was more aware of the seductiveness of apocalyptic redemptionism or its dangers than Moses Maimonides (1135–1204), the dominant figure in medieval Judaism.

But Maimonides also knew that some form of messianism, some hope and expectation of a redemptive end to the Exile and of the fulfillment of God's promises to his people in the Land of Israel, was a vital part of Jewish life. His solution was bold. To discourage false Messiahs, eschatological obsessions, and apocalyptic thinking, he taught that only God could bring about the advent of the messianic age, at a time that only God could know. No human being could calculate or advance the time of the redemption through mystical manipulations of the ineffable Name of God, *gematria* (numerology), prayer, or miracles. The true Messiah would, eventually, demonstrate his identity by following all the commandments, leading the Jewish people as a whole to perfect observance of Jewish law, and accomplishing the political and military tasks involved in reconstituting Jewish authority in the Land of Israel—regathering the Jews into their land and rebuilding the Temple on its ancient site. Maimonides intended such mundane but readily testable criteria, by their apparent impossibility, to prevent false Messiahs from attracting large followings among Diasporan Jews and to reinforce his fundamental message:

> No one is in a position to know the details of this and similar things until they have come to pass. . . . Therefore no one should ever occupy himself with the legendary themes or spend much time on Midrashic statements bearing on this and like subjects. He should not deem them of prime importance, since they lead neither to the fear of God nor to the love of Him. Nor should one calculate the end. Said the rabbis: "Blasted be those who reckon the end". One should wait [for his coming] and accept in principle this article of faith. [15]

Nonetheless, Maimonides' worst fears were realized in the late seventeenth century. After the massacre of 300,000 Jews in Eastern Europe by Cossack marauders, the most important of all postexpulsion false Messiahs emerged—Shabbatai Zevi. From 1665 to 1667 a wave of messianic enthusiasm swept over world Jewry. Responding to reports of the Messiah's appearance in Palestine in the person of Shabbatai Zevi, accompanied by "his prophet," Nathan of Gaza, majorities of Jews in virtually all major centers of the Jewish world—from Poland to Amsterdam, Italy, Turkey,

Yemen, and Persia—publicly repented of their sins and took other extraordinary steps to welcome the imminent redemption and honor the Messiah. While certain traditional fast days were abolished and new festivals proclaimed, extended personal fasts, flagellation, and other types of mortification were embraced as outward signs of repentance. Economic activity was suspended, and preparations to leave for Palestine undertaken. In feverish communication with one another, Jewish communities all over the world rejoiced in the excitement of the hour. Calendars were changed to mark the onset of the messianic age, gentiles were warned not to dishonor the name or person of the Messiah, and liturgies were rewritten. Rabbis and scholars who questioned the authenticity of Shabbatai Zevi as the Messiah, and the truth of the mystical framework within which his appearance and his words were being interpreted, were vilified.[16]

Concerned by unrest within his empire, the Sultan imprisoned Shabbatai. When presented with a choice of conversion to Islam or death, Shabbatai chose apostasy. While this resulted in bitter disillusionment on the part of most Jews, the Sabbatian movement continued, basing itself on mystical doctrines of the "repair of the world," which entailed processes of "Redemption through sin." A new Torah, the "Torah of Redemption," Sabbatians argued, would replace the old. Even the laws against incest would no longer apply. The Frankists, named after Jacob Frank, a late eighteenth-century Jew who proclaimed himself the reincarnation of Shabbatai Zevi, put elements of this antinomian system into effect in the orgiastic practices for which they became notorious.[17]

In the early nineteenth century Jewry still felt the effects of the spiritual earthquake of Sabbatianism. The rabbis had let their guard down. Most had allowed themselves to be caught up in the messianic enthusiasm surrounding Shabbatai Zevi and his apocalyptic message of imminent and miraculous salvation. The result had been deep schisms within the community, despair, mockery and persecution by the gentiles, challenges to the permanence and authority of the Torah, and bizarre mutations of Jewish belief and religiosity.

It is against the background of long-standing rabbinic opposition to active redemptionism and the rabbis' particular revulsion toward the Sabbatian movement and its consequences that Orthodox Judaism's negative reaction to political Zionism can be understood. David Vital, in his detailed study of the origins of Zionism, describes the "furious" resistance of leading rabbis. The great mass of Orthodox rabbis, he says, who at the turn of the century represented 90 percent of Eastern European Jewry, embarked upon a fight "aimed at the destruction or, at the very least, the crippling of the movement. It was maintained with great fixity of purpose and it was informed by deep, undisguised, and at times venomous hostility."[18] The rabbis interfered greatly with Zionist fund-raising activities and condemned cooperation with the secularist "sinners" who dominated the Zionist movement.

The overwhelming majority of early Zionists emphasized secular nationalist appeals and the simple need to rescue Jews from persecution to justify their program. They avoided metaphysical or religious appeals. Nonetheless, in a traditional Jewish context, no attempt to bring an end to the Exile of the Jewish people by returning them to the Land of Israel could be clearly distinguished from active redemptionism. Vital explains as follows.

> Orthodoxy's fundamental objection to Zionism was theological. It followed from the Zionists' intention to reverse the course of Jewish history and remake the Jewish people—in effect, to redeem them—through mere human agency. It was the settled Orthodox view that the condition of the Jews in their Exile, with its attendant miseries, had been divinely ordained and that to seek to alter it without divine sanction was blasphemous and, of course, futile. The Jews were, on the contrary, under a primary religious obligation to await redemption at the hands of the Messiah, in God's good time, with patience and submission.[19]

The most eminent Hasidic sage of the late nineteenth century, Rabbi Haim Soloveichik, wrote of the Zionists in 1899 that "each and everyone of them is of an evil reputation in his own locality. . . . And their purpose, as they have already announced and published it, is the uprooting of the foundations of the religion."[20] In a formal rabbinical proclamation at the time, the Zionists were vilified as "new deceivers," who teach the young "licentiousness and insolence" and who are "liable . . . to bring upon our nation a greater material disaster than all the disasters brought upon the people by false prophets and disseminators of lies about the redemption of Israel [in the past]."[21]

As Zionism developed in the early twentieth century, Orthodox Judaism's opposition remained strong. In 1911, Samson Raphael Hirsch, the founder of post-Enlightenment "neo-Orthodox" Judaism, warned that Jews must "attempt no action on their own initiative to restore their sovereignty, but must pursue their mission in Exile, awaiting the redemption solely through divine intervention."[22] Agudat Yisrael, the organization of "Torah-true" Jews established in 1912 partially as a counterweight to the World Zionist Organization, adopted the same position. Although some traditionalists were willing to support and even participate in practical programs to help Jews live observant lives in Palestine, Agudat Yisrael and the leading sages of traditional Judaism condemned political Zionism as a dangerous attempt to "push the end" and as a modern form of idol worship.[23]

Even that minority of Orthodox rabbis who initially supported Zionism did so despite grave misgivings about the appropriateness of working side by side with Jews who had abandoned observance of the halacha. When the Zionist movement added educational and cultural programs to its agenda, most of these rabbis left the movement. The majority of those who remained sought to emphasize an interpretation of Zionism as a mundane "rescue" effort for Jews based on the heightened need for a "secure refuge" that had become apparent amid renewed persecutions in Russia and Eastern Europe. Even religious Zionism, in other words, explicitly denied any spiritual significance to the Zionist program. Mizrahi voted in support of Theodore Herzl's 1903 proposal to accept Uganda as an alternative to Palestine. Although the state to be created might be governed by Jews, it would represent in the eyes of religious Zionists no more than another "host" environment within which the righteous remnant of observant Jewry, maintaining a more or less hostile attitude toward nonreligious Jews, could preserve its existence.[24]

This was a stance that most Agudists also came to adopt. During World War II the vast majority of traditionalist, or ultra-Orthodox, Jews was annihilated. Many survivors established themselves in Palestine. In this context even the Agudat Yisrael movement came to terms with the establishment of the Jewish state. In 1948 Agudat Yisrael and the Mizrahi movement (which became the National Religious Party) struck a bargain with the dominant Labor Zionist party, Mapai, according to which the question of the official status of religion would be deferred by dispensing with a written constitution; Orthodox rabbis would control marriage, divorce, and adoption; the state would honor the Sabbath; and kosher food would be served in state institutions. In return for commitments to preserve this religious "status quo," and even though Agudat Yisrael continued to oppose Zionism on ideological grounds and refused to join the World Zionist Organization, the religious parties agreed to join with secular parties in governing coalitions.

The majority of religious Zionists maintained this politically pragmatic attitude until 1967. To be sure, more than 200 Israeli rabbis signed a declaration published before the first parliamentary elections in 1949 characterizing the establishment of the state as *atchalta degeula* (the beginning of the redemption).[25] But after the first flush of excitement, life settled down to politics as usual, Tammany Hall–style, for the leaders of the religious parties, both Zionist and non-Zionist. The mobilization of religious sentiment along fundamentalist/redemptionist lines, representing a dramatic reversal of Orthodox Judaism's attitude toward Zionism, did not begin until after the catalyzing impact of the Six Day War and the Yom Kippur War.

Both opponents and supporters of the fundamentalist movement acknowledge the crucial influence of these wars. Many liberal and Labor Zionists argue that Jewish fundamentalism is a freak and tragic consequence of the wars, an unnatural distortion of what Zionism was meant to be—and would have been—in their absence.[26] But a longer perspective recalls the tendency of Jewish political life in the Land of Israel to attach itself to messianic themes, taking note of the chronic eruption of active, mystically based redemptionism, even in the Diaspora. The view that the emergence of Gush Emunim was a natural, if unintended, consequence of political Zionism's success is therefore at least as plausible as the perception that Jewish fundamentalism in Israel is a weird and accidental aberration of Zionist development.

Contemporary Origins of Jewish Fundamentalism

There is no doubt that the Six Day War was a watershed in Zionist/Israeli political history.[27] The juxtaposition of a terrifying period of siege and depression in May of 1967 with a lightning military victory and the dramatic, emotionally exhilarating reunion with the Old City of Jerusalem, Hebron, Beit-El, and other locations of biblical importance triggered an upsurge of romantic Zionist and religious sentiment. This corresponded with a challenge already under way by the National Religious party's Young Guard, who were dissatisfied with the logrolling and patronage-oriented politics of the party's aging leadership. In the vibrant aftermath of war, the Young Guard, led by Hanan Porat, Zevulon Hammer, Yehuda Ben-Meir, and Rabbi Haim Druckman, emerged as the dominant faction within the National Religious Party, and, hence, within religious Zionism. It did so by projecting images of patriotism, pioneering settlement, and religious observance.

Politically, if not organizationally, this was the beginning of Gush Emunim. The group's phenomenal success required unprecedented levels of cooperation between religious and nonreligious activists, dedicated to the practical political task of incorporating the whole Land of Israel into the State of Israel. This cooperation and Gush Emunim's success are in turn understandable only in the light of three interrelated factors:

—The ideas developed by the first chief rabbi in twentieth-century Palestine, Rav [Rabbi] Abraham Isaac Kook (1865–1935)

—The leadership and ideological elaboration of those ideas by his son, Tzvi Yehuda Kook (1891–1982)

—The political ascendance of Revisionist Zionism, under the leadership of Menachem Begin and his Likud coalition, dominated by the Herut party.

Rav Abraham Isaac Kook (Rav Kook the Elder). Most Jews in the national religious camp, following the lead of the Young Guard, now embrace Zionism and the State of Israel as the central factor in the long awaited process of redemption. In their minds this will eventually entail the return of all Jews to the Land of Israel, extension of Jewish rule over the entirety of the Promised Land, reestablishment of the legal dominance of the *halacha*, reconstruction of the Temple in Jerusalem, and the appearance of the Messiah. It is difficult to overemphasize the extent to which this fundamentalist, explicitly redemptionist stance, which ascribes sacred meaning to the consequences of Jewish political action, represents a revolutionary reversal of traditional Orthodox Jewish attitudes (whether non-Zionist or Zionist) toward political action as a whole, and toward Zionism in particular.

Though triggered by the events of 1967, this dramatic reversal has an important ideological basis in the thought and work of Rav Abraham Isaac Kook, appointed by the British in 1921 to serve as Palestine's Ashkenazic chief rabbi. He served in that capacity until his death in 1935. Rav Kook's efforts to give organizational expression to his radical reinterpretation of secular Zionism came to naught, but the legend of his saintly holiness and the power and originality of his ideas served more than thirty years after his death as the theoretical and ideological foundation for the contemporary emergence of Jewish fundamentalism.

Rav Kook articulated his approach in the vocabulary of the same long-standing but repressed doctrines of Jewish mysticism that surrounded the Sabbatian movement. He taught that the mundane, sensible world of ritual observance, rationality, and scientific inference is important as, but is no more than, a vehicle for preparing human beings to approach and eventually apprehend a much more fundamental spiritual reality. This other realm, immanent within the outer world of sensation and cognition, is pervaded by the pulsating illumination of the "Divine psyche."[28] For most peoples, at most times, the spiritual energy flowing continuously from this realm is displaced and distorted into various forms of idolatry because they cannot absorb "the light emanating from the universal spiritual psyche."[29] The "distinctive excellence" of the Jewish people consists in the presence of "the Divine sensitivity at the core of its being," which permits Jews, as individuals and as a collectivity, to experience and express the divine illumination in pure, nonidolatrous form.[30] Zionism, for Rav Kook the Elder, was significant as a movement of Jews returning from a long and spiritually purgative exile to reassume their "Divine vocation"[31] and achieve "the splendor of redemption." [32]

The repair of the world would naturally require contact with the mundane, if not the profane. Thus, "the external trappings of the nation's life," including language, political consciousness, and practical work, only set the stage for "a new surge of Divine inspiration."[33] After 2,000 years of exile, he welcomed a return of Jews to manual labor, physical culture, and military valor, even if most broke Torah commandments in the process.

> In times of redemption insolence is on the increase. . . . They rebel against everything . . . they break and they discard; they seek their nourishment in alien pastures, embracing alien ideals and desecrating everything hallowed. . . . These passionate souls reveal their strength so that no fence can hold them back. . . . Truly heroic spirits know (however) that this force is one of the phenomena needed for the perfection of the world.[34]

In sharp contrast to most observant Jews of the early twentieth century, Rav Kook was not disturbed by the flagrant rejection of Jewish religious law by secular Zionists, nor even by their often loudly declared atheism. Concerning young Jews who had left the tradition, attracted to revolutionary socialist and socialist Zionist causes, he scolded an unforgiving rabbinical colleague:

> To reject those children who have strayed from the ways of the Torah and religious faith, having been carried away by the raging currents of the times—I say unhesitatingly that this is not the way God wants. . . . The inner essence of Jewish holiness remains hidden in their hearts. . . . [35]

Rav Kook's willingness to tolerate, cooperate with, and even see positive value in secular Zionism made him a resource of inestimable value to the Zionist movement, eager to improve its credibility among the observant Jewish masses of Eastern Europe. Accordingly, its leadership honored him and welcomed his installation as chief rabbi. But while secular, mainly Labor, Zionism was seeking to use him; Rav Kook himself understood secular Zionism as, ultimately, an instrument of his brand of religious Zionism.

Secular Jews, he argued, had an important contribution to make to the redemptive process. Nor was it necessary for them to believe that what they were doing had or would have any divine meaning or redemptive value. Simply by settling in the Land of Israel, working its soil, and developing its potential for habitation by larger numbers of Jews, the Zionist movement was carrying out the divine plan—a plan to redeem not only the Jewish people, through its restoration in its own land and the coming of the Messiah, but, through them, the gentile nations as well. Eventually, in communion with religious Jews and with the Land of Israel itself, secular Zionists would begin to appreciate the true spiritual and redemptive meaning of their accomplishments.

> Resolute in body and spirit, and stirred by a deep and living passion, the young Israelite of the future, in viewing the renaissance of his people and his land, will speak proudly of the Holy Land, and glory in the God of Israel. A spiritual force of intense vitality will stir the dry bones that drew their sustenance from cold logic, lifeless metaphysics, and the decadence of skepticism. Then will be fulfilled the prophecy.[36]

Thus, forty years after his death, Rav Kook's thought and his celebration within the Zionist movement provided the intellectual and spiritual basis for Gush Emunim to integrate a substantial and highly motivated minority of secular ultranationalists within its predominantly religious framework. Gush Emunim's primary focus on redemption through the settlement, inheritance, and "redemption" of the "liberated areas" also echoes the singular importance and unique qualities that Rav Kook ascribed to the Land of Israel and the mystical significance of renewed contact between the Jews and their land.

> Eretz Yisrael [the Land of Israel] is part of the very essence of our nationhood; it is bound organically to its very life and inner being. Human reason, even at its most sublime, cannot begin to understand the unique holiness of Eretz Yisrael. . . . The hope for the Redemption is the force that sustains Judaism in the Diaspora; the Judaism of Eretz Yisrael is the very Redemption.[37]

> We are commanded to bite deeply into the delightful sweetness of the land of Israel's glorious, invigorating holiness. "That ye may suck, and be satisfied with the breast of her consolations; that ye may drink deeply with delight of the abundance of her glory." (Is. 66:11) And we must announce to the entire

world, to those who languish pitifully in dark exile, that the channel through which courses the full life, the abundant light and the pleasant holiness of our lively land has begun to open up.[38]

For Rav Kook, as, in a sense, for Labor Zionism, living and working in the Holy Land was a *mitzvah* (divine injunction) equivalent in value to all the other religious commandments combined. On this basis, religious Jews could joyously tolerate the lack of religious observance by most Zionists. They were confident that exposure to the Holy Land, complemented by their own sensitive and tolerant persuasion, would eventually lead the nonreligious Zionist majority to acceptance of the halacha and understanding of the redemptive meaning of Zionism. It is also on this basis that Gush Emunim can justify its program of de facto annexation, designed to force the majority of Israeli Jews into a permanent relationship with the entire Land of Israel, despite their refusal or inability, as of yet, to appreciate the rewards of that circumstance.

In one additional specific respect, Rav Kook the Elder's thought has had direct significance for the evolution of Gush Emunim. The rabbi emphasized the crucial role of charismatic personalities as conduits for spiritual energy, self-confidence, and redemptive guidance.

> . . . the functioning of spiritual inspiration will restore to the nation its ancient honor by restoring the patriarchal dignity of Israel's princes, who were distinguished by a personal spiritual quality of a high order. The adherence to *zaddikim* [righteous, charismatic men] with devotion and enthusiasm, through constant contact, raises the spiritual stature of the nation. The psychic fusion effected through the living contact of souls in the existential reality of life, merges the inner light in the psyche of the higher person, the true man of God, with the other souls that are attached to him . . . a personal influence that draws its inspiration from the domain of the spiritual in all its fullness which is fed by a surviving remnant of prophecy.[39]

In building a movement to lead the people of Israel toward goals to which the people as a whole did not yet even aspire, Gush Emunim activists benefited greatly from the validation for their activities provided by charismatic personalities, including rabbis, outstanding pioneer settlers, and gifted writers. Of all these, by far the most important was Rav Abraham Isaac Kook's son, Rav Tzvi Yehuda Kook.

Rav Tzvi Yehuda Kook (Rav Tzvi Yehuda). Secular Zionists honored Abraham Isaac Kook for offering a basis for cooperation between religious and nonreligious Jews. But they ignored his proposals for establishing institutions for the spiritual guidance of the Zionist enterprise. The yeshiva that the elder Kook had established in Jerusalem to carry on his work, Merkaz HaRav (the Rabbi's Center), slipped in stature not too long after his death; despite the presence there of his son, Tzvi Yehuda. Indeed, Merkaz HaRav barely managed to survive into the 1960s as an ordinary seminary with no more than twenty students.

However, in the mid-1960s the younger Kook attracted an important following among an elitist group of graduates of the Bnei Akiva. This secretive, exclusive fraternity of idealistic young men called itself *Gahelet* (Embers; the Hebrew is the acronym for Nucleus of Torah-Learning Pioneers). Gahelet contained a very large proportion of the future leaders of Gush Emunim, including Rabbis Haim Druckman, Moshe Levinger, and Eleazar Waldman.[40] Gahelet members, rebuffed in 1964 at their first effort to exert influence within the National Religious Party itself, gravitated toward Rav Tzvi Yehuda.

As his father had, Rav Tzvi Yehuda communicated to his followers a mystical, romantic interpretation of Zionism, redolent with the language of messianism and redemption. But he went substantially beyond Rav Kook the Elder by specifying the political and spiritual stages that the redemptive process would entail and the concrete steps that had advanced it and would advance it toward its glorious conclusion. His model of redemption was based on the traditional Jewish concept of repentance, involving a "turning" or "return." Although he warned his followers to expect setbacks and complex twists and turns in the process, Tzvi Yehuda identified three overall stages of redemption. The first stage, expressed by the [largely secularly organized] return of Diaspora Jews to the Land of Israel, was initiated out of a "repentance of fear," fear of physical danger in the Diaspora. This stage is well on the way to completion, but even while the Diaspora continues to exist, the next stage has begun. The second stage is made possible by the reunion of the Jewish people with the biblical heartland of Judea and Samaria. This stage is dominated by a dialectic of "national reconstruction" between the people of Israel and the Land of Israel. It entails the "complete resettlement in the Land and the revival of Israel in it . . . [and] the actual fulfillment of our inheriting the Land, of its being in our possession and not in that of any other of the nations nor in a state of desolation."[41] The third, and final, stage in the redemption process will require a "repentance of love," in which Jews whose spiritual health has been enlivened by their contact with the whole Land of Israel turn toward God and the observance of his commandments. In this stage, the Messiah and the final redemption will approach at a pace proportionate to the Jewish people's increasing level of religious observance.

Tzvi Yehuda's particular emphasis was on the critical importance of Jewish settlement on and political control over all parts of the land promised to the Jews by God, as well as the sanctity of the State of Israel itself as God's appointed instrument for returning the Land of Israel to the people of Israel.

> The State of Israel was created and established by the council of nations by order of the Sovereign Lord of the Universe so that the clear commandment in the Torah "that they shall inherit and settle the Land" would be fulfilled.[42]

What otherwise might be considered "mundane" Levantine politics is thus of cosmic significance. For it is the "rule of our own government" in the land that gives effect to the second stage of redemption.

> When this State of ours is in full control, both internally and externally, then the fulfillment of this mitzva of the Inheritance can be truly revealed—the mitzva that is the basis and essence of all of the mitzvot relating to settlement in the Land. It is these mitzvot that, by means of our rule, can accomplish the act of Redemption, and it is by their means that the vision of Redemption must be progressively fulfilled according to the word of the Universal King.[43]

Although the redemption of Israel would in principle lead to the redemption of all mankind, this theme was more prominent in Abraham Isaac Kook's thinking than in the much more parochially focused message of his son. "When Israel performs mitzvot other than for its own sake," wrote Tzvi Yehuda, "its merit reaches up to the heavens; when it does so for its own sake, its merit reaches above the heavens."[44]

An important incident that occurred some three weeks before the outbreak of the Six Day War helped instill in his disciples an incontrovertible belief in the divine source of the guidance they received from Tzvi Yehuda. His disciples recounted that on the eve of Israeli Independence Day the rabbi was delivering a commemorative sermon "in the midst of which his quiet tone suddenly rose to crescendo, bewailing the partition of historic Eretz Yisrael."[45]

> Nineteen years ago, on the very night that the decision of the United Nations to create the State of Israel was handed down, as the entire people rejoiced . . . I was unable to join in their happiness. I sat alone—quiet and depressed. In those very first hours I was not able to accept what had been done, that terrible news, that indeed "my land they have divided" had occurred! Yes, where is our Hebron—have we forgotten it?! And where is our Schechem, and our Jericho, where—will we forget them?! And all of Transjordan—it is all ours, every single clod of earth, each little bit, every part of the land is part of the land of God—is it in our power to surrender even one millimeter of it?![46]

Asked by his students if it was permissible to view the scheduled military parade in Jerusalem, Tzvi Yehuda is said to have responded, "Of course, know that this is the army of Israel that will liberate the Land of Israel."[47] This reply was interpreted and widely regarded within Gush Emunim as evidence of the rabbi's prophetic status.

Some have argued that the image of Tzvi Yehuda as a charismatic and quasi-prophetic figure was created by a self-serving core group of his students who realized they could trade upon their closeness to him to achieve a prominence within religious society that they could not have achieved by their own scholarly and spiritual accomplishments.[48] On the other hand, given Tzvi

Yehuda's impact on the imagination of many leading politicians, it is not difficult to understand why his leadership was accepted by so many national religious youth. One student at Merkaz HaRav describes an audience Tzvi Yehuda granted to Menachem Begin shortly after the latter's victory in the 1977 parliamentary elections.

> When Begin was chosen as Prime Minister he came to visit Tzvi Yehuda. He came as if to Canossa, as if this man, Tzvi Yehuda, was God's representative. Suddenly the Prime Minister kneels and bows before Tzvi Yehuda. Imagine for yourself what all the students standing there and watching this surrealistic scene were thinking. I'll never forget it. I felt that my heart was bursting within me. What greater empirical proof could there be that his fantasies and imaginings were indeed reality? You could see for yourself that instead of treating him as if he were crazy, people looked upon him as upon something holy. And everything he said or did became something holy as well.[49]

Tzvi Yehuda died in 1982. As we shall see, Gush Emunim is still feeling the effects of his passing. But while he lived Gush Emunim drew from him authorization for its belief that redemption was the crucial challenge facing Israel and the Jewish people, and that that challenge could be met by practical political accomplishments—most importantly, establishment of Israeli sovereignty over territories ruled until 1967 by Israel's Arab neighbors. Its efforts, however, would have had much less chance of actually shaping the course of events in the Middle East had 1977 not seen the election of an Israeli government fully committed to the permanent absorption of the West Bank and Gaza Strip.

The Rise of Revisionist Zionism. Most Labor Zionists accepted the British decision, implemented in 1921, to separate Transjordan (the East Bank) from the Palestine mandate and thus from the area within which the promised "Jewish national home" might be established. Within the dominant Labor Zionist movement, commitment remained strong to the principle of establishing a Jewish state in all of the "western Land of Israel" (that is, from the Jordan River to the Mediterranean Sea). But when, in 1947, Zionism was offered the possibility of a Jewish state in only part of this area, David Ben-Gurion and the pragmatic Mapai (Workers of the Land of Israel) party, in coalition with religious Zionists and the centrist General Zionists, accepted the proposal.

This acceptance was accomplished over the strenuous objections of more activist Labor Zionists and of the Revisionists. Within Labor Zionism, the activist approach was characterized by militant commitment to territorial expansion, tough policies toward Arabs, and maximal extension of Jewish settlement and sovereignty. The speeches and writings of its visionary leader, Yitzhak Tabenkin, were imbued with the imagery of romantic nationalism. Although explicitly secular, his message, and that of other activist leaders, featured authoritative references to the Bible and Israel's ancient past. The ethos of the movement also contained mystical overtones of communion between Jewish workers and fighters, and the soil of the Land of Israel. These ideas were most prominent within the Achdut Haavodah political party and its affiliated settlement movement, Hakibbutz Hameuchad.[50]

While the activist approach included many of the pioneering leaders of Labor Zionism, Revisionism developed wholly outside the socialist Zionist mainstream. The Revisionist party, under the leadership of its founder, Vladimir (Ze'ev) Jabotinsky, bitterly protested the separation of Transjordan from the Palestine mandate. In 1935 it left the World Zionist Organization and declared unswerving devotion to the principle of establishing Jewish sovereignty on "both banks of the Jordan." The military arm of Revisionism was the underground Irgun (National Military Organization) headed by Menachem Begin, who assumed the leadership of Revisionist Zionism with Jabotinsky's death in 1940.

From 1935 to 1967 the Labor party sought to protect its political paramountcy within Zionism and the State of Israel by ostracizing the Revisionist movement and its post–World War II leader, Menachem Begin. In 1948 the Irgun was forcibly disbanded. When Begin organized the Herut party and entered the parliamentary elections, Ben-Gurion, and other Labor leaders, denounced him as a fanatic, fascist, and a dangerous demagogue. As prime minister for most of the first nineteen years of Israel's existence, Ben-Gurion expressed his willingness to accept any political party as a partner in the government "except the Communists and Herut." Partly as a result of Ben-Gurion's policy, Herut remained at the margin of Israeli politics, participating in no governing coalitions and garnering no more than 14 percent of the vote in any of the five elections between 1949 and 1961.

One other important reason for the failure of Revisionism's political appeal in the first decades of Israel's existence was the disappearance of the territorial issue. With the return to the 1949 armistice lines after Israel's conquest of Sinai in 1956, those lines appeared to have crystallized into permanent borders. Old Revisionist demands, emphasizing maximalist territorial objectives, sounded strange and increasingly irrelevant to most Israelis. Even the ambitions of activist Labor Zionists regarding the need for Jewish sovereignty over all of Palestine, from the Jordan River to the sea, had faded from operational objectives to politically irrelevant, nostalgic slogans. Nor, between 1948 and 1967, did any substantial element within the national religious camp try to advance programs for radical change in the territorial composition of the state.

In 1965 Herut made its first important move toward power by joining with the center-right Liberal party to form Gahal. The new party received 21 percent of the vote in 1965. Thus, by the end of the Six Day War Begin was well positioned to exploit the reopening of the territorial question in Zionism. He benefited greatly from the wave of romantic enthusiasm for Israel's return "to the land of our forefathers." As the popular imagination shifted its attention from the State of Israel, built by the old guard of the Labor party, to the Land of Israel, Begin's loyalty to the greater Land of Israel and his distinctive appeals for Jewish solidarity on behalf of its ancient heritage, cast in emotional and grand historical language, struck much more receptive chords. Just as important for Begin's political ascendancy was that during the crisis preceding the 1967 war, he had been coopted into Levi Eshkol's cabinet as a full partner in the "emergency government." Although Begin left the government three years later in protest over the cease-fire agreement with Egypt, his participation in the Six Day War emergency government legitimized Herut's struggle for political power and paved the way for the electoral success of another alliance of right-wing groups led by Herut—the Likud.

Discredited by scandals and shaken by the losses suffered in the 1973 war, the Labor Party was voted out of office in 1977, and Begin became prime minister. Under his leadership, the Likud organized a coalition government with the National Religious Party dominated by Gush Emunim.

In the wake of severe economic difficulties, the Lebanon War debacle, and Begin's resignation in 1983 as prime minister, the Likud's electoral performance slipped. In 1984 it was forced into a "national unity government" with Labor. In October 1986, Yitzhak Shamir, Begin's successor as head of the Likud, assumed the premiership.

Immediately upon his election, Begin had gone to the Gush Emunim settlement of Elon Moreh on the West Bank. Holding a Torah scroll, he called for the establishment of "many more Elon Morehs." In the first Likud government, key ministries and other governmental and nongovernmental organizations connected to settlement and land acquisition were placed under the control of individuals strongly sympathetic to Gush objectives.[51] The densely populated Arab areas of the West Bank, intended as bargaining chips and kept largely clear of Jewish settlers by previous governments, were especially targeted for settlement—just as Gush Emunim had been advocating. Although the 1977 election campaign was not fought on the issue of the territories, virtually all Israelis knew that for Menachem Begin and a majority of the Likud leadership, there was no higher priority than consolidating Israel's permanent control of *Eretz Yisrael hashelema*, the completed (whole) land of Israel—referring especially to the West Bank and the Gaza Strip. During the 1981 campaign, which resulted in Begin's second electoral victory, he made sure there would be no doubt about his intentions, swearing by th names of his parents that while he served as Prime Minister there would be no Isreali withdrawal from Judea and Samaria, the Gaza District, or the Golan Heights.

From 1977 until the end of 1984 two Likud governments poured more than $1 billion into Jewish settlement in the West Bank and Gaza Strip and various support activities. In the West Bank alone nearly sixty new settlements were added. The number of Jewish settlers in predominantly Arab areas of the West Bank increased from a few thousand to over 38,000. Sweeping land requisitions and zoning restrictions were implemented to provide a land reserve for future settlements. Virtually open access to cabinet ministers was afforded to Gush Emunim leaders. Generous employment opportunities in governmental and quasi-governmental agencies responsible for religious and social life, infrastructural development, security, and other spheres of life in the settlements were provided to Gush activists. Thus, fundamentalists gained the economic and administrative resources to recruit new followers and sustain a wide range of intensive political and practical efforts in support of their program to transform the shape and direction of Israeli society.

In sum, Rav Kook the Elder provided the doctrinal basis for cooperation between religious and nonreligious Jews toward maximalist Zionist territorial objectives. For an idealistic but frustrated young religious elite, Rav Tzvi Yehuda provided charismatic leadership and authoritative imperatives linking specific political events (the Six Day War and the Yom Kippur War) and concrete political programs (Jewish settlement and annexation of the occupied territories) to the divine plan for the final redemption. Finally, the political ascendancy of the Zionist right wing provided Jewish fundamentalism with the status, self-confidence, and large-scale economic resources the movement needed to attempt the actual implementation of its program.

III

The Evolution of Gush Emunim

The Six Day War reopened the question of borders, re-kindled mass interest and excitement in the whole Land of Israel, and helped Menachem Begin escape from the political wilderness into the Israeli political mainstream. Thus, it served as the catalyst in the combination of factors, described in the previous chapter, that explain the emergence of a redemptionist, visionary, and territory centered Jewish fundamentalist movement.

Soon after the Six Day War discussions began among young rabbis and rabbinical students associated with Rav Tzvi Yehuda Kook as to how settlement in the "liberated areas" might be advanced. Such meetings produced little in the way of organized activity, but the urge to settle the West Bank for ideological reasons—as opposed to security purposes—led Moshe Levinger, a disciple of Rav Kook and a future leader of Gush Emunim, to establish a small, illegal presence in a hotel in the middle of Hebron during the spring festival of Passover in 1968.

The government was caught by surprise. Internally divided, depending for its survival on the votes of the National Religious Party, and reluctant to forcibly evacuate the settlers from a city whose Jewish population had been massacred thirty-nine years earlier, the Labor government backed away from its original prohibition against civilian settlement in the area and permitted this group to remain within a military compound. After more than a year and a half of agitation and a bloody Arab attack on the Hebron settlers, the government agreed to allow Levinger's group to establish a town on the outskirts of the city. That town is now one of the largest Jewish settlements on the West Bank—Kiryat Arba.

As a model for later actions by Gush Emunim to use the "creation of facts in the field" as a powerful political weapon, Levinger's success was important. But aside from Begin's Herut party, the only significant organized effort to push Israel toward permanent incorporation of the recently occupied territories was the Movement for the Whole Land of Israel.[1] This was an elite organization of well-known writers, intellectuals, poets, generals, kibbutz leaders, and other personalities prominent in the pre-1948 Zionist struggle. Founded two months after the Six Day War, it reflected the background of most of its organizers: militant, activist, romantic and focused on the Land of Israel. It adopted a platform calling for the rapid settlement and permanent absorption of all the territories. Its manifesto, filled with historical imagery, was devoid of religious language and sentiment:

> Zahal's (Israel Defense Force's) victory in the Six Day War placed the people and the state within a new and fateful period. The whole of Eretz Yisrael is now in the hands of the Jewish people, and just as we are not allowed to give up the State of Israel, so we are ordered to keep what we received there from Eretz Yisrael.
>
> We are bound to be loyal to the entirety of the country—for the sake of the people's past as well as its future, and no government in Israel is entitled to give up this entirety, which represents the inherent and inalienable right of our people from the beginnings of its history. . . .[2]

Despite the presence of one or two rabbis among this document's scores of signatories, the organization was a manifestation of secular ultranationalist Zionism. It aspired to be neither a movement of the masses nor a political party, but a respected pressure group whose main objective was to influence government policy through newspaper articles, books, and personal contacts with government ministers. After the 1973 war it was rapidly eclipsed by Gush Emunim, which did aspire to lead a mass movement, for the purpose not merely of changing government policies toward the territories, but of transforming the cultural and ideological foundation of society. On the basis of Kookist injunctions to tolerate the religious nonobservance of Jews active in the settlement and redemption of the Land of Israel, Gush Emunim absorbed many participants from the Movement for the Whole Land of Israel. By 1977 the latter organization and its newspaper, *Zot Haaretz,* had virtually ceased to exist.

The actual founding of Gush Emunim and the beginning of its serious effort at political mobilization took place in 1974. Gush Emunim's establishment is not inappropriately viewed as the religious expression of a wave of intense and pervasive discontent that swept Israel after "the earthquake"—the popular epithet adopted to refer to the Yom Kippur War. This emotional upsurge produced several reformist/populist movements. Unusual in Israel's highly institutionalized, party-dominated political system, these were loosely structured grass roots organizations, led by well-educated but disillusioned young army officers with impeccable credentials as war heroes. Focusing at first on technical errors made by military, intelligence, and political figures before and during the Yom Kippur War, these groups made short-lived attempts to build a political base for a technocratic, progressivist political movement.[3]

It was in that same atmosphere of crisis, of grass roots mobilization dedicated to remaking Israeli society in a manner that could justify the losses in the 1973 war, that Gush Emunim also arose. The Yom Kippur War was the first major conflict in which substantial numbers of Orthodox Jews participated within regular combat units. Famous for their knitted skullcaps, these soldiers came mainly from the recently created Yeshivot Hesder in which young religious Jews were permitted to integrate half-time study of sacred texts with regular service in the army. This participation gave religious Israeli Jews self-confidence and legitimacy within the wider secular society. Amid the psychological confusion of the period following the Yom Kippur War, a generation of young religious idealists, whose pride had always suffered by the honor granted to kibbutzniks and other secular Jews for serving in the army, felt empowered to offer their own analysis of Israel's predicament, and their own solution. But their analysis was not technocratic, it was theological. Their solution was a spiritual rejuvenation of society whose most important expression and source of strength would be settlement on and communion with the greater, liberated Land of Israel.

Early Activities of Gush Emunim. In 1973 a small group of religious zealots formed a *garin* (nucleus for a new settlement) called Elon Moreh. Its intention was to establish a Jewish settlement in the heart of Samaria, the northern bulge of the West Bank, densely populated by Arabs. In the spring of 1974, another, somewhat overlapping group of rabbis, religious war veterans, and hawkish Young Guard political activists, most of whom had been strongly influenced by Rav Tzvi Yehuda Kook, established an organization they named Gush Emunim. The express purpose of this "nonpartisan, extra-parliamentary" organization was to advance what one of their number, Hanan Porat, termed the Zionism of Redemption. After two unsuccessful but, for their supporters, inspiring attempts to establish a settlement near Nablus, the Elon Moreh garin agreed to join with Gush Emunim. In August 1974 a secretariat was formed, and a statement of principles and specific plans for political organization and action were approved. The immediate task was to mobilize mass opinion against the willingness of the Labor government to disengage from territories captured from Syria in the 1973 war. This, in turn, was seen as but the beginning of a struggle against Labor's policy, in the context of peace negotiations, to withdraw from territories Israel had held since 1967.

One of the group's first organized actions was to support a hunger strike staged by members of the Movement for the Whole Land of Israel to protest the government's apparent willingness to withdraw from Kuneitra, on the edge of the Golan Heights, as part of the disengagement agreement with Syria. When nonreligious supporters of this movement from a Golan settlement set up an unauthorized settlement in May of 1974, they were joined by Gush Emunim members wearing knitted skullcaps and determined to set a precedent of nonreligious-religious cooperation in the establishment of protest settlements.

But their primary focus was the West Bank heartland—Judea and Samaria.[4] Although the Labor party did invest substantial resources in settling the Golan Heights, the Jordan Valley, the greater East Jerusalem area, and the Gush Etzion area,[5] the government continued to resist Gush Emunim demands to create a large Jewish presence in the heavily populated highlands of the West Bank. The Labor party had intended to keep this area, as well as a corridor to Jericho through which Arab travel to Jordan was possible, free of Jewish settlement in anticipation of its eventual return to Arab rule.

From mid-1974 until the Labor Party's ouster from power in May 1977, Gush Emunim's primary efforts were directed toward challenging this policy and laying the groundwork for a Jewish settler presence in precisely those areas targeted for return to Arab hands. With the blessing and participation of Rav Tzvi Yehuda, the dramatic involvement of whole families, and the skillful use of the symbols associated with Jewish holidays and with the legendary illegal struggle by Labor Zionism to settle the Galilee during the British mandate, Gush members made eight attempts in 1974 and 1975 to evade army roadblocks and establish a settlement in the Nablus area. Seven times they were foiled by the army, but each time the numbers involved in the effort, the extent of media attention, and the level of public support grew. These attempts also attracted visits of support to the temporary Gush encampments by influential political personalities, including Menachem Begin, Ariel Sharon, and Geula Cohen. Finally, on the holiday of Hanukkah in December 1975, some 2,000 Gush supporters succeeded in establishing a settlement in Sebastia. After prolonged confrontation with the Labor government of Prime Minister Yitzhak Rabin and Minister of Defense Shimon Peres, the settlers received permission to maintain their presence in the nearby army camp of Kadum. Gush Emunim demonstrated its political muscle and mass base in May 1976 with the participation of 20,000 supporters in its first annual Independence Day March through the heart of the West Bank.

Gush Emunim and the Likud. Gush Emunim greeted the 1977 Likud victory with enthusiasm. Its expectations were heightened that the country was moving rapidly toward redemption. In fact, some Gush Emunim supporters appear to have felt that with the ascendance of a nationalist religious governing coalition, continued political activism on their part was unnecessary.

The new government immediately granted official status to several small Gush settlements that had received de facto recognition by the previous governments. In September 1977 Ariel Sharon, the new agriculture minister and head of the Israel Lands

Administration, announced a plan to settle more than one million Jews in the West Bank within twenty years. The plan redirected infrastructural investments, residential construction, and land acquisition away from Jerusalem and the Jordan Valley, and toward the highlands. The following year Mattitiyahu Drobles, chairman of the Land Settlement Department of the Jewish Agency, who was closely associated with Gush Emunim, issued the first version of a similar document, the "Master Plan for Judea and Samaria." Between 1977 and mid-1981 the Likud government spent $400 million in the West Bank and Gaza, built twenty settlements in areas considered off-limits by previous governments, and increased the number of settlers living in the West Bank, minus the Jordan Valley and East Jerusalem, from approximately 3,500 to 18,500. Following its second election victory in 1981, the Likud dramatically increased settlement-related expenditures and accelerated programs of land acquisition and infrastructural development beyond the already hectic pace achieved in the previous four years. By the end of Likud's second term, in August 1984, some 113 settlements were spread over the entire West Bank, including a half-dozen sizable towns. Some 46,000 Jewish settlers lived in the area (excluding expanded East Jerusalem), and housing and services were under construction to absorb 15,000 additional settlers each year.

Regarding the future of the West Bank and Gaza Strip, the objectives of Gush Emunim and of the Likud have largely coincided. But beyond this key issue and related questions, substantial differences have always existed. Gush Emunim is a fundamentalist organization. The Likud is a coalition of practical political parties. The former wants to transform Israeli society and bring redemption. The latter has something of an ideological agenda, but primarily wants to win elections and organize governments. As mentioned in chapter 1, both the Likud and the fundamentalist movement, particularly Gush Emunim, have sought to use each other to accomplish their own objectives.[6]

After a brief honeymoon, tensions emerged between Gush Emunim and the Likud government. With Egyptian President Anwar Sadat's visit to Jerusalem in 1977, the Camp David accords of 1978, the Egypt–Israel peace treaty in 1979, and levels of West Bank Arab political mobilization and anti-settler violence that

Gush considered intolerable, the expectations of many of its leaders and rank-and-file members were shattered. It was at this time, when relations between the Likud government and the fundamentalist movement were at a low ebb, that Gush Emunim's effectiveness as a pressure group on key issues of settlement, land acquisition, and Arab policy in the West Bank became most apparent.

Gush Emunim and the Circumvention of the Supreme Court: The Case of Elon Moreh. In the fall of 1979 Gush Emunim attacked the Begin cabinet for surrendering Sinai and setting the stage, with its autonomy plan, for what it feared would be the establishment of a Palestinian state in the West Bank and Gaza.[7] Gush stalwarts vigorously opposed the idea of Palestinian autonomy of any sort in the occupied territories, as described in the Camp David accords. In their view the most effective way to sabotage the American–Israeli–Egyptian autonomy negotiations, begun in 1979, was to spread Jewish settlements throughout those areas while sharply increasing their number and the number of Jewish settlers. An Israeli Supreme Court decision, handed down on October 22, 1979, severely threatened these objectives.

Agreeing with Arab petitioners that prevailing international law prohibited expropriation of private property for settlement purposes, the Court ordered that the Gush Emunim settlement of Elon Moreh, southeast of Nablus, be dismantled and the land returned to its Arab owners. Gush Emunim objected strenuously, condemning the government for its betrayal of Jewish rights to the Land of Israel. Movement leaders argued that unless applicable law or government policy were changed so that substantial amounts of Arab land could be transferred to Jewish control, the result of the Court decision would be "the collapse of the Jewish hold on Judea and Samaria."[8] Despite the embarrassment the protest caused the Begin government, the settlers threatened to resist evacuation of the site.

The fundamentalist movement's political clout was dramatically illustrated by the extent and solicitousness of reaction to the Gush campaign and its threats to oppose evacuation of Elon Moreh—an action that would have placed the Likud government in the same relationship to the settlers and their cause as that into which illegal

Gush settlement activity in the mid-1970s had placed the Labor government. Mattitiyahu Drobles, then director of the World Zionist Organization's land settlement department, expressed his "shock" at the Court decision and proceeded immediately to the prime minister's office to discuss the possibility of turning the site into a military base or rearranging the settlement in order to circumvent the decision.[9] On October 23 and 24, Gush Emunim members, led by Moshe Levinger, met with high-ranking sympathetic government officials, including Zevulun Hammer, a founder of the Young Guard and minister of education and culture; Yehuda Ben-Meir, another Young Guard leader and member of Knesset; Eliyahu Ben-Elissar, director of the prime minister's office; and Ariel Sharon, minister of agriculture. The government representatives offered alternative sites and an enlarged land area for the settlement and discussed various ideas for legislation to protect other settlements erected on privately owned land.[10] The following day, Zevulun Hammer met with Prime Minister Begin to discuss the issue. In response to a demand by the National Religious Party, a special cabinet meeting to deal with the problem of Elon Moreh in the broader context of land questions and the future of Jewish settlement was held on November 1.

After a debate over legal options that lasted five and one-half hours, the cabinet decided to comply with the Supreme Court decision but to find an alternate nearby site for the settlement of Elon Moreh. It also agreed to meet again to discuss long-term solutions to the legal vulnerabilities of Jewish settlement in the occupied territories. Ministers Sharon and Hammer expressed their dissatisfaction with the outcome of the meeting in terms similar to those of Gush Emunim leaders, who insisted on annexation or some other immediate change in the legal framework of settlement. Israeli radio reported that mothers on the site were warning that their families would fortify themselves against evacuation and that Gush Emunim intended "to enlist thousands of people on the eve of the evacuation and disrupt it."[11] On November 11, the cabinet met again. It decided to conduct a thorough study of the legal options open to the government in regard to the status of Jewish settlements in the occupied areas, but reaffirmed its decision to transfer the Elon Moreh settlement to a nearby location. It also announced its intention to expand Jewish settlement on "state land" throughout the West Bank, the Gaza Strip, and the Golan Heights, and to do so without limiting itself to security rationales.[12]

In an effort to head off a confrontation, Defense Minister Ezer Weizman met with Gush representatives for four hours, after which the latter reported their dissatisfaction and their insistence on a meeting with Prime Minister Begin himself. Amid warnings of the need to avoid civil war and threats from the National Religious Party that it would bolt from the coalition, thereby bringing the government down, if a confrontation with the Gush settlers ensued, yet another special cabinet meeting was called.[13]

The government's efforts to avoid a confrontation without categorically abrogating the Camp David accords (which prohibit change in the legal status of the territories except as the result of negotiation) intensified. In his capacity as acting foreign minister, Begin asked the attorney general to consider legal solutions to the problem advanced by Member of Knesset Haim Druckman on behalf of Gush Emunim.[14] Begin also met personally with the Elon Moreh settlers to discuss ways to avoid a confrontation over evacuation of the site. In December he promised Hammer, Ben-Meir, and Druckman that he would speed the land survey process in the territories designed to identify state land and facilitate Jewish settlement upon it.[15] The creation of a special inter-ministerial committee on settlement affairs, including Sharon and Weizman, but chaired by Begin, was made public. It met and announced the inauguration of an ambitious and systematic fleshing out of existing settlements in five "settlement blocs." At least two cabinet ministers (Simcha Erlich and Shmuel Tamir) opposed this decision because of its expense and because, they argued, it stemmed directly from pressure exerted by Gush Emunim and its political supporters in the National Religious Party.[16]

Finally, on January 17, the sixty members of the Elon Moreh settlement announced that they would peaceably move to the nearby site provided by the government. In their announcement they drew attention to the "serious situation regarding the legal status of the settlements" that had been uncovered. They stressed that their decision to abide by the Supreme Court's judgment was influenced by the impression gained from their meeting with Begin that he "would act to improve the situation" and by "a commitment undertaken by 30 Knesset members to act to change the legal situation in Judea and Samaria."[17] Indeed, within six weeks at least five proposals for change in the legal status of settlement in the occupied territories were under consideration by the cabinet and the attorney general's office.

But the transfer of the Elon Moreh settlement did not bring an end to Gush Emunim's campaign of political pressure with regard to land and settlement questions. Judging that implementation of the cabinet decisions was proceeding too slowly and that not enough land was being made available for Jewish settlement, and concerned about what they perceived as Defense Minister Weizman's moderating influence on the pace and extent of settlement, six heads of Jewish regional and local councils in the West Bank and Gaza (all members of Gush Emunim) began a hunger strike outside the Knesset on March 19, 1980. The strikers demanded immediate cabinet action in fulfillment of commitments made to the Elon Moreh settlers. Joined by other well-known Gush personalities, the hunger strike continued for more than six weeks. Prime Minister Begin was reported to have tearfully approached the strikers, trying to convince them to end their fast. In an interview he declared that they were not "seeking something that is contrary to the views of the government." The problem, said Begin, was that "this is a complex legal matter. The bill has to be worded clearly and we have to take all kinds of legal aspects under consideration. Therefore, this takes time."[18] Legal difficulties and opposition from Weizman resulted in a series of delays and postponements in the presentation of draft legislation to the Knesset. Nevertheless, on May 2 the hunger strikers declared an end to their fast. Yisrael Harel, speaking on behalf of the strikers and Yesha, explained that the fast had been concluded as a result of

> sufficient and unambiguous commitments . . . that a legal and immediate solution will be found for the problem of the existence, development and expansion of the existent settlements in Judea, Samaria, and the Gaza district and of settlements to be established in the future.

Harel continued as follows, apparently referring to Sharon and Begin:

... the guarantees are from determining factors in our state. Those factors have asked us time and again to stop the strike so that their final public decision is not made under the pressure of the strike. So far we did not have sufficient guarantees that the decision would indeed be made very soon. Now that we are in the possession of those guarantees—we have received very binding guarantees—we believe that the decision will be made. Then, the decision will be published by the factors making it.[19]

One week later the cabinet adopted the Attorney General's recommendation that a special ministerial committee be formed to develop administrative measures to safeguard existing settlements from legal challenges, provide land for seven particular settlements surrounded by privately owned Arab land, and create opportunities for expanded settlement and land acquisition within the legal constraints established by the Supreme Court. Sharon, Gush Emunim's most vigorous patron in the cabinet, advocated sweeping new legislation to change the legal framework in the territories. Accordingly, he cast the only vote against this cabinet decision. But he muted his criticism, since the cabinet had chosen him to chair the newly created committee. On May 15, the government announced a five-year plan for the establishment of fifty-nine additional settlements in the West Bank. Ten days later, frustrated in part with the government's responsiveness to Gush Emunim demands and the implications of that responsiveness for any positive outcome to the autonomy negotiations, Defense Minister Weizman resigned. Sharon then moved quickly to develop and implement an elaborate array of administrative devices to bypass legal restrictions enforced by the Court on the seizure of land for use by Jewish settlements. Combined with declarations of large areas as state land, these new procedures brought an effective, if not formal, end to the ability of Arabs to protect their lands from seizure by appealing to the Supreme Court. As a result, within a year and a half so much land was transferred to Jewish, and mostly Gush Emunim, control that the settlers virtually ceased raising the issue of land acquisition or the question of the legal status of the territories.[20]

The Elon Moreh episode clearly illustrates how relatively small numbers of Jewish fundamentalists, enjoying close political and personal ties with powerful figures in the Likud and the National Religious Party and possessing impressive public relations skills, were able to exert enormous influence. Important government policies were changed, careers of leading politicians were advanced or hindered, international negotiations were adversely affected, and the pace of de facto annexation of the West Bank and Gaza Strip was substantially quickened. Moreover, this influence was exerted while the fundamentalist movement lacked coherent overall organization, and while the party most closely associated with it, Tehiya (whose evolution is described below), was out of the government.

By this time, Gush Emunim had also entered an intense period of institutional elaboration and internal political realignment. In addition to the repeated disappointments it experienced vis-à-vis Likud government policy, it was seeking to address new kinds of issues created by progress in the actual implementation of its visionary program. Before 1979, although thousands of Israelis identified with Gush Emunim and shared a powerful commitment to the permanent incorporation of the whole Land of Israel within the Jewish state, an organizational basis for carrying out Gush programs or translating the fervent commitment of its activists into entrenched positions of political power was absent. To a large extent Gush leaders blamed their failure to prevent the Camp David accords and, the April 1982 withdrawal from Yamit on the absence of an effective, sophisticated political organization that could arouse masses of Israelis not directly involved in settling the territories.

The Social and Political Base of Jewish Fundamentalism. From 1977 to 1984 Gush Emunim developed from a rather loose association of settlement activists and ultranationalist rabbis, writers, and military figures into an umbrella movement containing an elaborate array of interdependent organizations, each specializing in particular aspects of the overall fundamentalist/redemptionist struggle or in appeals to one or another particular constituency. These organizations have drawn most of their recruits from a mass base composed of many overlapping segments of Israeli society.

The most visible part of this recruitment pool were the West Bank and Gaza settlers themselves. Few in number until the late 1970s, the young Gush Emunim settlements in Samaria, the Etzion bloc, and Kiryat Arba attracted the most idealistic and dynamic fundamentalist activists. The leaders and apparatchiks of the movement, operating in close contact with more senior spiritual/rabbinical guidance, were drawn mainly from the individuals attracted to these settlements. The decisive majority were young, Ashkenazic, well educated, upper middle class, and highly motivated. To be sure, with the emergence of relatively large urban settlements, the Jewish population in the West Bank, as well as in the Gaza Strip and the Golan Heights, has become increasingly diverse. But self-selection by new settlers and the common problems associated with living in occupied areas amid a majority of hostile Arabs have kept the settlements, which now contain nearly 70,000 inhabitants (excluding expanded East Jerusalem), a natural base of support for Gush Emunim.

Before 1948 the Yishuv educated most of its children in three separate school systems. The largest was the "socialist Zionist stream," operated by the Histadrut (the Labor Zionist Federation of Trade Unions). Another network of schools was sponsored by the centrist General Zionist party. The third was the Mizrahi school system. Shortly after the state was created the socialist Zionist school system was submerged, along with the General Zionist stream, within the "official" state educational framework. But a "state religious" school system and the traditional ultra-Orthodox schools were allowed to continue as separate entities. The influence of the fundamentalist-oriented Young Guard was felt relatively early in the state religious school system, which has included 25–30 percent of Israeli Jewish students. In contrast to the secular left, which lost the steady stream of youthful graduates of its partisan educational system when the socialist Zionist stream was absorbed by the state system, the religious sector has had its ranks replenished by individuals educated and socialized within a strong Jewish religious framework. The religious school system has thus been an important source of recruits for Gush Emunim, which is perceived by many of its graduates as religious Jewry's candidate to replace the socialists as leaders of the Zionist movement.

Closely associated with the religious school system has been Bnei Akiva. Founded more than sixty years ago, it presently has 25,000–30,000 members active in 150 branches. It operates thirty educational and other institutions and has helped found scores of cooperative and collective settlements, including many of those in the West Bank and Gaza. Bnei Akiva originated from the religious kibbutz movement, and a large proportion of its leadership traditionally has come from religious kibbutzim. But after the Six Day War, Bnei Akiva turned its energies away from traditional notions of "Torah and Labor" toward the question of the whole Land of Israel and the messianic ideas surrounding that question. Embodying the so-called generation of the knitted yarmulka, Bnei Akiva members and graduates have prided themselves on their idealism and their ability to combine patriotic duty, including military service and settlement, with religious observance and study. With the emergence of the Young Guard of the National Religious Party as its political inspiration, Bnei Akiva soon became a national political force to be reckoned with. In the mid-1970s Gush Emunim drew thousands of Bnei Akiva youths into its marches, demonstrations, and settlement actions.

Recruitment of religious school and Bnei Akiva graduates into Gush Emunim was facilitated by an institutional innovation adopted by the army, in cooperation with religious educators, the Yeshivot Hesder. Many teachers and directors in "national religious" yeshivas were eager to free themselves from a sense of inferiority relative to the ultra-Orthodox, even while moving toward more active participation, and more political power, in Israeli society. Frameworks were thus created within which religious high school graduates could fulfill their military service while stationed at religious seminaries located in the newly occupied territories. Modeled after the army's Nahal units, in which young Israelis interested in kibbutz life could join units whose work was divided between agriculture and military training, the Yeshivot Hesder, established after the Six Day War, permitted religious youths to divide their time in the army between military service and religious study. The overwhelming majority of the teachers in these yeshivas were oriented toward the outlook and policies that became associated with Gush Emunim. Indeed, it was expected that the majority of Yeshivot Hesder graduates would remain as settlers in the

occupied territories. Fourteen Yeshivot Hesder are now function-
ing, with an annual enrollment of approximately 3,500 students.
For an important segment of the national religious youth, they
have served to bridge the gap between adolescent education and
scouting activities and adult political commitment.

Two important segments of the nonreligious sector of Israeli
society have also provided Gush Emunim with substantial
numbers of recruits: the activist Labor Zionist movement and the
Herut party. Supporters of the former, as explained above, tended
toward expansive conceptions of the proper territorial extent of
Jewish sovereignty and were traditionally committed to the idea of
creating settlements as a means of determining future political
borders. Determined secularists, they yet found a common language with Gush organizers in their devotion to the Land of Israel
as the highest operational imperative. They provided Gush Emunim with large numbers of experienced settlers with agricultural,
organizational and military skills. They also provided a crucial
symbolic link between Gush Emunim's often illegal settlement
activities in the West Bank and Gaza and the Labor Zionist movement's famous "watchtower and stockade" illegal settlement campaign under the British mandate. Many of these supporters came
to Gush Emunim in the mid-1970s through the Movement for the
Whole Land of Israel.

In the 1930s two Revisionist Party members were accused of
murdering Chaim Arlosoroff, a leading Labor Zionist; Rav
Abraham Isaac Kook came to their aid. At least one leader of the
Irgun, David Raziel, spent some time as a student at Merkaz
HaRav during that period. Those ties and the similarly "visionary"
terms, centered on the Land of Israel, in which both Revisionists
and Kookists think of Zionism may help explain the close relationship that developed after 1967 between Herut circles and Merkaz
HaRav.[21] Nor did it hurt these relations that Begin himself began
regularly to employ religious imagery and display outward signs of
religious observance. Once the Likud came to power, Gush activists enjoyed easy and direct access to cabinet ministers and high-
level bureaucrats. Gush Emunim has drawn some of its most
articulate publicists, such as Israel Eldad and Eliezer Schweid, and
its best-known political patrons, including Ariel Sharon, Geula
Cohen, Yitzhak Shamir, and Menachem Begin himself, from the

ranks of the Revisionist movement and the veteran members of the prestate dissident undergrounds, Lehi (Freedom Fighters for Israel, also known as "the Stern Gang") and the Irgun. As we shall see, in the wake of the Egypt–Israel peace treaty, a number of leading personalities within Herut deserted that party and joined with some religious leaders of Gush Emunim to found Tehiya.[22]

While the above groups have provided skilled activists and powerful supporters to Gush Emunim, the electoral strength of the Likud, translated into support for the program of the movement, has been based largely on the votes of Sephardic Jews (those whose families came to Isreal from the Middle East or North Africa) who have entered into Israeli politics. In the late 1970s their resentment at being effectively excluded from the Labor- and Ashkenazic-dominated Israeli establishment found increasing expression in their adoption of maximalist, anti-Arab political positions.

The Organizational Elaboration and the Exercise of Power. The closest thing Gush Emunim has had to an overall representative body has been Yesha. Based in the Gush settlement of Ofra (in the West Bank, northeast of Ramallah), Yesha began as an association of representatives from various regional councils established by groups of West Bank and Gaza settlements with the assistance of the Ministry of Interior. It developed into an important coordinative organization that lobbies on behalf of settler interests and Gush programs with government ministries, the military government, and Jewish Agency offices; provides administrative resources and political guidance to settlements; and has played a key role in the design of zoning and development plans for the expansion of Jewish settler access to land and the regulation of Arab municipal growth.

In December 1979, Yesha launched *Nekuda* (Point), a monthly journal edited to this day by Yisrael Harel, a professional journalist and Gush activist who has also served as Yesha's general secretary. The first issue dealt extensively with the Supreme Court decision, a month and a half earlier, that had dismantled the Elon Moreh. The next few issues dealt with a variety of issues facing Gush Emunim—protests against settlement expenditure by Jewish slum dwellers, relations with the Arabs, the autonomy plan, and the hunger strike organized by Gush leaders in protest against what they perceived as the crisis in land acquisition brought on by the 1979 Supreme Court decision. *Nekuda* quickly developed into the primary forum for expression of settler opinion and the in-house deliberation of all salient issues confronting Gush Emunim.[23]

When the Camp David Accords were signed in 1978—a move that Gush Emunim bitterly opposed—it precipitated a crisis for Gush supporters within Herut and the National Religious Party, both of which officially backed the accords. One result was the formation of Tehiya, the first political party traceable to Gush Emunim, though neither officially endorsed by it nor supported by a majority of Gush members. Tehiya was founded as an independent party comprised of both religious and nonreligious ultranationalists. Instructively, it originated in a meeting held in March 1979 at the home of Rav Tzvi Yehuda Kook that was attended by several key religious figures in Gush Emunim, some prominent members of Herut, and leaders of what was left of the Movement for the Whole Land of Israel. Discussions focused on the implications of Begin's "betrayal" of the cause and the failure of Gush Emunim and other ultranationalist elements to prevent it.

Rav Tzvi Yehuda's endorsement of Yuval Neeman—Israel's leading nuclear physicist and a secular ultranationalist—to head the new party, as well as his emphasis on the overwhelming significance of the Land of Israel dimension of the redemption process, overcame both severe personal rivalries and religious differences within the group.

> The Land of Israel is neither religious nor secular. It belongs to the whole Jewish people. The religious and secular frameworks should be discontinued. Today the Land of Israel is the focal point for the redemption. Both the religious and secular camps should compromise on any controversial issues.[24]

On this basis, and without any religious language or mention of religious law beyond a vague call for "return to our Jewish heritage and a revival of the spirit . . . of pioneering Zionism," Tehiya was formed. In the elections of 1981 it received 44,500 votes and placed three deputies in the parliament: Yuval Neeman, Geula Cohen, and Hanan Porat. In 1984 its vote total rose to 83,000, resulting in a Knesset delegation of five deputies.

In addition to Tehiya, two other organizational manifestations of Jewish fundamentalism, staffed largely by individuals active within Gush Emunim, need to be considered: Amana and the Movement to Halt the Retreat in Sinai.

Amana was actually begun in 1976 as Gush Emunim's own small settlement organization. As such, it marked the beginning of Gush's transition from a fringe group specializing in protest demonstrations and illegal political events, to a broad movement including within its purview practical efforts to establish and consolidate viable Jewish settlements. In the spring of 1980, however, with Gush Emunim's informal secretariat of leading personalities effectively disbanded, and with settlement and land acquisition activities rapidly accelerating, Amana announced that for all intents and purposes *it* was Gush Emunim and could speak on its behalf.[25]

Amana played a particularly important role in the months before the May 1981 elections, as a debate raged within Gush Emunim over which, if any, of the political parties deserved support. Sharing the Likud's fear that a Labor victory would revive the Allon Plan, both Amana and Yesha cooperated closely with the Likud government to establish as many settlements and to seize as much land as possible before the elections. Much to the relief of Gush Emunim, the Likud won the elections, but that did not interrupt the government's intention to complete the withdrawal from Sinai by April 23, 1982, including the evacuation of 5,000 Jewish settlers from the Yamit district, in fulfillment of the Egypt–Israel peace treaty. After the shock of Yamit's evacuation, Gush Emunim formally reconstituted its secretariat, but Amana remained. By the spring of 1983 Amana had ten full-time staff members, representatives in Europe and the United States, and an annual budget approaching $2 million.

Indeed, it was opposition to the evacuation of Yamit that led to the establishment of another important organization related to Gush Emunim, the Movement to Halt the Retreat in Sinai. The first groups to mobilize against the withdrawal were businessmen and farmers living in Yamit. Having moved to the district with official encouragement and lavish government assistance, they had established a comfortable and profitable life. Their organized opposition dissolved, however, amid prolonged and, for Gush Emunim, embarrassing negotiations over just how generous the relocation and compensation packages awarded by the government would be.[26]

In the spring of 1981 the organization was formed. Leading roles were taken by two overlapping groups: Gush activists from Tehiya and Yesha, fearful that evacuation of Jewish settlements in Sinai in return for peace would set a dangerous precedent for the West Bank and Gaza, and a number of rabbis committed to the principle that Yamit was an integral part of the Land of Israel, the abandonment of which would severely interrupt the process of redemption. The organization's primary objective was to stop the withdrawal through mass mobilization of public opinion. The fallback position, if the primary objective proved impossible to achieve, was to engineer such a dramatic and painful clash between the government and settlers opposing withdrawal that the memory of the psychological and political trauma would inhibit any future government with inclinations to evacuate settlements elsewhere.

In August 1981 Yesha passed resolutions urging West Bank and Gaza settlers to join actively in the organization. Hundreds of Gush settlers from the West Bank infiltrated into Yamit, taking up residence in houses evacuated by settlers who had accepted compensation. In September the organization launched a countrywide petition campaign to express what it claimed was the opposition of most Israelis to implementing the withdrawal from Sinai. The petition was widely circulated, but the movement's declared goal of one million signatures apparently was not met.[27] In March 1982 an antiwithdrawal rally at the Western Wall in Jerusalem drew more than 40,000 demonstrators. The final stage of activity was an attempt to concentrate 100,000 opponents of withdrawal in Yamit itself to confront the army on April 22, when it was to receive the order to complete the evacuation.

In its effort to rally wider sections of the public, the organization employed appeals designed to obscure the spiritual/redemptive ideology that actually motivated most of its leadership. Its propaganda and public statements instead focused on the security dangers that would be associated with the withdrawal, the undependability of Egyptian and American guarantees, and the contradiction of Zionist pioneering values that abandonment of the settlements would represent.[28]

However, truly widespread public support to halt the withdrawal process was not forthcoming. In the weeks preceding April 22, the Movement to Halt the Retreat in Sinai managed to concentrate no more than several thousand supporters (mostly yeshiva students) in Yamit to resist the army. Fully televised confrontations occurred, including some pushing and shoving, but despite reports that extremist groups were ready to resist with arms and explosives, and despite threats by supporters of Meir Kahane to commit suicide if the operation was not halted, the evacuation was completed by unarmed soldiers without serious injury. Many of the evacuees, including such leading Gush figures as Beni Katzover, Moshe Levinger, and Haim Druckman, formed a new organization Shvut Yisrael (Israel's Return), dedicated to returning Jewish rule to Sinai. The Yeshiva Hesder located in Yamit and several groups of Yamit settlers belonging to Shvut Yisrael were reestablished in settlements across the border in the Gaza Strip.

In subsequent years Gush Emunim has attempted to turn the anniversary of the "uprooting of Yamit" into a national day of remembrance and rededication. But neither the "national trauma" it sought to inflict nor the yearning for a return to Sinai it has sought to engender has taken hold beyond its own ranks.

Gush Emunim and Related Groups in the Aftermath of Yamit and the Lebanon War. Within Gush Emunim the failure of the Movement to Halt the Retreat in Sinai *was* traumatic. It occurred just six weeks after the death of Rav Tzvi Yehuda and just six weeks before the outbreak of the Lebanon War. Both of these events sharpened emerging divisions within the movement. In this context, the evacuation of Yamit precipitated a severe crisis of confidence within Gush Emunim, a reevaluation of the movement's hitherto primary focus on the establishment of "pioneering" settlements, and another series of organizational experiments.

In symposia sponsored by Gush Emunim to discuss the meaning and implications of the Yamit disaster,[29] some argued that the failure was due to the overconfidence displayed by many religious leaders that in the end, God would intervene to prevent the evacuation. Others argued that it was the spiritual imperfection of the Yamit settlers that explained the debacle. Others interpreted it as the inscrutable will of God.

The political conclusions drawn from the episode were of two opposing varieties. Many Gush militants identified the key problem as a failure to integrate the fundamentalist movement's efforts with the concerns of the Israeli mainstream. They advocated a broadly gauged campaign of political and cultural outreach to Israelis not actively involved in the fundamentalist movement. The second kind of conclusion emphasized the undependability of the government and the Israeli public where matters of redemption were concerned. This analysis stressed the imperative of acting purely and decisively to establish or destroy political facts according to the will of God, regardless of the temporary opposition of most Israelis or the government.

These two conclusions strengthened two opposing trends in the development of Jewish fundamentalism in Israel in the 1980s—political and cultural outreach, and direct action and violence.

Political and Cultural Outreach

According to the first interpretation, the failure in Sinai was due to the isolation of Gush Emunim from the wider Israeli public. This isolation explains why Gush was caught off guard by the enthusiasm with which so many Israelis greeted Sadat's visit to Israel and the subsequent Camp David Accords, and why the effort to "save Sinai" did not get off the ground until it was too late. To prevent the repeat of Yamit in Judea and Samaria, much larger numbers of Jews had to be persuaded to settle in the territories than could be mobilized from the ranks of Gush Emunim itself, and a great deal more emphasis had to be placed on effective political organization and ideological and cultural outreach within Israeli society as a whole.

This focus on increasing the number of Jewish residents in the West Bank beyond some decisive point received enthusiastic and generous support from the Likud government, which energetically implemented policies in support of this objective from the fall of 1982 through the winter of 1984. These programs entailed the investment of truly gigantic amounts of public money in the subsidization of garden suburbs in the West Bank and Gaza Strip. By offering spacious homes at cut-rate prices, and rapid transportation to jobs located in metropolitan areas the government could attract tens, and eventually hundreds, of thousands of non-ideological, upwardly mobile Israelis to live in those areas.[30]

The strategy of political outreach also entailed a flurry of attempts to revitalize Gush Emunim's organizational structure and to create new political parties that could mobilize broader support for fundamentalist goals. Rabbi Haim Druckman played a central role in these personal and political maneuvers. Druckman is credited with having coined the name Gush Emunim at a meeting of its early leadership in his home in February 1974. A fervent, very observant, and mystically inclined leader of the Young Guard, he was number two on the National Religious Party's list for the 1981 Knesset elections, but opposed his party's support of the Camp David accords. He played an active role in the Movement to Halt Retreat in Sinai and threatened as early as January 1981 to bolt from the National Religious Party in protest against the planned evacuation. In March 1983 Druckman left the party to establish his own party, Matzad (the Religious Zionism Camp). Druckman's appeal was directed to the yeshiva wing of the National Religious Party, the participants in the Yeshivot Hesder. Early in 1984 Druckman was joined by Hanan Porat, who left Tehiya because of its secularist stance and who failed in his own short-lived attempt to found a new political movement in the spirit of the Kooks—Orot (Lights). Attempting to build a more broadly based religious ultranationalist movement, Matzad joined with an ultra-Orthodox party, Poalei Agudat Yisrael (Pagi), whose fiercely anti-Arab stance and support of settlement in the West Bank were allowed to compensate for its officially "non-Zionist" character. This new alliance entered the July 1984 parliamentary elections under the name Morasha (Tradition), emphasizing the religious side of Gush Emunim's appeal. In head-to-head competition with Tehiya and the Likud, it received 21 percent of the votes cast by Gush settlers in 1984, but many more votes from Israelis within the green line. Although it placed two deputies in the Knesset, Morasha was disappointed by its performance.[31] In July 1986 the party came to an end with its redivision into Matzad and Pagi.

The secularist emphasis in Tehiya, which prevented Druckman from entering that party and drove Porat from it, was strengthened by its alliance with Tzomet (the Movement for Zionist

Renewal), founded in 1983 by superhawk Rafael Eitan, who had just retired as chief of staff. The 1,300 activists who formed Tzomet were drawn from the ranks of activist Labor collective and cooperative settlements. The movement's platform emphasized its commitment to Jewish sovereignty over the whole Land of Israel, including the Golan Heights, the need to respond to the "traitorous" behavior of the dovish left during the Lebanon War, and a Spartan philosophy of militarism, discipline, and pioneering austerity. In 1984 Tzomet and the Tehiya party formed a joint list for the Knesset. Eitan was placed in the number two position, between Yuval Neeman and Geula Cohen. Thus, the first three positions in Tehiya's 1984 Knesset list were held by secular ultranationalists. Rabbi Eleazar Waldman, in the fourth position, was the most prominent religious figure still associated with the party and the only one elected to the Knesset on the Tehiya ticket in 1984. Gershon Shafat, another Gush Emunim stalwart and also religious, was the fifth candidate elected to the Knesset that year. Tehiya received 23 percent of the votes cast in Gush settlements.[32]

By 1984, then, little was left of Gush Emunim's original principle forbidding the active participation of its leadership in political parties. Still, in the wake of the Yamit disaster and the gradual withdrawal from Lebanon, Gush Emunim made repeated attempts to construct some sort of overall administrative-political framework, including a major effort following the political fragmentation of the fundamentalist movement in the 1984 elections. In August of that year 1984 Yesha adopted a wide-ranging and detailed list of bylaws specifying its political objectives and institutional structure. It identified the Yesha Council as "representing the settlers and settlements of Judea, Samaria, and Gaza, in the public political arena on a non-partisan basis."[33] In February 1985 Gush Emunim announced it had formed a fifty-person secretariat and ten-member action committee, and had appointed a new general secretary, Daniella Weiss, a member of the original Elon Moreh garin and a religious activist in Tehiya. It also announced plans for an educational council of rabbis and other learned men were. In its editorial praising these developments, *Nekuda* noted just how disorganized Gush Emunim had become.

The public as a whole responded to these developments with surprise. It appears that Gush Emunim, even in the absence of orderly and coordinated activities, is seen in the eyes of the public as gigantic, well-organized, and ideologically influential. . . . It appears that only within the movement itself was it known that in recent years Gush Emunim carried out no organized activities and that most of the key personalities who served as its leadership had found other political or public frameworks within which to pursue their spiritual and political objectives.[34]

The immediate catalyst for the creation of the Gush Emunim secretariat, and the most divisive issue to emerge within the Jewish fundamentalist movement since its inception, was the question of the organized use of illegal violence. According to official Gush spokesman Noam Arnon, had it not been for the new organizational effort, the arrest of the Jewish terrorist underground in April 1984 would have destroyed the movement.

The bitter controversy that erupted within our camp following the arrests was liable to have been, God forbid, the final split, the decisive schism, from which we would not have been able to recover as a broad, united movement. . . . But at the last possible moment, and with the help of God, Gush Emunim revived itself.[35]

Analysis of the continuing debate inside of Gush Emunim over the origins, consequences, and implications of the machteret will provide valuable insights into the Jewish fundamentalist worldview and the range of acceptable disagreement within it. In the balance of this chapter, I provide the background for that analysis.

Direct Action and Violence

The second kind of conclusion many Jewish fundamentalists drew from the Yamit episode led not in the direction of mass settlement or conventional political and educational action to mobilize political support and build a new Israeli consensus, but toward confrontational postures combined with dramatic and, especially, violent actions. The proliferation of groups implementing such strategies reflects the deep distrust toward the Likud government that the Camp David peace process as a whole, and the Yamit evacuation in particular, engendered within the Jewish fundamentalist movement. The general intent of those who have responded to the events of 1982 in this manner has been twofold: to eliminate opportunities for a negotiated peace agreement that otherwise might be exploited by what they would consider fainthearted or traitorous Israeli governments; and to do so by means of actions that would themselves advance the process of redemption. Of particular importance in this context were the rise of Meir Kahane and his extremist Kach movement, a dramatic escalation in attacks by underground Jewish terrorist groups against Arabs and dovishly inclined Jews, and a burgeoning campaign to change the political and religious status quo in sensitive locations such as the city centers of Nablus and Hebron and the Temple Mount in the Old City of Jerusalem.

The existence of various vigilante and terrorist groups within the fundamentalist movement can be traced to the shocked reaction of many of its activists to the Camp David accords and the implementation of the withdrawal from Yamit.[36] In 1979, at the behest of Chief of Staff Eitan, Jewish settlers in the West Bank and Gaza Strip were integrated into regular reserve units responsible for patrolling local Arab areas. With weapons, ammunition, and training readily available, and a sympathetic political climate created by Chief of Staff Eitan and Defense Minister Sharon, attacks on Arabs and Arab property became commonplace. In June 1980, following an Arab attack on Hebron settlers that left six Jews dead, car bombs severely injured the mayors of Nablus and Ramallah as well as one border policeman. The Yamit evacuation, frustrations associated with the Lebanon War, and rising levels of Arab militancy in the territories accelerated the activities of the Jewish terrorist underground, setting the stage for another major action in July 1983, in which three Arabs were killed in an attack by masked gunmen on the Islamic College in Hebron.

But these were only the most spectacular events in a wave of less serious vigilantism and terror that swept through the West Bank and Jerusalem from 1980 through 1984. During that period the Israeli press reported more than 380 attacks against individuals, in which 23 were killed, 191 injured, and 38 abducted. Hundreds more attacks were directed at property—automobiles, homes, and shops. Forty-one attacks on Muslim and Christian religious institutions were counted.[37] Broadly speaking this violence was carried out by three distinct but inter-related groups.

Meir Kahane and "Kach". Meir Kahane is a fiery American-born rabbi, who founded the Brooklyn-based Jewish Defense League. Under investigation by the FBI, he left the United States in 1971 and created another movement in Israel—Kach. In 1980 he was arrested and held in administrative detention by the Israeli authorities for six months, reportedly on suspicion of participating in a plot to destroy the Muslim shrines on the Temple Mount. He endorsed and is suspected of having been behind the activities of a shadowy group or groups known as TNT (Terror against Terror), which claimed responsibility for a long series of violent attacks against West Bank Arabs, Christian missionaries in Jerusalem, and dovish Israeli Jews. He has publicly praised violent attacks against Arabs and has led his followers repeatedly to Arab villages, addressing the residents as "dogs" and warning them to leave the country.

In three unsuccessful campaigns for election to the Knesset he appealed to Jewish voters on an overtly racist platform, proposing laws that would forbid intimate contact between Jews and Arabs and promising to rid the country of its Arab population through intimidation, discriminatory legislation, and enforced servitude. Then, in 1984, drawing support mainly from poor, undereducated Sephardic Jews, he received 29,907 votes, sufficient to put him into the Knesset. Although Kach has established two small settlements on the West Bank, it received only 3–6 percent of the vote in Gush Emunim settlements.[38] But in 1985 Kahane had enough support in Kiryat Arba, the largest of all Gush settlements, to give Kach two seats on the local council and a role in its governing coalition.

Activities of Temple Mount Related Groups. The small plateau behind the Western Wall in the Old City of Jerusalem is reputed to be the biblical Mount Moriah, where, according to Genesis, Abraham offered Isaac as a sacrifice. It is where both Solomon's Temple and Herod's Temple were built. Indeed, the Western Wall itself is a retaining wall for the courtyard of Herod's Temple, the only portion of the structure that remains intact. The plateau is sacred for Muslims as well as for Jews. Mohammed is said to have ascended to heaven from it. The magnificent Dome of the Rock was constructed upon it to mark the exact spot of his ascent. The el-Aksa Mosque, also located on the plateau, is the third holiest shrine in Islam—following those in Mecca and Medina. While Jews refer to the area as the Har Habayit (Temple Mount), Muslims call it Haram el Sharif (Noble Sanctuary). The halacha bars religious Jews from setting foot on the Temple Mount plateau since the exact location of the Holy of Holies, into which entry by anyone other than the High Priest was strictly forbidden, is unknown. Supervision of the Muslim shrines has thus been left largely to Muslim authorities in Jerusalem.

Since 1967, however, at least five separate groups, with a total estimated membership of 1,500, have sought to change that.[39] Their objectives range from building a Jewish synagogue on the site to exercising full Jewish sovereignty, restricting Arab/Muslim access to the area, and even replacing the Muslim shrines with a rebuilt Temple. Most of their activities are peaceful, but in addition to two acts of arson and murder on the Temple Mount by deranged individuals in 1969 and 1982, a number of illegal, sometimes violent, attempts to change the status quo on the Temple Mount have been made.

In May 1980 the police uncovered a plot to blow up the el-Aksa Mosque. A large cache of explosives was discovered on the roof of a yeshiva in the Old City of Jerusalem. The conspirators were two soldiers with links to Kach and to Gush Emunim. Roni Milo, a leading Herut politician, defended them at their trial. It was at this time that Meir Kahane and one of his lieutenants were arrested and held for six months in administrative detention.

In March 1983 several dozen religious zealots were arrested after a Muslim guard on the Temple Mount heard digging underground. Equipped with arms, shovels, and diagrams of the underground passageways leading to the area, the group appears to have planned to seize the Temple Mount and hold public prayer services there. Participants included soldiers and yeshiva students from Kiryat Arba and Jerusalem. Most of those arrested in connection with the incident were discovered in the home of Rabbi Yisrael Ariel, a prominent activist within Gush Emunim, known for his extreme views. Ariel was the number two candidate on the Kach list in the 1981 elections. Hanan Porat, Moshe Levinger, Eleazar Waldman, and other Gush leaders who appeared to have had prior knowledge of the operation criticized its modus operandi, but expressed support for the group's objectives.

On the night of January 27, 1984, an Arab guard interrupted a small group of unidentified intruders in the immediate vicinity of the Muslim shrines. When police reinforcements arrived, the intruders had escaped, but their intentions were apparent from what they had left behind—thirty pounds of explosives, fuses, detonators, and twenty two grenades. Bombs had been prepared with considerable expertise, suggesting the participation of army veterans with demolition experience.

The Gush Emunim Underground. By far the best organized effort to destroy the el-Aksa Mosque and the Dome of the Rock was undertaken by a group of Gush Emunim activists from the West Bank This plot was carefully and systematically developed between 1978 and 1982. An army officer with a high level of expertise in explosives was involved, and sufficient munitions to carry out the operation were stolen from the Israel Defense Forces. The plan was aborted following the group's failure to gain explicit approval from leading Gush rabbis.

Details of this conspiracy were uncovered after the arrest, on April 27, 1984, of twenty-five Gush activists, mostly West Bank settlers, who were charged in connection with the placement of bombs under five Arab buses. The police had thwarted the bombings at the last minute. During the interrogation and trial of the accused, their responsibility for the attacks on the Arab mayors and the Islamic College was established. Several among this group were also charged and convicted in connection with the 1978–1982 plot to destroy the Temple Mount.

What is so significant about this network of Jewish terrorists is that virtually all of them were respected members of the Gush Emunim mainstream, with close and in some cases very personal ties to the leadership of the movement. They included one rabbi (director of a religious school in Kiryat Arba), a former general secretary of Gush Emunim, a former member of Gush Emunim's secretariat, the head of the Committee for Renewal of Jewish Settlement in Hebron, several officers in the army reserve, the son of one of the Gush founders, a *Nekuda* reporter, and a certified war hero. Indeed in their backgrounds as soldiers, pioneering farmers, political activists, and observant Jews, they corresponded in almost every detail to the Gush Emunim ideal. And, apart from one or two individuals, they expressed no serious regrets about their deeds. One of the organizers of the network, and its leading theoretician, was Yehuda Etzion, who began serving a seven-year prison sentence in 1982 for his role in the attack on the Arab mayors and in the conspiracy to blow up the Temple Mount.[40] At his trial Etzion said that he had been "privileged to cut off the legs of some of the murderers."[41]

The initial public reaction of Gush Emunim to the arrests was one of stunned silence and official statements, by the Yesha Council, of the unacceptable nature of the alleged behavior of the accused, the importance of emphasizing the government's responsibility for controlling Arab violence, and the need for a thorough process of soul-searching within the movement to determine how terrorist attacks on Arab women and children could be carried out by "good religious boys"—"some of our best comrades."[42]

But as details of the activities and histories of the accused became known, it became clear to most observers that leading figures within Gush Emunim, including Moshe Levinger and Eleazar Waldman, must have provided at least tacit approval for their actions. Indeed, rather quickly the publicly expressed sentiment within Gush Emunim and the wider publics from which it has drawn support shifted. The activities of the underground were portrayed as an understandable and perhaps even necessary reaction to the failure of the authorities to provide for the personal security of Jewish settlers—particularly in regard to stone throwing against settler vehicles on the roads of the West Bank. Settlers and politicians from Tehiya, Morasha, and the Likud flocked to the prison where the accused were held to express their sympathy and support. An organization of settlers quickly formed to provide legal and financial assistance to the defendants and their families. Debates continued for a long time inside the movement over the implications of the affair. But within two months the Yesha Council and the editorial board of *Nekuda* admitted that they had come under severe attack from within Gush Emunim for their "hasty" condemnation of the machteret. They immediately threw their support behind the effort to provide moral, financial, and political support to the defendants.[43] In July 1985 both Yesha and *Nekuda* joined the families of the defendants in a demand for a blanket pardon. From July 1984 to April 1986 *Nekuda* published a series of five lengthy articles by Yehuda Etzion, written in his prison cell, presenting an elaborate ideological, political, and theological justification for his actions.

The material presented so far suggests how complex are the various components of ideology, organization, tactics, and leadership that have made up the Jewish fundamentalist movement in Israel. The period since 1974, when Gush Emunim was formed, has been a tumultuous time in Israeli politics, and it has been no more stable for the fundamentalist movement than for any other segment of Israeli society. Though Gush Emunim has formed its ideological and organizational core, several of the groups and many of the individuals who have played a prominent role in the advancement of fundamentalist objectives cannot be identified as belonging to Gush Emunim per se. Nor has one organization, including Gush Emunim at its most coherent, ever included within its scope all the radical national-religious and secular-ultra-nationalist activity that must be considered part of the fundamentalist phenomenon. In the next chapter, however, I will show that elements within the worldview of Jewish fundamentalism give the movement a coherence that might seem surprising, in light of its organizational fragmentation and the heterogeneity of those groups within Israeli society from which it has drawn support.

IV

The Worldview of Jewish Fundamentalism: The Breadth of Consensus

To understand the Jewish fundamentalist movement, one must remember that the perceptual and ideological categories shared within it do not serve some ethereal, symbolic purpose, but actually guide interpretation of daily events. They are the basis for political calculation and action. For this reason, the shape and the boundaries of the fundamentalist belief system must be established. The worldview of Jewish fundamentalists in Israel is also worthy of careful study precisely because it is so radically different from that of most Americans, and even of most Israelis.

In this chapter I will present an overall depiction of Jewish fundamentalist ideology. It is convenient and, as should be apparent from the previous chapter, only marginally inaccurate to refer to contemporary Jewish fundamentalist ideology as "the ideology of Gush Emunim." In the next chapter I will analyze the range of *disagreement* within the Jewish fundamentalist movement. The points that everyone in the movement *agrees* on will be implicit in the issues they consider significant and in the ways they argue use with one another over those issues. This analysis will also provide a basis for comments in chapters 6 and 7 about present trends and future prospects.

There are good reasons why Gush thinking is not understood outside its own circles. The very content of the belief system discourages attempts to explain it to non-Jews. Furthermore, most Israeli/Jewish intellectuals and journalists are so repulsed by its tenets that they avoid analysis of it or focus only on its most sensationalist aspects.[1] Nor did its most authoritative spokesman, Rav Tzvi Yehuda Kook, produce a systematic presentation of his approach to Zionism and the redemption process. Apart from scattered published lectures, essays, and newspaper articles, most sources of Rav Tzvi Yehuda's teachings have been notes to his homilies and lectures. A tightly knit circle of his disciples, including Hanan Porat, Moshe Levinger, Eleazar Waldman, Shlomo Aviner, Yoel Ben-Nun, Yaacov Ariel, and Haim Druckman, formed the ideological and political core of Gush Emunim's leadership. The authoritative nature of Rav Tzvi Yehuda's thinking is evidenced by the regularity with which they, and virtually all other Jewish fundamentalist leaders, frame ideological and tactical disputes as disagreements over accurate interpretations of his opinions. Shlomo Aviner, one of Gush Emunim's most prolific and influential ideologues, reflects the central importance of the Rav's thinking and the effective political use his students have made of their privileged access to him in his conclusion to "Messianic Realism," an article often cited in fundamentalist circles.

In conclusion, this writer wishes to disclaim any pretension to originality in the views and sentiments expressed in this article. These were drawn exclusively from the teachings of Rav Kook, and more directly from the comments of his son Rav Tzvi Yehuda and his disciples, to the best of the author's grasp.[2]

Jewish fundamentalist thinking is grounded in seven basic beliefs. Although expressed in terms consistent with Zionist rhetoric, in fact they represent a categorical rejection of certain key tenets of Zionist ideology. One of the most satisfactory ways to explain and document these beliefs is to examine the ideas of Rav Tzvi Yehuda Kook. However, in addition to published writings and lectures of Rav Tzvi Yehuda and interpretive articles by those of his students prominent in the leadership of Gush Emunim, I will use two sources—the work of Rabbi Menachem Kasher and of Harold Fisch.

Kasher was a renowned scholar who died in November of 1984, in his nineties. His messianic tracts are well known to many yeshiva students and Gush activists and are reported to have had "an enormous impact upon those who formed the core and periphery of Gush Emunim."[3] Following both the Six Day War and the Yom Kippur War, Kasher published treatises arguing that both Jewish law and the opinions of the great European rabbis of the last two centuries justified his classification of the contemporary period as the Great Era—the beginning, or even the middle, of a redemption process that will culminate in the inauguration of the messianic age.

Fisch, formerly rector of Israel's sole religious university, Bar-Ilan, is the only member of Gush Emunim's core religious elite to have published a systematic presentation of the fundamentalist worldview. Based directly on the ideas of Kook and Kasher, Fisch's book has appeared in two slightly differing versions: the English original, published under the title *The Zionist Revolution* in 1978, and a Hebrew edition, *The Zionism of Zion*, published in 1982.

The Abnormality of the Jewish People. Zionism arose simultaneously in the late nineteenth century in both Eastern and Western Europe. The analysis of the "Jewish problem" and its solution, propounded independently by Leo Pinsker in czarist Russia and Theodor Herzl in Austria, Germany, and France, was anchored in the bold conviction that anti-Semitism could be utterly eliminated if Jews were granted the opportunity to become a "normal" people. In the Hebrew phrase, Jews were to become *goy kekol hagoyim,* a nation like all other nations. What set Zionists apart from Jewish advocates of socialist, Yiddishist, religious, and assimilationist solutions to the gathering crisis of European Jewry was that Zionists ascribed anti-Semitism and its tribulations to the structural "abnormality" of Jewish existence as a diaspora people. Living scattered among other peoples, a minority everywhere, Jews appeared to gentiles as a weird, mysterious, and even ghostly presence. Anti-Semitism was therefore traceable to an abnormal mode of existence and to the fears and passions that, under the circumstances, Jews naturally provoked among gentiles.

According to this view, Jewish life had been distorted on both the individual and the collective levels by the abnormality of diaspora existence and the degradation and persecution associated with it. By assembling in their own land, where they would constitute a majority of the population, Jews could undergo a process of normalization that would result in a national culture and personality no different in their fundamentals from those of any other. With remaining Jewish minorities in other countries standing in the same relationship to their "host" countries as, say, that of the German minority in France to the French people, anti-Semitism would fade and eventually disappear.

In unusually explicit terms, Fisch articulates Gush Emunim's radical *reversal* of these basic Zionist propositions. The idea, he says, "that the Jewish nation is a normal nation and ought to be treated as such by the so-called international community . . . is the original delusion of secular Zionism."[4] Authentic Zionism, for Fisch, entails rejection of classical Zionism's use of other nations as models for how the Jewish people should behave and what it might and should become. Jews are not and cannot be a normal people; they are, in fact, irrevocably abnormal. The eternal uniqueness of the Jews is the result of the covenant God made with them at Mount Sinai—a real historical event with eternal and inescapable consequences for the entire world. Fisch gives particular prominence to biblical quotations that remind the Jews of their unique covenanted status in the eyes of the Lord of the Universe, such as the following:

> And I will establish my covenant between me and thee and thy seed after thee in their generations for an everlasting covenant, to be a God to thee and to thy seed after thee. And I will give to thee and thy seed after thee the land in which thou dost sojourn, all the land of Canaan for an everlasting possession; and I will be their God.[5]

Not surprisingly, fundamentalists embrace the notion of Jews as an *am segula* (a chosen, or "treasure," people) to refute the classical Zionist idea of Jews as a normal people. This is clearly apparent in what one might have thought to be the most unlikely of places—the propaganda of the World Zionist Organization. In a workbook for study purposes issued by the organization's Department for Torah, Education and Culture in the Diaspora, traditional Zionist teachings of normalization are completely absent. Instead of posing the problem of Jews as a nation that, via Zionism, will be normalized and join the stream of history as a nation like any other nation, this booklet takes as its point of departure not only that Jews are unique, as every nation is unique, but that the Jewish people, endowed with a divine and special destiny, is different in kind from every other nation that has existed, does exist, or will exist. The question for study is, then, not whether the Jews are normal, but whether their special, abnormal qualities are to be understood as evidence of "intrinsic superiority," as the reason why God chose the Jewish people, or as the result of their being divinely chosen.[6]

The implication of chosenness is that the transcendental imperatives to which Jews must respond effectively nullify the moral laws that bind the behavior of normal nations. In "Messianic Realism," and other articles, Aviner considers the relationship between history, politics, and redemption. He argues that divine commandments to the Jewish people "transcend human notions of national rights." He explains that while God requires other, normal nations to abide by abstract codes of "justice and righteousness," such laws do not apply to Jews.

> Ours is not an autonomous scale of values, the product of human reason, but rather an heteronomous or, more correctly, theonomous scale rooted in the will of the Divine architect of the universe and its moral order.[7]

> From the point of view of mankind's humanistic morality we were in the wrong in (taking the land) from the Canaanites. There is only one catch. The command of God ordered us to be the people of the Land of Israel.[8]

Thus does Jewish fundamentalism utterly reject the traditional Zionist image of Jews as a normal people, bound by and rewarded according to the same laws and principles of national self-determination applicable to other nations.

The Meaning of Arab Opposition to Israel. As befits an abnormal nation, the conflicts Israel encounters with its neighbors are not normal either. In their analysis of the Arab conflict with Israel, if not always in their propaganda, most Israeli leaders have sought to explain Arab hostility in practical terms—as a conflict that stems from misperceptions or specific circumstances. Accordingly, as those perceptions and circumstances change, opportunities for ending the conflict can materialize and should be awaited, identified, and exploited.

Gush Emunim views the conflict with the Arabs in a radically different way—as the latest and most crucial episode in Israel's eternal battle to overcome the forces of evil. This stance is illustrated in the words with which Eleazar Waldman—head of the Kiryat Arba Yeshiva, Member of Knesset for the Tehiya party, and prominent student of Rav Tzvi Yehuda—reassured fundamentalist Jews troubled by the outcome of the Lebanon War. By fighting the Arabs, Waldman reminded his audience, Israel carries out its mission to serve "as the heart of the world, in contact with every organ, and with the world understanding that it must receive the blood of life from the heart."[9] Arab hostility springs, as does all anti-Semitism, from the world's recalcitrance in the face of Israel's mission to save it. Thus, the very ferocity of the Lebanon War should be seen as evidence of the advance of the redemption process.[10]

Many Zionists, especially on the left, have not only come to recognize the legitimate rights of Palestinian Arabs, but have even noticed similarities between the historical experiences of Jews and Palestinians. Jewish fundamentalists' assumptions about the world, however, make it essentially impossible for them to see Jews and Palestinians in comparable terms. Nor can fundamentalists acknowledge any real tie between the Palestinians, or any human group other than the Jewish people, and the Land of Israel. To do so would contradict the prophecy that the Promised Land would "vomit out" any other people that tries to live there, and that only with the return of the Jews would the land again "shoot forth branches, and yield fruit,"[11] as a sign of the beginning of the messianic age. Hence, historically unsupportable notions that only under Jewish cultivation did Palestine become a productive country and that most Palestinian Arabs arrived in the area only within the past century are treated as incontrovertible.[12]

Fisch dismisses the Palestinians as the exact opposite of the Jewish people. The Jews are authorized by the living God and creator of the universe as a legitimate, eternal people with unalienable rights to the entire Land of Israel. The Palestinians have absolutely no legitimate claim to nationhood or to any part of the country. They have experienced no real suffering, and have drawn together as an entity only out of opposition to the Jews. Theirs is a "suicidal" struggle for the elimination of the state and people of Israel. As such, Israel must recognize the Palestinians as the most destructive and dangerous emanation of Arab hostility, and stand ready to destroy them as they seek to fulfill their collective "death-wish."[13]

The image of the Palestinians as doomed and suicidal in their opposition to Jewish rule in the Land of Israel corresponds to a more fundamental categorization of them. Gush rabbis and ideologues regularly refer to the local Arabs as "Canaanites" or "Ishmaelites," and weigh the implications of the terms Joshua offered the Canaanites before his conquest of the land, or the circumstances under which Abraham expelled Ishmael, for the determination of policy in current circumstances. Thus Rav Tzvi Yehuda cited Maimonides to the effect that the Canaanites had three choices—to flee, to accept Jewish rule, or to fight.[14] These are the choices, both suggest, that frame the appropriate attitude for Jews to take toward Palestinian Arabs. Of course, the decision by most Canaanites to fight ensured their destruction. The same fate awaits present-day non-Jewish inhabitants of the land who choose to resist the establishment of Jewish sovereignty over its entirety. Similarly, addressing the Arab problem on the "ethical dimension," Hanan Porat points out that since God "heard the voice of the boy (i.e. Ishmael)," obviously Arabs, as individuals, must be treated humanely. But "when Ishmael laughed, the Holy One Blessed Be He led Abraham to heed Sarah's demand to expel that mother (Hagar) and her son.'" Humane treatment is appropriate, Porat emphasizes, "only for those Arabs ready to accept the sovereignty of the people of Israel." From this general principle he infers a duty to make merciless war against Arabs in the Land of Israel who reject Jewish sovereignty and the specific requirement to deport the families of Arab juveniles who throw stones at the passing automobiles of Jewish settlers.[15]

Fisch's image of the Palestinians as suicidal, therefore, does not reflect a consensus within Gush Emunim that they must inevitably be destroyed. Insofar as they try, violently or otherwise, to resist the extension of Jewish sovereignty over the whole land, Palestinians will indeed be uprooted or destroyed—thus is their political struggle suicidal. However, should they accept the establishment of Jewish rule over the whole land, various formulas of subordination, for arranging relations between Jews and non-Jews in a Jewish-ruled Land of Israel, can be discussed. Although some of these formulas offer Arabs more than others, all share one fundamental principle—that whatever rights may be accorded to Arabs as individuals *in* the land (rights to own property, earn a livelihood, be treated respectfully, and so forth), no group, people, or nation may be recognized as having any rights *over* any portion of it. This distinction is the most common element in fundamentalist discussions of "the Arab problem." It was the dominant theme in the contributions made to a special Jewish–Arab relations issue of the fundamentalist journal *Artzi* (My Land). A key point of departure here, as elsewhere, is the teaching

> of our master and teacher Rabbi Tzvi Yehuda Kook (of blessed memory), who distinguished clearly between relations toward an Arab national entity in the Land of Israel, for which no place at all exists, and relations, so to speak, to Mustapha and Ahmad, since Arabs are also created in his image.[16]

Israel's International Isolation as Proof of Jewish Chosenness. The biblical characterization of the Jewish people's relationship to the gentile nations Gush supporters most often cite is found in Numbers 23:9: "a people that dwells alone and that shall not be reckoned among the nations." This reflects a deep-seated belief that very nearly the only distinction worth making among human groups is that between Jews and gentiles. Thus, fundamentalists interpret what they consider the wildly irrational opprobrium heaped upon Israel by the world community as yet more evidence of the Jewish people's special, divine destiny—according to Fisch, "a theological sign of election."[17]

In the worldview of Jewish fundamentalism, the traditional Zionist slogan—"What counts is not what the gentiles think, but what Jews do!"—is replaced by something quite different— "What counts is not what gentiles do, but what Jews *are!*" Israel's maximal territorial and political ambitions are therefore right because Jews are the chosen people of God. Given that, the State of Israel, by attracting outrage and persecution, merely continues the traditional role of the Jew in world history—that of a "barometer for registering the moral state of the nations."[18]

In a long, didactic article written in dialogue form for the first issue of *Artzi,* Shlomo Aviner explains to Gush stalwarts the unending persecution of the State of Israel. A question is posed:

"All the world knows that the Land of Israel is connected to the people of Israel, as it is written in the Bible, so why do they make so much trouble for us?" Because the concept of an ontologically based opposition between Jews and gentiles is so central to fundamentalist thinking, Aviner's answer to this question is worth quoting at some length:

> ... we experienced the opposition of the goyim (gentiles) to the state of Israel even before it was established. The enmity which the peoples of the world show toward the Jewish people has been present throughout history. Its like has not been shown to any other people ... it goes beyond all historical or rational explanations. Various economic, sociological, etc., explanations have even been advanced to explain the European holocaust. We don't deny them, but they certainly do not suffice. It simply must be recognized that there is an inner instinctual enmity on the part of the nations of the world toward the Jewish people. ... Hitler, may his name be blotted out, expressed openly this essential enmity that he felt toward the Jewish people, an enmity that went far beyond any rational explanation. Said the despised one: "The Jewish people and I cannot exist in the same world." The source of this kind of enmity is that in the final analysis our moral values contradict the basis upon which the peoples of the world build their lives. In our essence we negate their values. If we are right, that means the foundations of their lives are shattered. We have no intention of harming them, but we do negate their way of life, and this fact causes them to be our enemies.[19]

Classical Zionism considered the gentiles essentially rational, and explained anti-Semitism as the natural response of rational people to an irrational mode of Jewish existence. Out of his belief in gentile rationality, Herzl even approached leading anti-Semites for assistance in building the Jewish national home. While classical Zionism argued that anti-Semitism would gradually disappear with the creation of a normal state for a normal Jewish nation, Jewish fundamentalism expects rationally unwarranted persecution of Jews and the Jewish state to continue until the culmination of the redemption. In the context of these basic assumptions about the intrinsic and pervasive antagonism between Jews and gentiles, instances of gentile goodwill can be explained only supernaturally, as the result of the direct intervention of God. Thus does Menachem Kasher account for what might otherwise appear to be the puzzlingly supportive behavior of the United States during the Yom Kippur War.

> All the nations of the world well know that the goal of the Arabs is to destroy the people of Israel, God forbid, and nonetheless they take their side. All except the United States of America, who stands by the side of Israel; *truly this is a miracle from heaven.*[20]

The Impossibility of Arriving at a Negotiated Peace. The scale and pervasiveness of gentile hostility to Israel, reflecting as it does the underlying spiritual tension that God introduced into the world via his covenant with the Jews, cannot be assuaged through negotiation or compromise. It makes no difference whether the political efforts to achieve peace entail direct contacts between Jews and Arabs or whether there is some sort of international mediation or orchestration of the peace process. All efforts, no matter how structured or under whose auspices, are bound to fail.

Those Israelis who have pursued what they believe to be options for peace based on compromise make the silly mistake of thinking that the conflict is a normal one, about borders and political rights. In fact, territorial and political problems are but superficial aspects of the metaphysical struggle being waged. In the short run, negotiated compromises may appear to be successful. But by obscuring the ever-present threat of annihilation and by abandoning territories, they not only weaken and endanger Israel, but contradict the imperatives that God has placed upon the Jewish people to inherit the land. This, in turn, delays the eventual redemption not only of Israel, but of the entire world.

From this perspective, two kinds of peace are possible. The first is a temporary peace based on Arab and international perceptions of Israeli power. This kind of peace cannot last forever, because it does not signify Arab abandonment of the destruction of the Jewish state; but it can be maintained without negotiations involving territorial or political concessions. This is precisely the sort of peace Menachem Begin predicted when, at the height of Israel's apparent success in the Lebanon War, he declared that the land would enjoy the biblically ordained "forty years of peace" because of Arab fear and disarray.

The second kind of peace, "real peace," is that which will accompany the completion of Israel's inheritance of the whole land and will precede the coming of the Messiah to rule over the reunited people of Israel. As part of this process of redemption, all nations "will marvelously acknowledge the truth which it is Israel's task to bring to the world, that message of justice and peace of which the holy mountain is the visible symbol."[21]

In homilies quoted by the editors of *Artzi* to introduce the journal's first issue, Rav Tzvi Yehuda Kook decried the Camp David peace talks, and the Egypt–Israel peace treaty they presaged:

> The Guardian of Israel will defend us and save us from every disgrace of these generations that are confused by a false "peace." He will provide us with the courage for a true-peace (*Shalom-emet*) that will last, in our land, for all eternity.[22]
>
> God will give strength to his people and bless his people with peace. And only thus, through the strength which He will give to his people, will we be blessed with peace. Accordingly, any sort of peace which does not result from the strength which he will give his people, the real power of its faith, religion, wisdom, and holiness, will be an amputated, temporary, peace and a curse for generations to come.[23]

In the absence of true peace, as Eleazar Waldman explained while the Israeli army was still occupying much of Lebanon, wars are to be seen as a natural and expected, if unfortunate, part of the redemption process. "It is impossible," in fact, "to complete the Redemption by any other means."[24] In accordance with this process, anti-Semitism and the wars it precipitates will cease only when Israel's territorial and political destiny is fulfilled.

The Redemption is not only the Redemption of Israel but the Redemption of the whole world. But the Redemption of the world *depends* on the Redemption of Israel. From this derives our moral, spiritual, and cultural influence over the entire world. The blessing will come to all of humanity from the people of Israel living in the whole of its land.[25]

The Cardinal Importance of the Land of Israel. Gush Emunim's semiofficial slogan is "The Land of Israel, for the People of Israel, according to the Torah of Israel." The primacy of the land in this triple commitment is also a prominent theme in Fisch's book, whose Hebrew title, *The Zionism of Zion,* refers to the motive of Jewish return as a positive expression of the Jews love of the land of Zion, rather than a desperate attempt to find a refuge from persecution. The covenant between God and the Jewish people, according to Fisch, is actually a contract with three partners:

> The Covenant rests on a triad of relationships: God, land and people. The land is holy only because God chooses to dwell in it and chooses that we should dwell in it with him. Take away the theological dimension and Zionism itself turns to ashes.[26]

Gush Emunim's critics among Orthodox Jews often remark on the fundamentalists tendency toward "idolatry" in their approach to Eretz Yisrael as the supreme value in Jewish life. Indeed, for fundamentalist activists No longerwho are not religious, the land, in combination with the Bible and historicist notions of the "destiny of the Jewish people," does play a role functionally equivalent to that of God in the belief system of religious fundamentalists: it is the source of transcendental imperatives. For all Jewish fundamentalists, however, an irreducible attachment to the Land of Israel, in its entirety, is at the core of their worldview. *Artzi* quotes Rav Tzvi Yehuda:

> The Land was chosen even before the people. . . . The chosen land and the chosen people comprise one completed, divine unity, *joined together at the creation of the world and the creation of history.* They comprise *one vital and integral unit.*[27]

Other nations may feel special ties to the beauty of their homelands or monuments built there. Some even feel that theirs is a special, divinely favored land. In particular, Fisch mentions the belief by many American pioneers that by moving westward they were "responding to a divine call, fulfilling a divine destiny."[28]

Though these sentiments may be genuinely felt by others, according to Fisch, *only* the Jews in fact have a relationship to their land that is divinely ordained. Hanan Porat has made this point with particular clarity:

> Israel's national connection to the Land of Israel is unique among the nations—it is (radically different) from the ties binding the French, English, Russian, and Chinese peoples to their lands. . . . For us the Land of Israel is a land of destiny, a chosen land, not just an existentially defined homeland.[29]

One implication of this belief is that political debates over territorial questions are understood to be of direct, cosmic significance.

> The covenant between the people of Israel and its God, which includes the promised land as an integral part, is an important objective within the entire scheme of creation. It is from this fact that the linkage between the people of Israel and its land is rooted—in the transcendental will of God who created all in his honor.[30]

In this context, arguments in favor of trading territory for peace, or for a more homogeneously Jewish state, are absurd. But also inappropriate, and even dangerous, are justifications advanced by some Israelis for the need to maintain Jewish rule of this or that piece of the land. The world must never think that Jews believe their right to the whole land is based on essentially changeable, conditional, considerations such as security or economic or demographic necessities. The entire Land of Israel is the Promised Land, to be "conquered, possessed, and settled." That fact, and that alone, is what Jews must rely on in the face of Arab and gentile opposition to its habitation and rule by Jews.

Among themselves, Jews should stop making distinctions that portray some parts of the land as more important than others. Arguing that such discussions only invite gentile pressures and Arab terror, Hanan Porat advises against the use of any sort of "apologetic arguments."

> *There is no moral blemish in our declaration, once and for all, that the Land of Israel is the land of the Jewish people*

by virtue of God's command engraved in iron and blood, as Rabbi Kook of blessed memory has said.[31]

To express the intimate and unbreakable bonds they feel to the land, fundamentalists commonly invoke images of the Land of Israel as a living being. Territorial concessions and destruction of settlements then become equivalent to the tearing of flesh. Haim Druckman's speech in the Knesset condemning Israel's withdrawal from the Yamit district of northeastern Sinai was replete with these images.

Who does not feel the shock that has gripped every settlement in the Land of Israel, every family on the land, and every true pioneer? Who has not heard their cries, the cry of the land, over the sons that are about to be separated from her? . . . the uprooting of settlements in the Land of Israel is the severing of a limb from a living body. These settlements are the essence of our existence and flesh of our flesh. We shall not accept the amputation of our living flesh.[32]

Current History as the Unfolding of the Redemption Process. A key element in Jewish fundamentalism, as in any fundamentalist movement, is its adherents' belief that they possess special and direct access to transcendental truth, to the future course of events, and to an understanding of what the future requires. For Jewish fundamentalists, history is God's means of communication with his people. Political trends and events contain messages that provide instructions, reprimands, and rewards. Political and historical analysis, properly undertaken, is equivalent to the interpretation of God's will. In combination with religious texts this analysis guides the continuing struggle toward redemption. In his own analysis of Jewish fundamentalism's governing ideology, Eliezer Schweid, one of Gush Emunim's most sophisticated polemicists, stresses this principle.

The weight of the opinion of those who know the truth about the burgeoning of Redemption, a truth discerned through study of the Torah, is greater than the weight of the opinions of leaders who do not see anything but what exists in the present and can only guess at the future.[33]

This general approach to the relationship between history, political action, and the special understanding available to fundamentalist elites, is well illustrated by the messages they discern in three key events: the Holocaust, the Six Day War, and the Yom Kippur War. Harold Fisch characterizes the Holocaust, the destruction of six million Jews by Nazi Germany during World War II, as an example of God's discipline—"a commandment written in blood upon the soil of Europe."[34] God thereby instructed his people that the emancipation, in which so many Jews had placed their hopes for a future of equality within a liberal democratic Europe, could not provide them with an escape route from the burdens of their covenant.[35] Referring to the refusal of most rabbinic authorities to give their blessing to Zionism before the onset of the Holocaust, Fisch expresses the hope that present day rabbis "have learned to hear the voice of the God of Israel speaking to us from the fire of history."[36] If they have, they will not make the same mistake again, by minimizing the cosmic significance of contemporary political struggles, especially the struggle to achieve permanent Jewish control over the whole Land of Israel.

Thus, the Holocaust is seen as God's way of coercing his chosen people back to the Promised Land and of convincing them of the cosmic urgency of its complete reunification—the whole people of Israel in the whole Land of Israel. Best known for this interpretation of the Holocaust is Menachem Kasher, who argued that by entailing the destruction of more Jews than the loss of the First and Second Temples combined, the Holocaust must be understood as the "birthpangs of the Messianic Age (which) fell upon our generation and thus opened for us the way to Redemption."[37]

Kasher combines an elaborate exegesis of biblical and Talmudic sources with a detailed interpretation of Israel's wars in an effort to determine precisely what stage the redemption process has reached. He employs the distinction between the Messiah Son of Joseph, who will settle the land and win victories but ultimately fail in his struggle for redemption in the war of Gog and Magog, and the Messiah Son of David, who will subsequently and miraculously lead Israel and the world to complete redemption. Kasher, and most fundamentalists, sees the Arab–Israeli wars as part of the period of the Messiah Son of Joseph, during which "miracles are shrouded in natural events."[38] Whether religious or nonreligious, the soldiers who died in Israel's army during these wars died as martyrs "for the sanctification of the Name [of God]."[39] Kasher's hope was that Jewish casualties in 1948, 1967, and 1973 were sufficient to warrant the Yom Kippur War's categorization as the third and last of the wars of Gog and Magog. Otherwise, he contended, it must be considered the first of the three, and he predicted that two much more terrible wars will occur before the appearance of the Messiah Son of David.[40]

In general, Jewish fundamentalism considers the wars of 1967 and 1973 to show that it is not "only in darkness and disaster that the God of Israel speaks, demanding an answer. He speaks also through great acts of deliverance."[41] Thus, Fisch compares the Six Day War to the Israelites' crossing of the Red Sea on their way out of Egypt. The war was "a truly religious moment," containing "the experience of miracle, of sudden illumination." It was, according to Fisch, "a triumph . . . by which (the Jews) were not only delivered from mortal peril but also restored to Jerusalem and to the cities of Judah."[42] Through the Six Day War, God awakened Israelis to feel themselves as Jews, separated from and threatened by the gentile world, but reconnected to their land, hearkening to "the revelation . . . of the full meaning of the Jewish calendar which binds us to a past echoing with ancestral obligations and a future of promise and redemption."[43]

Fisch interprets the 1973 war as God's admonition to his people to reconcile themselves to the abnormality of their condition, their radical separation from the gentile world, and the acceptance of a "covenant destiny."[44] Emphasizing the date of the attack—on Yom Kippur, the Day of Judgment, or Day of Atonement—the world-wide isolation of Israel that Fisch argues attended the oil embargo, the genocidal intent of the "Arab onslaught," and the United Nations General Assembly resolution equating Zionism and racism, Fisch interprets the conflict as an unappealable contradiction of the political stance of Israelis who had argued for territorial compromise as a path to peace with the Arabs.

> Launched on Yom Kippur, at the most sacred hour of the Jewish year, it was a challenge to the Jewish calendar and all that it stood for, namely, the whole historical pilgrimage of the Jewish people, its covenant destiny. A metaphysical shudder, as it were, passed

through the body of Israel. . . . No longer was it possible to affirm with any confidence that we were engaged in a normal conflict with a normal enemy.[45]

No matter what precisely the Six Day War and the Yom Kippur War may have signaled about the schedule of redemption, the assumption is that all events reflect the will of God and that the center of his interest in the world is the unfolding redemption of the land and people of Israel. According to Rav Tzvi Yehuda:

It is God, and no other, who created the world and who creates peoples and kingdoms. It is He who was the immediate cause of all the great upheavals that have occurred on this earth during the last fifty years. He destroys kings and makes kings. None of this is by accident! There is no mysticism here, rather open eyes that can see the hand of God. Our holy land, that was exhausted and asleep, its power blocked up, has arisen as a result of all the wars that have taken place during these last fifty years, beginning with the war which destroyed the Turkish government. And now, with the help of God, the land is in our hands, and the Temple Mount is in our hands. . . .

The world is not filled with randomness, but ordered by the hand of the master of the universe. For centuries He has been "angry" at this land, and the air was filled with malaria. Now it is healthier and healthier: can this be some arbitrary coincidence?![46]

The Faith and Ideological Dedication of the Jews as Decisive Factors. Despite the dominant role that God is seen to play in shaping human history, Jewish fundamentalists are not fatalists. Their call for sustained political mobilization is based on a view of the Jewish people as God's chosen assistants in the process of *tikkun olam* (repair of the world)—a process that will culminate in complete redemption and establishment of the messianic kingdom. Accordingly, a key element in the fundamentalist worldview is the belief that the success of efforts to accomplish redemptively necessary political objectives will be determined by the vision of Jewish leaders, their sensitivity to the imperatives of the hour, and, especially, the single-minded faith and spiritual discipline of the Jewish people as a whole. Virtually all political contacts with the international environment are therefore construed not as opportunities to adjust demands or resources to changing circumstances, but as tests of the vision, courage, and will of the Jewish people and its leadership.

Fisch's interpretation of the significance of the Israeli debate over peace negotiations and the disposition of the occupied territories reflects this perspective. As noted previously, Fisch does not believe that opportunities for reaching a negotiated peace with the Arabs exist. From a practical standpoint, the deep division within Israeli society between hawks and doves is therefore irrelevant for the prospects of peace or war. The internal contest over the future of the occupied territories *is* nonetheless of critical importance. It represents a struggle between authentic Zionism, which accepts the lonely destiny of the Jews as God's covenant people and embraces the "scandal of biblical reality," and a Zionism that distorts and abandons Jewish history in a vain search for normalcy.[47] Only if the Jewish people can pass this and other tests of their faith and commitment, by rejecting apparently pragmatic compromises in pursuit of their historic mission, will the redemptive process move forward.

In view of this repeated testing of the nation's spiritual fiber, only a "fuller Zionism, one that includes in itself the mystery of holiness and the dream of salvation," can provide the Jews of Israel with the strength they will need to survive against a hostile and unredeemed world.[48] A renewal of such faith will require secular Jews in Israel to emerge from the "complex spiritual crisis" presently afflicting them, and to return, if not to Orthodox Judaism, then to an inspired and providential understanding of the Zionist mission. Pseudosophisticated political calculations must be cast aside in favor of a purer, simpler faith in the destiny of the Jewish people to rule the whole Land of Israel and thereby to fulfill the terms of its convenant with God. This will entail abandoning "cheap imitation of the culture of the West," and ignoring "world opinion."[49] No Jewish fundamentalist leader has been clearer about the decisiveness of Jewish action and belief, and the need to resist any gentile influence on the formulation or implementation of Jewish national policy, than Rav Tzvi Yehuda.

There is no reason to pay attention to all the confusion of mankind produced by the transient nations of the world. Such petty confusions—who takes account of them? Think not of what happens outside, only put ourselves and our land in order, hearkening to the word of God and of his prophets.[50]

No state nor council of states has any right or authority whatsoever to interfere in the internal affairs of our state or in our settlement of our land. Our state has armed forces praised and admired throughout the world; neither do we depend on aid or intervention by any foreign power. . . . Our wonderful army is ready to fulfill its mission and insure the success of all our efforts to strike roots in the land, to settle in all parts of the land of our fathers, the sovereign state of which our prophets foretold, with no intervention by any other government in the military and political arrangements which we establish across the breadth of our land. And the Lord of hosts, the God of Jacob, will be with us and protect us. Selah.[51]

Writing in 1978, only four years after the founding of Gush Emunim by Rav Tzvi Yehuda's students, Fisch identified that movement as the force within Israeli society that represented the reformulation of Zionism in covenantal terms. Rejecting the search for a "reasonable accommodation to circumstances," he wrote, Gush activists "avow the absoluteness and transcendence of the Jewish bond with the Holy Land and the Holy City, and affirm, even in defiance of current political trends, that history will finally justify them."[52] Despite what appear to be enormous obstacles to Gush Emunim's struggle to achieve the "spiritual rehabilitation" of the Jewish people, eventually success will come. Thus do Jewish fundamentalist exhortations for greater effort and more sacrifice most commonly conclude with an appeal to remember that whether God's word (or the imperatives of Jewish destiny) is successfully fulfilled is *talui banu* (dependent on us).

As noted at the outset, it is this intimate connection between what is felt as transcendentally imperative and what is perceived as one's personal, political duty, that is the distinguishing mark of a fundamentalist political vision.

V

The Range of Disagreement
within Jewish Fundamentalism

The assumptions about history and politics outlined in the previous chapter form the ideological basis of Jewish fundamentalism. They are the points of departure, the terms of discourse, for the discussions within what Gush Emunim speakers and writers refer to as *tzibur shelanu* (our public). But even among activists within the movement there is a substantial range of disagreement on most important issues. More importantly, the debates within the movement reveal the forces that drive it, the stresses to which it is subject, and the trajectories it may trace in the future.

I have chosen for analysis six issues that together encompass most of the critical disputes within Gush Emunim between 1982 and 1987. For each issue I will identify mainstream opinion and characterize the support for it in comparison with opposing views, located along a continuum appropriate to the issue under discussion. These issues are as follows:

- Leadership and source of transcendental authority
- Territorial scope of the whole Land of Israel
- Pace and political dynamics of the redemption process
- Attitudes toward international and Israeli opposition
- Policy toward and eventual status of local Arabs
- Prospects for peace

Leadership and Source of Transcendental Authority. Until his death in 1982 Rav Tzvi Yehuda Kook was acknowledged by most Gush Emunim activists as the leader of the movement. Through him, authoritative interpretation of his father's writings—particularly the latter's magnus opus, *Orot* (*Lights*)—was possible. As noted in

91

chapter 2, many of his followers understood and reported his words as akin to prophecy.[1] His advice and guidance were sought on issues pertaining to where and how to establish illegal settlements, what political frameworks to construct and support during elections, and how to manage relations between nonreligious and religious Jews within the movement. Tzvi Yehuda taught that deciphering the circuitous route that redemption would take and the particular actions God desired of his people required spiritual vision and rigorous religious training. Combined with his father's endorsement of charismatic leadership, this teaching encouraged his followers to rely on and accept his leadership.

But Tzvi Yehuda was very old and wrote very little. His manner of speaking was elliptical and filled with allusions to rabbinic texts and authorities unfamiliar to most Israelis, and even to most Gush supporters. Consequently, even during his lifetime he served more as a charismatic focus for the respect and devotion of activists within the movement than as its effective leader. Since his death, various leading elements within Gush Emunim have used anecdotes about his life, his commentaries and homilies (as transmitted by his students), as well as the writings of his father to support contradictory positions on many issues.

The leadership vacuum within Gush Emunim that Tzvi Yehuda's death created has been widely acknowledged. In May 1983, a year after the Yamit evacuation, an important Gush conference was held to discuss the movement's future. Rabbi Yaacov Ariel, head of the yeshiva in the settlement that hosted the conference, spoke of the need to shift from dependence on a charismatic leader who was no longer present to some form of collective leadership.

> As long as Rav Tzvi Yehuda was alive, there was a natural leadership, but since his death, and perhaps since he stopped giving his opinion on specific matters, controversies began. . . . The fact that most of those invited (to our conference), are here, shows that there are plenty of opinions. After the death of Rav Tzvi Yehuda it is not possible to find a single leader, rather all together our public may perhaps be able to do what formerly one man could do.[2]

Most activists within the movement find their own leaders among the pioneering elite who founded the first West Bank settlements, such as Hanan Porat from Gush Etzion and Beni Katzover from Elon Moreh, and among the rabbis who teach in their yeshivas or who live among them in the settlements. Indeed, many rabbis whose influence as spiritual leaders over Gush activists is very great do not occupy public positions. Nor do their names commonly appear in the media. The intimate relationships they build with their students and followers are based on regular contact, constant study of sacred texts, and close consultation in matters of religious and personal life. These relationships also create opportunities for them to wield enormous influence over their followers in matters pertaining to politics and the advancement of the struggle to settle and annex the West Bank and Gaza Strip. But a number of rabbis, mostly students of Tzvi Yehuda, have become public personalities—for example, Haim Druckman, Moshe Levinger, Eleazar Waldman, Yoel Ben-Nun, Yisrael Ariel, Yaacov Ariel, and Shlomo Aviner. Despite substantial differences among them, each claims to be transmitting the authentic message of Abraham Isaac and Tzvi Yehuda Kook; a statement by Aviner to that effect was quoted in chapter 4.[3]

In fact, the work of both Kooks has been subject to a wide range of interpretation within the fundamentalist movement. The debate over the Yamit debacle entailed intricate discussions of what Tzvi Yehuda *had* said about the issue in an effort to agree on what he *would have* said had he lived to the time of the evacuation.[4] A prolonged and fervid debate took place in 1984 and 1985 over whether the Jewish terrorist underground represented a distortion of the Kooks' message or an expression of it.[5] The extraordinary range of interpretation among those seeking the "authentic" teaching of the Kooks is also exemplified in the contrasting views of Eleazar Waldman and Yisrael Yaacov Yuval regarding Abraham Isaac Kook's attitude toward war and its relationship to the redemption process. Waldman quotes *Orot* as alluding to the biblical book Song of Songs, which Jewish mystics considered an allegory of love between God and the people of Israel pertaining to the messianic age. Waldman quotes Rav Kook as follows:

When war breaks out, the power of the Messiah is aroused. The time of the nightingale has arrived; she sings in the boughs. The wicked ones disappear from the world, the earth is perfumed, and the voice of the turtle-dove is heard in our land.

"On the one hand," comments Waldman, "war is accompanied by destruction and death, on the other hand, it increases the power of the Messiah. . . . Unfortunately it is still impossible to achieve the completion of Redemption by any means other than war."[6]

In sharp contrast to this view that Rav Kook sanctioned war as necessary to Israel's efforts to advance the redemption process, Yuval learns from *Orot* about "the dangers inherent in extremist nationalism." He quotes from that same source as follows:

. . . until such happy times as it will be feasible to conduct an independent national policy without recourse to vicious and barbaric practices . . . it is not in the interest of Jacob to wield sovereignty, when this entails wholesale bloodshed and ingenuity of a sinister kind.[7]

More broadly, the rabbis of Gush Emunim legitimize their opinions on the basis of their interpretation of both halacha and *aggadah*[8] (the major rabbinic glosses and commentaries on the halacha). In addition to key biblical passages, the writings of Maimonides and of the scholar and mystic Rabbi Moshe ben Nachman, or Nachmanides (1194–1270), are cited more often than any other sources by both rabbis and religious fundamentalist laymen to validate particular positions within their universe of discourse.

As noted in chapter 2, Maimonides' discussion of messianism was designed to discourage thinking about apocalyptic matters. By stipulating that only earthly political success by religiously observant leaders—not mystical intuition or reputations for miraculous behavior—could validate action to advance the coming of the Messiah, Maimonides hoped to make redemptionist-oriented activity virtually impossible. But Zionism's success in ending the Exile for at least part of the Jewish people, and the establishment of Jewish rule over most of the Land of Israel, has, ironically, made his "practical" approach to messianism a legitimizing resource of enormous importance for Gush Emunim rabbis seeking authentication of their efforts to push the end. The prominence of Nachmanides as an authority is even more understandable in light of the principles with which he is most closely associated: that the

Land of Israel is "equal in weight to all the commandments put together," and that all the commandments were *taluyot ba aretz* (tied to and dependent on the Land of Israel).[9]

The significance of these sources for the communication of transcendental imperatives is expressed not in precise agreement on what they mean, but in the extent to which they are used to articulate and justify quite different positions on questions of importance within the fundamentalist movement. For example, Shlomo Aviner declares that "there is an absolute Torah prohibition against the transfer of any portion of our holy land to foreign rule" and that those who even discuss territorial concessions are committing the sin of "profanation of the Name of God."[10] Portions of the Land of Israel not yet ruled by Jews must, he writes, be acquired at any cost:

> We must settle the whole Land of Israel, and over all of it establish our rule. In the words of [Nachmanides]: "Do not abandon the land to any other nation." If that is possible by peaceful means, wonderful, and if not, we are commanded to make war to accomplish it.[11]

Thus, Aviner argues that the principle of *pikuach nefesh* (preserving life rather than following halacha) does not apply to the commandment to conquer, possess, and settle the land. Rabbi Yehoshua Zuckerman quotes the same words from Nachmanides to prohibit any cession to a neighboring state of parts of the Land of Israel already under Jewish rule, without also suggesting a positive commandment to conquer areas not under Jewish rule.[12] Yaacov Ariel, on the other hand, while accepting Nachmanides' classification of any war over the territorial boundaries of a Jewish state in the Land of Israel as a *milchemet mitzvah* (commanded war), is unsure, citing Maimonides, whether or not such wars belong to the category of *yehareg velo ya avor* (to be fulfilled even if one's life is at stake). While prohibiting any consideration of convenience or comfort in the formulation of policies toward territorial issues, he is also unsure, on the basis of Maimonides' teachings, whether in dire circumstances military and political experts might be authorized to cede territory.[13]

Relying mainly on Nachmanides and Maimonides as well are Rabbis Avraham Elkana Kahana-Shapira and Yehoshuah Menachem Ehrenberg, who reject the notion that portions of the Land of Israel could be ceded in order to preserve good relations with the United States or to prevent the outbreak of war. They do suggest, however, that in principle and in extremis, military and political experts could decide to cede territory rather than continue in an utterly hopeless military and political predicament.[14]

Also reflective of the authority attributed to these sources was a debate conducted over whether the Jewish terrorist underground was wrong in principle or only in method or timing—a debate that centered on the question of whether or not the government of Israel was to be considered a representative of heaven on earth. Citing both Tzvi Yehuda and Maimonides, Yisrael Ariel defended the *machteret* against the charge that they were "rebelling against God." Ariel wondered whether without a king, a halachically proscribed revolt can take place at all. Moreover, according to Maimonides, Ariel reminded his readers, a Jew who "does not hear" the commands of a king who breaks the law of the Torah, "even a king of Israel," cannot be considered in "rebellion against the authority of God."[15] In response, Yehuda Zoldan, quoting Nachmanides and Tzvi Yehuda, challenged Ariel's distinction between the "state of Israel" and any particular "government of Israel." He argued that "as long as, and only as long as, the government's acts are not obviously against the Torah," the democratically elected government of Israel must be obeyed as the halachic equivalent of a king.[16]

In a related set of discussions, Rabbi Yitzhak Shilat cited Maimonides' practical messianism to support his own position that direct actions can be taken for the explicit purpose of advancing the messianic process. If the machteret was perhaps an inexpedient means of achieving redemptive goals, it was wrong—but only on tactical grounds, not in principle. Shilat stressed that according to Maimonides, Rabbi Akiva's proclamation of Bar Kochba as the Messiah, though mistaken, was not in principle unwarranted; he thus implied that Gush Emunim should remain alert to the possibility that one of its number is indeed the Messiah.[17] In direct contrast, Yoel Ben-Nun vigorously condemned the Jewish terrorist efforts to destroy the Muslim shrines in Jerusalem as contrary to the teachings of Maimonides and of the Kooks.

Whoever thinks that he need not take account of the results that were liable to flow from the destruction of the Dome of the Rock, because he believes he is acting according to the "Laws of Redemption," and is thereby not constrained by regular laws, cuts himself off not only from [Maimonides], but also from Rav Kook and from Rav Tzvi Yehuda and exposes himself to the "trivial laws" that the representatives of the people implement to protect the public welfare. . . . "Laws of Redemption" that give rise to actions like that are a Sabbatian distortion.[18]

But if most Jewish fundamentalists think and act according to transcendental injunctions mediated through role models, the guidance of spiritual leaders, and the semiauthoritative interpretation of sacred texts, some claim authority to act out of a more direct sort of contact with God's will. The most significant and influential example is Yehuda Etzion—the ideological spokesman for the most prominent segment of the Jewish terrorist underground.

Etzion is a veteran of Ofra, one of the earliest Gush Emunim settlements in the West Bank; he is not a rabbi. At his trial for his role in the attacks on the two Arab mayors and the Islamic College in Hebron, and in the plot to blow up Temple Mount, he proudly admitted the truth of the charges, but challenged the right of the court to pass judgment on his acts. In his statement to the court, reprinted in full in *Nekuda,* Etzion explained his motives and those of his fellow conspirators as grounded in their belief that God had given them a personal responsibility to advance the redemption process through radical action. Referring to the rebuilding of the Temple, Etzion declared:

I have seen myself as responsible to carry out actions which I would characterize as the purification of the Temple Mount, the only holy place of the people of Israel, from the structure now located upon it, on the site of the holy of holies, the building known as the Dome of the Rock.[19]

In long articles published in *Nekuda,* Etzion argued that the divine imperative for Jews to build the Temple could not be ignored. His response to God's "painfully obvious" commandment to do so, he wrote, is comparable to Abraham's unhesitating willingness to offer his son Isaac as a sacrifice when God commanded him to do so, even though Abraham could see no useful or rational purpose to his action.[20]

Though quoting Rav Kook the Elder as the inspiration that guided him to the realization of his responsibility, Etzion characterized his actions and those of his comrades as directly authorized by God through the Torah, and proven to be so by the purity of their intentions.

> The commandment that pounded in the heart of Joshua and the generation who captured Canaan, in the heart of David and Solomon, and their generation, the word of God in his Torah, is thus, as it was first purely stated, what motivates us.[21]

> The source of our authority will be our volunteering for the holy because we only come to return Israel to its true purpose and destiny of Torah and Holiness . . . we are looking for the complete renewal of the true official authority—the Sanhedrin and the anointed from the House of David—we are those who nurse from the future, from which we gain our authority for the generations.[22]

Etzion's commitment to radical and violent action to push the end places him on the extreme edge of the fundamentalist movement in terms of the directness with which transcendental authorization is experienced and the immediacy with which divine commandments are to be implemented.[23] Since he received directly from God the "commandment that pounded in the heart of Joshua" he was much less willing than other fundamentalists to accept scriptural or rabbinic constraints against pursuing his cosmically prescribed objectives. The prominence his articles were given in *Nekuda* triggered considerable criticism from more mainstream writers; nonetheless several authors expressed strong support for his views and his tactics. Herzl himself was considered irrational and crazy when he proposed the idea of a Jewish state. So argued Aviva Segal, rejecting calls for "realism" and predicting that when the Temple is rebuilt, Etzion will be honored as a prophet.[24]

At the other end of the spectrum with regard to the source of the transcendental imperative is the nonreligious wing of the fundamentalist movement. Although it includes no more than 20 percent of Gush Emunim activists, the secular ultranationalist camp has produced some of the leading fundamentalist ideologues, polemicists, and politicians—including Geula Cohen, Rafael Eitan, Israel Eldad, Eliyakim Haetzni, Yuval Neeman, Eliezer Schweid, Moshe Shamir, and Zvi Shiloach.[25] This group saw in Rav Tzvi Yehuda Kook a leader whose emphasis on the Land of Israel and settlement, as opposed to religious observance, created valuable opportunities to harness the efforts and devotion of tens of thousands of religious Jews in support of their maximalist Zionism, but essentially secular, program. Indeed, as noted earlier, Tzvi Yehuda was instrumental in establishing Tehiya—the party with which most secularly oriented fundamentalists are affiliated.

Following Tzvi Yehuda's death, latent tensions pertaining to the level of personal religiosity of Gush Emunim leaders and settlers surfaced. Haim Druckman's efforts to establish Matzad as a political alternative to Tehiya and Hanan Porat's decision to abandon Tehiya in favor of a religiously oriented political framework were reactions to the domination of Tehiya by secular activists who refused to incorporate reference to God or the Torah in the charter and political propaganda of the party.

On the other hand, Tehiya is not antireligious. It supports efforts to establish mixed religious and nonreligious Gush settlements, and Tehiya policy forbids desecrating the Sabbath in public. Rabbi Waldman, ranked fourth on Tehiya's list for the Knesset in the 1984 elections, is a prominent member of the party. Religious imagery including the vocabulary of redemptionism and holiness, if not explicit appeals to the Torah, is common in the discourse of its leading personalities. "All members of Tehiya," Geula Cohen has said, "believe that we are living at the beginning of Redemption even if no one knows its exact definition."[26] She and other secular ultranationalists have acknowledged that the devotion and spiritual confidence of religious Jews, derived from their faith in God and their belief in the Torah, is a more effective ideological basis for the fundamentalist movement as a whole than the integralist or romantic nationalism they represent.[27]

As is true of the religious majority, the nonreligious minority within the Jewish fundamentalist movement seeks rapid and comprehensive change in the shape and substance of Israeli society in direct response to its perceived transcendental imperatives. It possesses the same basic worldview (the abnormality of the Jewish people, the implacability of Arab hostility, the primacy of the cleavage between Jew and gentile, the highest priority of the Land of Israel, and so forth) as the religious majority. Nonreligious fundamentalists participate in most of the same organizations and pursue virtually the same political objectives as their religious counterparts. In some sectors, such as Amana, secularists have predominated. But although these secular ultranationalists accept the binding and immediate implications of a transcendental imperative, they do not accept the direct word of God, the authoritative interpretation of sacred writings, or the exegetical virtuosity of revered rabbis as the legitimizing basis for belief and action. They rely instead on individual interpretations of the requirements of the "Jewish national renaissance"; on heroic models such as Abraham (Yair) Stern, founder of Lehi, and Yitzhak Tabenkin of Ahdut Haavoda; and on the rhapsodic, evocative work of numerous writers and ideologues.

Secular Jewish ultranationalists consider Uri Zvi Greenberg the greatest Hebrew poet of the contemporary era. The theme of nation worship, the glorification of the boundless but untapped strength of the Jewish people restored to their land, and the employment of terminology traditionally associated with religious beliefs are typical of his work and the discourse of most nonreligious fundamentalists. Each is illustrated in this short passage from Greenberg's poem "Ode to the Nation."

O NATION, HOW GREAT YOU ARE!

. . .

What shall they do here today,
Your sons and daughters,
In the fullness of their vigour,
With the storm of their dammed-up fury,
The force of revolt within them?
What shall they do
With the pulse of battle pounding in their blood?
Bid them conquer the land,
Scale the peaks with standards flying;
Storm the walls of Titus, raze Bastilles;
As rebels they will go forth,
And you shall hear them, singing their song

Of freedom and conquest and redemption,
Full redemption![28]

Also typical of this conception of the nation and its destiny as the source of transcendental meaning are the writings of Israel Eldad, who was originally active in the Revisionist movement and later became a leader of Lehi. A well-known writer and historian, Eldad was one of the founders of the Movement for the Whole Land of Israel, and is an important participant in the theoretical and ideological debates within Gush Emunim. His ultranationalist interpretation of the source of ultimate authority, his embrace of religious motifs, and the historicist nature of his thinking are reflected in his description of the discovery by archaeologist Yigal Yadin, a former army general, of letters from Bar Kochba to his army:

> The letters of Bar Kokhba, the last commander of the Jewish army, thus reached the first commander of the new Jewish army after one thousand eight hundred and twenty years, as if by personal delivery . . . an extraordinary feat, bordering on the sublime. If you associate this experience with the visionary siting of Herzl's tomb between the Memorial to the holocaust and the military cemetery, perhaps you will no longer look upon the Israeli army as an army like any other . . . anybody who dares talk about Israel's "militarism" is blaspheming . . . committing an act of profound impiety. . . . Can there be anything more sacred than the fighting force of this people?[29]

The extent to which religious and nonreligious fundamentalists share the same "sacred" discourse is illustrated by a poll of 539 Gush Emunim settlers in which 11 percent identified themselves as nonreligious. The two groups gave virtually identical responses to the halachically framed question of whether "withdrawal from Judea and Samaria falls under the principle of *ye'horeg v'al ya'avor* (that a Jew should give up his life rather than allow the area to be ruled by non-Jews)"—17.3 percent and 17.0 percent, respectively, disagreed or strongly disagreed; 62.1 percent and 66.8 percent, respectively, agreed or strongly agreed.[30]

The transcendental imperative to which nonreligious fundamentalists feel themselves responding is most precisely understood as a teleological conception of the course that Jewish history is required to take. The unique destiny of the Jewish people and the unique destiny ascribed to the Land of Israel are to fulfill each other. Reunited with its whole Land, the people of Israel attain a central place, if not *the* central place, in the consciousness of humanity. Realization of this vision demands concentration of the Jewish people in the Land of Israel; extension of Jewish settlement and sovereignty over as much of the Middle East that was ever under Jewish rule as possible; replacement of Western, Christian, "pseudodemocratic" values taken from Europe and America with authentically Jewish political forms; and a "national renaissance" expressed in cultural, technological, and spiritual spheres. Non-religious fundamentalists understood the Bible, as the historic product of the Jewish people's creative genius, to provide both lessons of realpolitik to contemporary Israel and, in its description of the Davidic kingdom, an image of a powerful, united Jewish people bringing the world hope, and a kind of salvation, through its social, cultural, and technological accomplishments.[31]

Eldad identifies the exact character of the Jewish people's contemporary struggle to establish the "physical and economic basis for the nation's spiritual renaissance."[32] It is instructive that he does so in terms strikingly similar to those used by Harold Fisch, in a religious framework, to describe the "divine drama" in which Israel plays an inescapable and leading role.[33] This generation of Jews, according to Eldad, "has the potential of being the greatest of all," if only the Jewish people plays the part history has assigned it with full vigor.[34]

> Israel's army is again facing the Egyptian army in the very same place where the first exodus took place under the leadership of Moses. . . . The role of Egypt the enslaver has in our times been filled by Nazi Germany and by Stalinist and Neo-Stalinist Russia. . . . The first scene of the drama—Joseph's days of greatness in Egypt—is being re-enacted elsewhere, in America. . . . Thus on the contemporary stage all three acts of our ancient drama are being produced simultaneously: Prosperity in a foreign land; Enslavement; Exodus and the liberation of our country. We are re-living the days of Joseph, Moses, Joshua and David, all at once.[35]

To be sure, the absence of a personal God, or of binding religious law, requires that nonreligious fundamentalists' notions about the source of transcendental imperatives differ from those of their religious counterparts. To understand how the nonreligious fundamentalists yet operate rather comfortably within a political, ideological, and organizational rubric that is so heavily religious, it is crucial to understand that the ultimate values of each group lead to essentially identical operational objectives. In addition, both religious and nonreligious fundamentalists believe that their counterparts are serving a useful purpose. Each ignores the metaphysical differences between their positions, while considering the other's theological views to be wrong, but temporary or irrelevant. Although many day-to-day problems exist between religious and nonreligious members of Gush Emunim, particularly in mixed settlements, ideological differences have not been an important problem. Because they share the political imperatives regarding the land, settlement, and the rejection of "normal" Western-democratic oriented Zionism, issues that otherwise might seem likely to challenge the integrity of the movement dissolve into each segment's acceptance of the other's different names for the same things.

As noted previously, another stream within Zionism, very prominently represented among nonreligious Gush activists and supporters, is activist Labor Zionism, particularly the Achdut Haavodah party and its affiliated kibbutz movement, as those institutions were shaped by their historic leader—Yitzhak Tabenkin. The following excerpt from an interview with Ephraim Ben Haim, a disciple of Tabenkin active originally in the Movement for the Whole Land of Israel, and now in Tehiya, illustrates how, even for those not mystically inclined, common political objectives help to dissolve differences over the religious or nonreligious character of the transcendental imperatives involved.

> *Question:* Doesn't all the talk of divine promises and messianic redemption bother you?
>
> *Ephraim Ben Haim:* I'll tell you how I deal with all that. For me the Bible is the holy thing. In my eyes it is more holy than in those of a religious man. Because it is the fruit of the Jewish genius. Perhaps the word

"holy" is not correct, but I don't know how to express this any better.

Regarding the promised borders: I don't believe that God said anything to Abraham. I see in the promised borders the geopolitical mission of the people of Israel for its generations. . . . it doesn't bother me that they (the religious) believe their source is divine.

Now, the matter of redemption: first of all you should know that . . . some of the religious, the enlightened ones, such as Akiva, rejected the idea that only the angels could bring redemption. . . . That is to say the days of the Messiah are not a mystical thing, abstract. . . . I certainly think that we are living in a special period. If someone sees it as a messianic period, and if in his heart of hearts has some mystical feeling about it, that doesn't bother me.[36]

Territorial Scope of the Whole Land of Israel. Many of the most extreme positions with respect to the destined borders of the State of Israel are espoused by members of the nonreligious wing of the fundamentalist movement. Israel Eldad is famous for his advocacy, throughout the 1950s and 1960s, of a Jewish state stretching from the Nile to the Euphrates. In the early 1970s he still argued for a territorial minimum that included Jordan (and Sinai) under Jewish sovereignty. Judging that "the map of the Middle East is still very much in a state of flux" and that many Arab states rest on "ramshackle foundations," Eldad predicted that Israel "will yet help many an oppressed minority to attain its independence and in turn redraw the map." Accordingly, he refused to indicate what he thought Israel's proper borders should be.[37] Although in recent years Eldad has scaled down his objectives to focus on those areas Israel currently controls, other secular ultranationalists continue to pursue their vision of an Israel stretching broadly across the entire Fertile Crescent.

One of these is Yaacov Feitelson, former mayor of Ariel (the largest settlement in the northern bulge of the West Bank) who recently abandoned Herut to join Tehiya. Taking a stance similar to Eldad's former position, Feitelson has refused to place specific limits on Israel's eventual borders, but envisions its domain as stretching across the entire region.

> I am speaking of a tremendous vision. We are only in the infancy of the Zionist movement. . . . Israel must squarely face up to the implementation of the Zionist vision—a vision that has not changed since the days of Herzl. As is known Herzl never indicated what the borders of the state were to be . . . in his time the settlement of the Syrian desert was discussed. I say that Israel should establish new cities throughout the entire area. I mean really the whole area of the Middle East, without limiting ourselves: we should never say about any place: here we stop.[38]

Yuval Neeman, leader of the Tehiya party, has advised the following:

> If we are attacked by Jordan, I would annex the Red Mountain (east and south of the Dead Sea), which is relatively unpopulated, and which has great importance for the development of the southern part of the country. We would also thereby create a border with Saudi Arabia from which we could threaten the oil fields. . . . In the North—if the conflict in Lebanon should begin again, I advocate maintaining control over the Litani.[39]

Among religious fundamentalists, debate over the appropriate borders of the Jewish state focuses mainly on the various biblical descriptions of the Promised Land and on different interpretations of what is required or allowed in the conquest, settlement, and inheritance of it. One of the most respected scholars in Gush Emunim, Yehuda Elitzur, has outlined several more or less concentric territorial shapes for the Jewish state on the basis of biblical sources. He considers the "promised," or "patriarchal," boundaries—extending to the Euphrates River, southern Turkey, Transjordan, and the Nile Delta—"the ideal borders." The borders as reflected in the lands conquered by the "generation that left Egypt"—including northeastern Sinai, Lebanon and western Syria, the Golan Heights, and much of Transjordan—are the lands Israel is required eventually to conquer and settle. The boundaries of the "returning exiles from Babylonia" encompass southern

Lebanon, southwestern Syria, half of Transjordan, the northern Negev, and northeastern Sinai, but not large parts of the coastal plain. Neither these borders nor the smaller ones described in Ezekiel, which include the Jordan River on the east, are to be considered candidates for permanent boundaries. Elitzur suggests that Ezekiel's borders, which more or less correspond to the territory Israel presently rules, were meant to describe the shape Israel would take during the "dawn of redemption," a shape that would be expanded as the redemption process advanced.[40] In general, Elitzur concludes, public settlement of Jews devoted to inheriting the land, in any part of the territory ever conquered by or promised to the ancient Israelites, is sufficient to transform that territory into a part of the "holy Land of Israel."[41]

Territorially ambitious rabbis and religious leaders differ according to which direction they emphasize for expansion and the means they suggest as mandatory or permissible to accomplish this expansion. At one extreme are those who characterize wars of liberation, in virtually any direction, as required under conditions deemed favorable by political and military elites. Shlomo Aviner represents this group:

> We have been commanded by the God of Israel and the creator of the world to take possession of this *entire* land, in its holy borders, and to do this by wars of defense, and even by wars of liberation.[42]

Support for this position is easily found in the writings of Tzvi Yehuda Kook.

> We are commanded both to possess and to settle. The meaning of possession is conquest, and in performing this mitzvah, we can perform the other—the commandment to settle. In our eternal Torah we are commanded to settle the desolate land, meaning also the portions of the land that are spiritually desolate. We cannot evade this commandment. . . . Torah, war, and settlement—they are three things in one and we rejoice in the authority we have been given for each of them.[43]

Somewhat less aggressive positions are taken by rabbis and lay leaders who specify conditions to be met before expansion can take place. Only with a "qualitative improvement of the spiritual climate" within Israel, Rabbi Uzi Kelcheim has argued, will the "quantitative extension of the territory of Eretz Israel" occur.[44] Without advocating wars of conquest, others speak in practical terms of opportunities they believe may or will arise. "We must prepare ourselves," said Hanan Porat in the immediate aftermath of the Yamit evacuation (but before the Lebanon War), "in terms of our consciousness and by establishing new settlement nuclei, to settle those portions of the Land of Israel that today are still not in our hands . . . nuclei for the Litani area, Gilead, Transjordan, and Sinai."[45]

Other fundamentalists focus their expansionist ambitions on one particular geographic area. Traditionally, most such aspirations have been directed toward the East Bank of the Jordan, where the Israelite tribes of Reuven, Gad, and Manasseh were located. Thus, Eleazar Waldman opposes the idea propounded with much fanfare by Yitzhak Shamir, Ariel Sharon, and some nonreligious fundamentalists that the East Bank, now ruled by King Hussein, become the Palestinian homeland. Waldman and the religious majority of the movement may acknowledge that such proposals have some tactical utility, but they oppose any *formal* agreement to relinquish the East Bank to non-Jewish rule, since it is clearly part of the Land of Israel.[46]

But if Transjordan has been the primary focus for Gush Emunim's expansionist ambitions, the Lebanon War encouraged many others within the movement to discuss Biblical imperatives toward territorial expansion in other directions as well. In September 1982, at the climax of the war, *Nekuda* published a transcript of a study session in Ofra led by Yehuda Elitzur that identified the most serious distortion of Israel's true borders to be in the north—in Lebanon.[47] The following month Jewish fundamentalists made this position public in a book entitled *This Good Mountain and the Lebanon*. Rabbis Dov Lior, Yaacov Ariel, and Yisrael Ariel were among those who declared southern Lebanon to be the lands of the Israelite tribes of Zevulon, Naphtali, and Asher. Yisrael Ariel characterized the borders of the Land of Israel to include Lebanon up to Tripoli, Syria, part of Iraq, part of Kuwait, and Sinai.[48] In October 1982 he called for the annexation and settlement of most of Lebanon, regardless of the cost.

Beirut is part of the Land of Israel—about that there is no controversy, and being that Lebanon is a part of

the Land of Israel we must declare that we have no intention of leaving. We must declare that Lebanon is
flesh of our flesh, as is Tel Aviv or Haifa, and that we
do this by right of the moral power granted to us in
the Torah. Our leaders should have entered Lebanon
and Beirut without hesitation, and killed every single
one of them. Not a memory or a trace should have remained. . . . We should have entered Beirut at any
price, without regard to our own casualties, because
we are speaking of the conquest of the Land of Israel. . . . We should immediately divert the waters of
the Litani to the Jordan. . . . [49]

In response to the peace treaty with Egypt and Israel's gradual
withdrawal from Sinai, some fundamentalists sought to focus
irredentist sentiment there. But despite the loyalty with which
Gush Emunim commemorates the uprooting of Yamit, and the
official and undisputed status Sinai holds within the fundamentalist movement as an integral part of the Land of Israel, this demand
is not highly salient. The organization created to work toward this
objective, *Shvut Sinai* (Return to Sinai), seems to have disappeared.

Most within the movement appear to be uncomfortable with
public appeals to biblical or halachic imperatives to justify so-
called wars of liberation. The rabbis who raised territorial demands during the Lebanon War were severely criticized for doing
so, though, as we shall see, mainly on tactical grounds. The general
perception within Gush Emunim is that recognition of Arab
political rights in Jordan and Lebanon represents a painful, if
temporary, compromise of Jewish territorial claims. Yoel Ben-
Nun's remarks in this respect are representative.

We shall not forget "our Transjordan," but we know
well that the people of Israel, in its current circumstances . . . is hardly able to integrate the western Land of
Israel, that we have in our hands (to say nothing of
the lands of Naphtali and Asher in Lebanon!). That is
hard to understand and to swallow, but "This also is
the word of God."[50]

The dominant view within the Jewish fundamentalist movement is that the task of this generation is to ensure the establish-

ment of permanent Jewish control of Judea, Samaria, the Gaza District, and the Golan.[51] For virtually all of those referred to as "our public," the "western Land of Israel"—the area between the Jordan River and the Mediterranean Sea—is the irreducible minimum for fulfilling the purpose of Zionism, carrying out the obligation to settle and inherit the land, and advancing the redemption process. Aspirations to extend Jewish rule over Sinai, parts of Lebanon, and much of the East Bank should not be forgotten, and may some day become politically relevant. In the meantime, direct action to achieve these objectives may be postponed in the effort to consolidate Jewish rule west of the Jordan.

Within this mainstream view, the most important point of disagreement is on whether or not to move quickly toward formal annexation. The declaration of Israeli sovereignty in Judea, Samaria, and Gaza is a formal part of Tehiya's platform, and the party has introduced resolutions to that effect in the Knesset. But many within the movement, if not most, prefer to wait until a very substantial shift in the demographic balance is achieved through massive Jewish settlement and Arab emigration.

What may be termed a "dovish fringe" also exists within Gush Emunim. Shaken by the losses that many Yeshivot Hesder sustained in the Lebanon War, a number of rabbis and other well-known leaders of the movement began speaking of the need to consider peace and the saving of Jewish lives as valid reasons to delay demands for exclusive Jewish rule of all the territories. Among those who have taken positions of this nature are Zevulon Hammer, Yehuda Ben-Meir, Rabbi Yehuda Amital, Yochanan Ben-Yaacov, and Rabbi Aharon Lichtenstein. The positions they favor range from granting administrative autonomy for West Bank and Gaza Arabs without establishing formal Israeli sovereignty as a more or less permanent solution, to relinquishing certain densely populated Arab areas to Jordan or Egypt.[52] Though hedged about with many conditions, these views do involve acceptance of the principle of *pikuach nefesh* as applicable to territorial questions, belief that security *might* someday be enhanced and not degraded by compromise, and emphasis on the value of the people of Israel as greater than the Land of Israel. In the words of Amital:

> If opportunities for a genuine and final peace with the Arabs materialize, after which emigration of Jews from

the Land might stop and a massive immigration of Jews might begin, and if we are faced with the choice of more Jews in the Land of Israel, with less holy land under Jewish rule, or fewer Jews in the Land of Israel and more holy land under Jewish rule, we should choose the first option.[53]

The radical character of such beliefs in the fundamentalist context is reflected in the banning of Zevulon Hammer, minister of education and culture in the Begin government, from most Gush settlements after he made remarks suggesting that although settlements should never be abandoned, autonomy and other negotiated arrangements to bring peace to the area should not be ruled out. Amital's opinions triggered a wave of angry letters and articles denouncing his views as a contradiction of the basic premise of Gush Emunim, challenging his right to be considered part of the movement, and attacking the editors' decision to allow such heresy to appear in the pages of *Nekuda*.[54] Indeed, insofar as these individuals have arrived at positions that include compromise and delay in the implementation of transcendental imperatives, they must be considered as substantially less fundamentalist than the vast majority of Gush Emunim leaders and activists.

Pace and Political Dynamics of the Redemption Process. Both religious and nonreligious Jewish fundamentalists believe that Israel's role in the contemporary period has world historic significance. Most think of it in terms of a process of redemption that has begun and will culminate in the establishment of *malchut Yisrael* (the restoration of the authority of the house of David over the whole Land of Israel). For the religious, this will include the arrival of the long-awaited Messiah, and even some nonreligious fundamentalists embrace the vision of a rebuilt Temple in Jerusalem, state enforcement of the halacha, and a unifying "spiritual revival."[55] Cutting across the religious divide are intricate debates over the exact schedule of events in this redemptive process, the extent of human involvement in its advancement, and its overall length.

For religious fundamentalists the debate is, on one level, theological. Some argue that individual spiritual repentance and increased religious observance will be necessary before the process can move toward completion. Others contend that God welcomes any action necessary to advance the process, and will respond to it, whether or not individual Jews repent. The esoteric elements in this debate are not as important as the dramatically different political stances for which differing theological and philosophical interpretations are offered as justification. The crucial distinction within Jewish fundamentalism as a whole is between "vanguardists," or "truth tellers," on the one hand, and "consensus builders" on the other.[56]

The vanguardists believe that although the process of redemption has begun, and may be completed in the near future if the proper steps are taken, its fulfillment is in serious jeopardy. Therefore, dramatic action is often required to "create facts" necessary for the continuation of the process, even if the vast majority of Jews oppose such action as irrational or illegal. It is imperative that the truth be spoken, no matter how unsettling or unpopular it is, so that the people learn to trust Gush Emunim as an organization of zealots dedicated above all to redemption, unsullied by considerations of political expediency. The government of Israel, argue the vanguardists, is neither holy nor authoritative, and if its decisions contradict the destiny of the people and Land of Israel, and what they see as the Zionist mission of the state, those decisions must be defied. Nonreligious vanguardists state their position as follows:

> We must distinguish very clearly between state and government. The first is given in trust to the second. The Knesset acts only as a custodian. The state is not the property of the Knesset and the government rather the latter administer the affairs of the state *in trust,* and on condition that they remain faithful to that trust.[57]

Their religious counterparts make the same argument in halachic terms.

> When a king of Israel behaves in a manner contrary to the Torah—his authority as a king of Israel is cancelled . . . similarly we must distinguish between the concept of "state," that has supreme value, and the concept of "leader of the people." This latter status depends on different conditions which, if not met, mean that neither the "leader" nor the "government" can be considered "authoritative" in the halachic sense.[58]

Most vanguardists emphasize the decisive role of human effort in fulfilling God's will. They tend to reject the notion that certain aspects of the process, such as the restoration of the Sanhedrin or the rebuilding of the Temple, must await the miraculous intervention of God or his angels. With bold action rooted in faith, and justified on the basis of their appreciation of the higher law to which they are responding, the vanguardists claim to act in the tradition of authentic Zionism, a minority movement that ignored accusations of unrealism to make divinely supported visions a reality. Rather than wait the generations it would take to convince Israelis to act decisively, the vanguardists see the function of Gush Emunim as responding to true, but as yet unappreciated, messianic imperatives.

> The establishment of Gush Emunim settlements across the Green Line, and the effective erasure of that line, required a few to take upon themselves the responsibility for determining the fate of the western Land of Israel in our generation . . . without the permission of the elected government of Israel, and even in the face of its bitter opposition.[59]

Drawing on Talmudic sources, as well as on the writings of the Kooks and Menachem Kasher, they emphasize that just as Rabbi Akiva judged that the outcome of the revolt against Rome would determine the advent of the messianic age, so too must Gush Emunim, despite the absence of obviously miraculous signs, understand its pursuit of concrete political objectives and the liberation of the entire Land of Israel from foreign rule as a direct struggle to complete the redemption process.[60]

Politically, many of the vanguardists are associated with Tehiya. Within Gush circles, they have argued against the principle of voting for the Likud in parliamentary elections as the "lesser of two evils." Before the 1981 elections the Likud came under heavy criticism for officially supporting the idea of Arab autonomy in the West Bank and Gaza, though an even greater fear was that a Labor victory would curtail the resources available for Jewish settlement in the areas. Beni Katzover, a religious vanguardist prominent in Tehiya, argued against calculations of political expediency.

> Our strength must be that we speak the truth, our truth, to the people. We must concentrate on the ends

[and] not the means. . . . If we say that the Likud is a
lesser of the evils and therefore we should support it,
this means we accept [Arab] autonomy. How can we
say to the people that we are speaking our truth when
we can be seen to accept autonomy? . . . The biggest
enemy of the Land of Israel is confusion, blurring of
the truth.[61]

Similarly, Eleazar Waldman agrees that the truth must be told to
the Jewish people that "they are not yet what they were created to
be."[62] But Waldman, among other vanguardists, also emphasizes
the importance of telling the truth to non-Jews.

We do not struggle for the Land of Israel only by dis-
regarding the Arabs or the gentiles, but, in fact, we do
so out of *our responsibility* to the gentiles. Based on our
faith that "You have chosen us from among all the
families of the earth," we must publicly, and without
fear, declare our truth. And we must be ready to struggle on behalf of the truth that we speak.[63]

Another belief typical of the vanguardist approach is that settlement in the territories does not yet suffice to prevent their return to
Arab rule. Thus, Katzover, who was a member of the original Elon
Moreh settlement nucleus, which eventually settled in Sebastia,
has repeatedly called on Gush Emunim to "return to Sebastia"—
that is, to the strategy of spectacular and extralegal actions designed to create facts, raise the consciousness of the people, and
sabotage what he and other vanguardists see as the all too likely
possibility that a territorial compromise will be reached.[64]

Vanguardists were in the forefront of the struggle to stop the
withdrawal from Yamit, favoring explicit and implicit threats of
violence. Yisrael Ariel, who had been arrested himself for urging
soldiers at Yamit to disobey orders, warned:

Don't wait for the exterminator to sneak up on the settlements of Judea and Samaria, perish the thought.
Don't wait for the moment when the cranes arrive at
Kedumim and Elon Moreh. Take Yamit as an example . . . and the moment that they come to uproot a
planting, to attempt to demolish houses, let every individual abandon a house and do battle in Yamit in or-

der to save Judea and Samaria, in order to save all of the Land of Israel![65]

One of the most articulate spokesmen for the vanguardist camp is Eliyakim Haetzni, an attorney and fiery polemicist in Kiryat Arba whose writings appear in *Nekuda* more often than those of any other author. In 1985 Haetzni founded Elisha (Citizens for Judea, Samaria, and Gaza), whose purpose was to mobilize political opposition to the Hussein–Peres peace initiatives under way at that time. And in his book, *The Shock of Withdrawal from the Land of Israel,* he argues that Jews faithful to the Land of Israel have the right to resist and even overthrow the State of Israel if it betrays Zionism and the Jewish people by agreeing to relinquish portions of the homeland to Arab rule.[66]

Haetzni is a founding member of the Yesha Council, and in October 1985 the council passed a resolution reflecting his views:

The proposals and plans of the Prime Minister [Peres] constitute a clear and absolute abrogation of Israel's role as a Zionist state. . . . We warn any regime in Israel which implements such proposals that we will relate to it as an illegal regime as General de Gaulle treated the Vichy regime of Marshal Petain, which betrayed the French people.[67]

Haetzni and others have leveled withering criticisms at Gush Emunim leaders for failing to fulfill their vanguard function. Rejecting the official Gush argument that the Jewish terrorist underground arose in response to a failure of the government to protect settlers from Arab violence, vanguardist Dan Tor blamed the underground on the leadership vacuum in Gush Emunim. According to Tor, the movement failed completely at Yamit, abandoning its revolutionary mission for a business-as-usual approach in which its so-called leaders served as government lackeys.[68] By refusing to speak the truth about the liberation of the lands of Zevulon and Naphtali in Lebanon it demonstrated that "whoever betrayed the southern portion of the Land of Israel will not have the moral strength to conquer its northern portion."[69] Another vanguardist, Baruch Lior, has attacked Yesha for its reluctance to emphasize demonstrative settlement in the most sensitive locations as the most effective means of pushing the end.

> It is possible that we will be in the minority . . . then
> we must emphasize that the truth does not derive from
> majorities . . . we must focus the tremendous debate on
> three places—Hebron, Shechem (Nablus), and the
> Temple Mount—with acts of settlement and a wide-
> ranging propaganda effort.[70]

If such efforts should not succeed in preventing movement
toward a territorial compromise, Lior advocates a kind of uni-
lateral declaration of independence by the settlers.

> We will deny the country's right to the name "State of
> Israel." We will continue to maintain a state of the
> Jews in the heart of our land and engrave on its flag
> the duty of ingathering the exiles and of settlement.[71]

However, the vanguardists' very attacks on the leadership of Gush
Emunim reflected the fact that after 1982 the center of gravity
within the movement shifted from vanguardism to consensus
building. In late 1986 one vanguardist complained bitterly about
this trend.

> The Six Day War rejuvenated the term "redemption."
> Many of those who, as a result of the war, went to set-
> tle in the liberated areas did not refrain from using it
> daily to explain, with one word, the meaning of their
> deeds. Parallel to this historic reorientation, over these
> past twenty years, a reaction against it has crystal-
> lized. . . . Even among many students of Rabbi Tzvi
> Yehuda, may he rest in peace, and also in the Chief
> Rabbinate of Israel, a trend exists toward moderation
> and reduction in support for the process of "redemp-
> tion." Every catalyst for the process of national advan-
> cement is repressed. . . .[72]

In contrast to the vanguardists, who conceive of the redemption
as a relatively rapid process (hence their common identification of
the present period as the "generation of the Redemption"[73]),
consensus builders portray it as a process likely to take decades.
Responding to those for whom the continuing delay in the completion of the process has raised doubts about its reality, Shlomo
Aviner asked whether

> anyone could think that only fifty years were needed to
> repair this people?! Sometimes it takes a single man

fifty years or more to repair defects in his own soul. Is
it reasonable that for an entire people fifty years would
suffice? Whoever thinks that understands nothing.
Generations will be necessary to enlighten this people![74]

Other fundamentalist leaders have used stages in biblical history to
suggest the length and rhythm of the redemption process.

Our kingdom, like the entire process of redemption,
we build little by little . . . from the conquest of the
land by Joshua (to the Kingdom of Saul, David, and
Solomon), hundreds of years passed . . . and we don't
even yet have all of the Land of Israel nor the Kingdom of David. This is only the beginning of the Kingdom—a Jewish government—as if in the period of the
Judges.[75]

But despite its length, the consensus builders consider the
process of redemption to be well under way. They express confidence that the settlements established and under construction in
the territories have made territorial compromise all but impossible. The task that remains for Gush Emunim is to help the
majority of Israelis to accustom themselves to the new reality, to
prepare them—spiritually, ideologically, and politically—for the
unfolding process of redemption, and to provide leadership and
inspiration during the setbacks that are bound to occur. This
means avoiding extremist slogans and confrontational actions,
which alienate many Israelis and impede the creation of a new
consensus supportive of Jewish sovereignty over the whole Land
of Israel as an objective more important than peace or a high
standard of living.

This approach also entails characterization of the State of Israel
per se as "the primary stage in the process of the Redemption of
Israel."[76] In part to discourage vanguardist acts of defiance, consensus builders regularly affirm those aspects of Rav Tzvi Yehuda's
teachings that ascribed literal holiness to the state, government,
and people of Israel, regardless of their shortcomings. Although
he has a reputation for vanguardist actions and attitudes, Moshe
Levinger emphasizes this and other themes associated with the
consensus-building approach.

In light of the great mission of the State of Israel . . .
dedicated to the final victory of good over evil . . . the
State of Israel is holy. The Torah, the Yeshivas, and the
synagogues, as well as buildings, industry, agriculture
and all productive enterprises—all are holy, even
though there are different levels of holiness. But also
the responsible governmental institutions are holy . . .
as are, in a special way, the army and the police,
who guard the state.[77]

The most important slogan of the consensus builders is a traditional phrase whose use in this context is attributed to Tzvi
Yehuda—*kima kima* (little by little). The position of Rabbi
Yehoshua Zuckerman, director of the Merkaz HaRav Yeshiva in
1984, is typical.

Remember the teaching of our Rabbi, Rav Tzvi
Yehuda Kook, may he rest in peace, concerning faith
in our state. This faith does not permit slogans such as
"Messiah now," "peace now," or "holiness now." The
Redemption comes kima kima, by the same power that
created our state, and we shall work, managing to
move forward along the path toward it, despite all its
complexities.[78]

Rather than speaking the truth at all costs, most Gush spokesmen and strategists emphasize the need to "say only that which can
be heard" by the public at large. The primary task, in their eyes, is
an ideological/educational one that must be performed gently,
over a long period of time. By mid-1983 most leaders of the
movement agreed that during the Lebanon War, great damage had
been done by those of its members who had spoken loudly of the
importance of settling and annexing those portions of Lebanon
that Gush Emunim considers within the promised borders of the
Land of Israel.

Today our problem is how to educate the people. . . . It is very important for our youth to learn
where the borders of the Land of Israel are, but the
transmission of this truth must be gradual. We must
return to what we have learned in the house of study
from Rav Tzvi Yehuda, little by little. . . . In order to
bring our ideas to the public, it is impossible to ex-

press them in all their fullness . . . the ear cannot hear too great a noise.[79]

It is time, according to Yosef Ben-Shlomo, chairman of the Jewish philosophy department at Tel Aviv University, for Gush Emunim to establish its hegemony over the entire Zionist movement. This will entail maintaining a low profile for some long-term goals, elaborating an "ideological manifesto . . . highlighting only those objectives that the people of Israel agree with deep in its soul," and then launching a comprehensive educational, ideological, and cultural campaign for the final defeat of secular, dovish Zionism.[80] Moshe Levinger has made similar consensus-building arguments for dissimulation in regard to the unliberated areas in the north, and for patient confidence in the inexorable pace of redemption. In view of the unpopularity of the Lebanon War, he advises against discussing the question of whether or not Lebanon is a part of the Land of Israel.[81] Levinger has also tried to reassure Jewish fundamentalists that despite the Yamit evacuation, budget cuts for settlements, the outcome of the Lebanon War, and the Labor Party's participation in the government, the future is secure.

> The public that is faithful to the Land of Israel has begun to worry. Perhaps, in spite of everything, the danger is real that the Yamit precedent will be repeated, God forbid, in parts of Judea, Samaria, and Gaza. I must say, taking full responsibility, that such simplistic and absolutist comparisons between what happened in Sinai and the infrastructure we have established here in the heart of our forefathers' inheritance: Judea, Samaria, and Gaza, are exaggerated and totally unjustified.[82]

Levinger proceeds to argue for continued support of the Likud's participation in the national unity government (despite an apparent settlement freeze), intensified efforts to convince all Israelis of the ideological and spiritual centrality of the Land, calm faith in the future, and dedication to building a normal life in the territories without recourse to needless confrontation with the authorities.

Uri Elitzur is often referred to as one of a half-dozen activists who might be candidates for a formally elected leadership position in Gush Emunim. After a lengthy series of conversations between

Amos Oz (a leading Israeli author and dovish activist) and Gush Emunim stalwarts appeared in *Nekuda,* many fundamentalists objected to the publication's giving so much attention to Oz's views. Elitzur's consensus-building approach, including his judgment of the importance and the difficulty of building the necessary consensus, is reflected in his response to those who objected to the debate with Oz.

> *The most difficult political or international problem with which we are now faced, and which it is now proper for us to address, is to persuade Amos Oz. I have no illusions that it will be possible to achieve this goal in the next five years, but I believe that in fifty years it will be done.*[84]

The most prolific exponent of the consensus-building approach, and the most sophisticated, is Yoel Ben-Nun. Alone among Gush leaders, Ben-Nun has been a regular contributor of articles to the left-wing press.[85] For Ben-Nun the lesson of Yamit is that "it is impossible to succeed without the support of the decisive majority of the people. We must go With the people and not against it—nor against large parts of it."[86] The process of redemption, he counsels, is a long one, dependent ultimately on the will and miraculous action of God to bring it to completion. Gush Emunim's contribution cannot be discovered halachically, but can be determined only on the basis of pragmatic political concerns.[87] Given the enormous progress made by the settlement movement, the primary task at the present juncture is to engage in a prolonged Kulturkampf with the dovish left, aimed at constructing a new consensus on the boundaries and character of the Jewish state. Simple declarations of Israeli sovereignty over the occupied areas will not do what only the ideological conversion of masses of Israelis to the cause of Jewish fundamentalism can accomplish.[88]

Thus, "the days of Sebastia and Yamit," when Gush Emunim's mission was to act as a vanguard, "are gone and will not return."[89] By panicking over every problem, agitating fiercely for more and more money for settlements, exaggerating threats to the personal security of settlers, and justifying actions by the Jewish terrorist underground, the vanguardists discourage more settlement and cause Gush Emunim to appear as a special-interest group, separated from the mass of Israelis. This endangers the fulfillment of the redemption by interfering with the political task of building a new consensus.[90] Confident of the long-term strength of Gush Emunim, Ben-Nun condemns all Gush elements that support independent or radical actions based on challenges to the legitimacy of the state in pursuit of redemptionist ends. He asserts instead the decisive importance of engaging in a wide-ranging, respectful dialogue to reconstruct a consensual basis for the authority of the state. "There is nothing more urgent at this stage than to renew the authority of the state based on a public consensus."[91]

Attitudes Toward International and Israeli Opposition. As emphasized in chapter 4, Jewish fundamentalists conceive of a radical distinction between the Jewish and non-Jewish worlds and assume a basically antagonistic relationship between them. Fundamentalists consider Jewish messianism "not only our responsibility to ourselves but to all the families of man."[92] Thus, Jewish conflict with the gentiles, and even wars against them, is "for their own good,"[93] because in the long run the reunification of the people of Israel with its whole land hastens the redemption of all mankind.

At least until that time arrives, however, few if any Jewish fundamentalists consider gentiles dependable friends or partners. "For us," Moshe Levinger has declared, "the gentiles can be divided into two types: those who hate us and those who would be indifferent to our destruction."[94] Despite such rhetoric, however, there are real differences within the movement over what distinctions are worth making among gentiles, the cultural and political threats they represent, and the appropriateness of political models associated with the western democracies.

All Jewish fundamentalists reject the notion of a "Judeo-Christian tradition" which constitutes the basis for a Western civilization in which Jews authentically share. In fact, in discussions on Jewish relations with non-Jews living in the Land of Israel, many Gush Emunim rabbis have distinguished Muslims from Christians, insofar as the former are "unquestionably monotheistic," whereas the belief of the latter in the Trinity suggests they be regarded as "idol-worshippers."[95] Still, Rav Tzvi Yehuda was willing to acknowledge that "the great gentiles," such as novelist George Eliot, "know that the Land of Israel is joined to the people of Israel."[96] Most fundamentalists, however, tend to think that even if all gentiles are not actively opposed to the renaissance of the Jewish people in its land, they cannot possibly understand it. The following passages are quoted from a nonreligious and a religious fundamentalist, respectively.

The historical connection of the people of Israel to Judea and the Mountain of Ephraim is something no foreigner can ever understand. One cannot begin to explain it with routine political concepts . . . these are things that are outside the realm of formal, realistic discussion, as might be proferred in a meeting of the Security Council or an international court.[97]

The Torah took pains to explain to us God's motive in taking a land from one people and making it the home of another. There is no problem here of "being in the wrong," or being in the right. The question is the source from which the words came. There is a qualitative difference between the Torah morality of the people of Israel and the moral laws of other peoples spread over the earth which are derived from anthrocentric worldviews in which man stands at the center of law and is the highest value. In contrast, the Jewish worldview is theocentric. For the believer the source of both action and belief is the command of God.[98]

Whether religious or nonreligious, Jewish fundamentalists contrast the materialism and shallowness of the Christian West with the discipline, historicity, and spiritual depth of Judaism. Democracy and equality, regardless of race, religion, or ethnic background, may be appropriate values for Europe and America, but they do not apply to Israel.

If in Europe and the United States a moral and democratic mission requires equality of rights for all, it is clear and obvious that in Israel what must determine rights to vote and to be elected to public office must be identification with and participation in the struggle of the people of Israel to accomplish its mission.[99]

Beyond this rejection of political models imported from Europe and America, a very substantial body of opinion within Gush Emunim identifies the influence of Western, liberal democratic culture on the Jewish people as the source of its current problems.

The most fervent exponent of this viewpoint is Moshe Ben-Yosef (Hagar), who has written, "There is no Western culture—neither American, Russian, German, nor French—that is not foreign to the culture and history of Israel."[100]

Along with Haetzni and Ben-Nun, Ben-Yosef is one of the most published authors in *Nekuda*; for several years he has had his own column. For Ben-Yosef, the European Enlightenment, which "emancipated" the Jews, was actually a great catastrophe, making it "impossible for Jews to live in any foreign land" while simultaneously "thrusting upon the Jewish people the experience of self-annihilation (via assimilation)."[101] By destroying the organic religious and social unity of the past, eighteenth-century Europe's new liberal democratic culture exposed Jews, as an ancient God-centered tribe, to a new form of systematic anti-Semitism, which culminated in the Holocaust.[102] Tragically, the Zionist movement adopted liberal nationalist norms, in vain imitation of the West. Gush Emunim and maximalist Zionism remain the Jewish people's last and only hope to preserve its unique culture and destiny[103] by conducting a "war of extermination against Western culture, which has brought the greatest of holocausts upon us— the Liberal holocaust."[104] This will require severing as many ties with the West as possible. In Ben-Yosef's words:

> We must finally put an end to the kind of Zionism which rejects the implementation of real Zionism—the future of the people is in danger! Otherwise, by means of a bureaucratic democracy transferred from the Western industrial countries, the beggars who live off the wealth of others will build, from Eilat to Metula [within the green line] a boutique for strictly European merchandise. That is to say, by means of the dictatorship of the secretariat of the party they are seeking favor in the eyes of the intellectuals of the Behemoth— from the left and the right—in the lands of the uncircumcised.[105]

Ultimately, what is required to save the Jewish people from the cultural imperialism of the West is to force the halacha and maximalist Zionism upon them, using state power to do so.

> Our survival as a sovereign Jewish national kingdom . . . requires a different approach to the imple-

mentation of the halacha in a democratic society and, indeed, a revolutionary understanding of the halacha itself. For this we shall need an uncompromising leadership . . . that lives the Zionist revolution from its very sources and also understands the Western conception of the world in which we have become trapped.[106]

Accordingly, Ben-Yosef saves his most vitriolic language not for gentiles, but for Israeli opponents of Gush Emunim, especially those who object to the fundamentalist movement on liberal democratic grounds.

It is a mistake to think we can avoid the catastrophe of a kulturkampf, we are already engaged in it . . . the main representatives of cultural degeneracy in the Land of Israel (in addition to the media and the educational establishment) are "Shinui" and the Movement for Citizen Rights [dovish civil libertarian political groups]. They are typical of the decadence of a society that has disowned the Biblical tradition—by means of scientific progress, aesthetics, and the most elaborate and costly ethical system in history. Instead they demand that permissiveness be established as the cultural reality of Israel.[107]
Kahanism is but a festive overture to the real fascist dictatorship that is being prepared for us in the academies of anarchism by the big brothers of the left. . . .[108]

Although religiously nonobservant himself, Ben-Yosef believes a reformed halacha, springing from nationalist/tribal imperatives, can and should be imposed within Israel, and blames the official rabbinate for impeding the process.[109] While few opinion leaders within the Jewish fundamentalist movement are as vituperative as Ben-Yosef or as willing to discuss publicly the establishment of a theocratic dictatorship, even fewer take issue with his attacks on Western culture. Eliyakim Haetzni, Tzvi Shiloach, Meir Kahane, Amiel Unger, Israel Eldad, and many others regularly condemn Israeli doves as "Meists," "nowists," "Hellenizers," "fifth columnists," "traitors," and carriers of Western materialism and spiritual decadence.[110] Peace Now is widely considered representative of a categorical abandonment of Zionism and as the source of apathy and loss of will among Israeli Jews.

With great sorrow we witness today an accelerating process, under the guise of "sane" Zionism, of dehistorization and de-Zionization, a process encouraging Jews to fold their hands and undermining faith in the justice of our cause. . . . *Zionism was always based on anti-Nowism, and in all the years of the Exile it stood in revolt against its essence, which was "nowism."* In exile the life of Jews was entirely submerged in the bleak and uncertain "now."[111]

Against a background of Labor party efforts, from 1984 to 1986, to exercise the "Jordanian option," i.e. a territorial or administrative division of the occupied territories between Israel and Jordan, before the Likud's return to power, the expression of such sentiments was extended to include the personal vilification of Shimon Peres, Abba Eban, Ezer Weizman, and other leading foreign policy moderates, as well as discussion of the inevitability of, and even the need for, civil war.

Haetzni, for example, portrays Peres as the "second Reheboam," referring to the son of Solomon, whose policies triggered a civil war and the secession of ten tribes from ancient Judea.[112] Haetzni relies heavily on the precedent of the Maccabean War against the Syrian Greeks as, first and foremost, a *"civil war, between Jews and Jews* (Hellenizers vs. those faithful to the land and culture of Israel)."[113] He also insists that any government ceding territory would thereby negate Zionism and its own claim to legitimate authority, warning that if

the state withdraws the army, the police, and the Israeli administration from Judea, Samaria, and Gaza—scores of thousands of Jews will remain, perhaps joined by thousands more from within the country and the Diaspora, in an emergency mobilization to save the land. . . . And if, amidst the shedding of blood, the government tries to evacuate 100,000 Jews from their homes by force, a civil war will break out.[114]

Among the large number of Gush adherents who share Haetzni's views, most would express them less explicitly.[115] They tend to emphasize the horror of the possibility of "a split in the people," even while warning that the excesses of the dovish left could well bring it about.[116] Within this body of opinion, debate is over tactics—for example, whether to take up arms against Israeli troops enforcing a withdrawal order, engage in violent provocations in order to sabotage the process, or remain behind to be slaughtered with great drama by the Arabs.

Beneath the surface of these debates over appropriate tactics in the face of "traitorous" or "blasphemous" political options that present and future Israeli governments might seek to exercise, there lies a more fundamental disagreement within Gush Emunim over the meaning and value of democracy. This issue came to light after the arrest of the Jewish terrorist underground in the spring of 1984. Although most of the soul searching within Gush Emunim triggered by those arrests focused on tactical and educational questions, Eliezer Schweid argued that two more basic questions had to be confronted:

> 1. Do we see democracy as having value in and of itself, or only as a means? . . . Is the halachic sanctity of the state of Israel attached to the fact that it is the state of the Jews, with no connection to the nature of its government?
>
> 2. . . . Do we prefer the absolute and enforced authority of the halacha, which would follow its formal establishment as the law of the state, to a basis of humane and moral sentiments? Or do we fear the halacha, unrestrained in its enforcement, would not stand the test of our moral sentiments and human values, and that its formal establishment would in fact result in hurried and unconsidered rationalizations of it?[117]

With the partial exception of Moshe Ben-Yosef, no one has systematically attempted to answer these questions. However, occasional references by both religious and nonreligious fundamentalists to the "inauthenticity" of majoritarianism in Jewish tradition suggest the direction the debate would take should it ever get under way. Thus, Rabbi Yehuda Hankin reminds his readers that "if democracy means that authority is derived from the public, then Judaism, as is the case with most religions, is not democratic."[118] Rabbi Moshe Tzuriel notes that "apart from disputes within the Sanhedrin . . . there is no basis in the halacha for pitting a majority against a minority, rather the arguments involved are to be weighed objectively."[119] Eliyakim Haetzni makes the same point from a biblical, historicist, but purely nonreligious perspective:

> Even if 100% of the Jewish inhabitants of Israel should vote for its separation from the Land of Israel, that "hundred percent consensus" would not have any more validity than the "hundred percent consensus" that prevailed within the people of Israel when it danced around the golden calf. The fate of those dancers around the golden calf, and they represented a massive "democratic" majority, was branded as with a hot iron into the genetic code of the Jewish people. The same is true of the fate of the spies [sent by Moses into Canaan] who were ready to abandon the Land of Israel, ten of the twelve of them at any rate, a solid "consensus," the fate of whom is also deeply engraved on the historical consciousness of the people.
> . . . The history of Israel is the history of the minority, of Joshua son of Nun and Caleb son of Yephunah, who said: "Let us arise and take it; we shall succeed." In the end the consensualist majority turned on its heels and died in the desert while these two did enter the Land.[120]

Jewish fundamentalism's ambivalent attitude toward Israeli democracy is most apparent in its variety of opinions about the extent to which rehabilitation of its Jewish opponents is possible. Most fundamentalists are prepared to write off the Peace Now leadership, the small liberal parties, and what is often termed the "secular left" as totally cut off from their roots and more than likely to emigrate or assimilate.[121] Yet the movement as a whole seems undecided as to whether or not the Labor Zionist movement, previously the bedrock of Israeli society, is salvageable. Compare the tone of these two quotes from editorials published in *Nekuda*.

> Now that Gush is entering its second decade, its greatest challenge and responsibility is to renew the battle for the support of the people. . . . But not only to reinvigorate Likud supporters and supporters of Gush Emunim. We must redouble our efforts within the ranks

of the Labor settlements, where there exists a silent
majority that continues to appreciate the pioneering
work of Gush.[122]
The Labor Party has been transformed into an out and
out leftist party that supports the establishment of a
Palestinian state. . . . Labor's explicit hostility toward us
is destroying the basis for dialogue . . . the Labor
Party, that was the leading institution in critical areas
pertaining to the upbuilding of the state—settlement,
immigration, and security—today, in almost every area,
adopts positions of retreat and faithlessness . . . indeed
the Labor Party has now endorsed the right of the Palestinians to the Land of Israel.[123]

While the contributions and promise of Labor Zionism and of the
Jewish left in general are emphasized by some, others emphasize
their irremediable abandonment of authentic Jewish and Zionist
values. Thus, while Menachem Froumin reminds his readers of all
the deadly seriousness of the threat posed by the left, he admon-
ishes Gush Emunim to remember that Moses, in his struggle with
Amalek, had to raise both his hands, right and left, to achieve
victory.[124] Abraham Mintz, a Gush veteran, responds that the
"leftists" are

ready to abandon the Land of Israel simply to serve
fewer days in the reserves . . . and just as we should
not allow hatred to blind us, nor should we let love
blur our vision. We are ready to have good relations
with anyone, to honor and love him. We are even
ready to restore sinners to our midst, but not when
they hold a knife in their hands.[125]

Disagreements within the movement over whether antifunda-
mentalist Israeli Jews should be considered criminal or merely
benighted are also expressed by uncertainty regarding the limits to
be imposed on intra-Jewish conflict. This was illustrated by
Yesha's 1986 prudent but confused reinterpretation of its contro-
versial 1985 declaration of intent to resist any government move
toward territorial compromise.[126]

Gush Emunim supporters who espouse the most moderate
position on this issue refuse to subordinate "love of all Israel" or
"the unity of the people" to consolidation or expansion of Jewish

sovereignty over the whole Land of Israel. Strongly criticizing Gush rabbis who endorsed the war in Lebanon as a means to "liberate" large areas of the homeland, at the expense of Jewish lives and risk to the well-being of Diaspora Jewish communities, Yehuda Amital warned that

> there is a hierarchy of values in Judaism, and . . . those who fail to distinguish holiness from holiness will in the end fail to distinguish between the holy and the profane. We must consider the relative priority of three values: *Israel, Torah,* and *the Land of Israel.* The interest of the people of Israel precedes that of the interest of the Land of Israel.[127]

Consistent with this view, Amital and other rabbis have criticized threats of violent opposition to the government on ideological as well as tactical grounds. Indeed, though a minority view in any case, such sentiments appear to be more common among religious leaders than among the secular ultranationalists. Amital, Yoel Ben-Nun, and Aharon Lichtenstein have expressed such strong concern for maintaining the safety and unity of the people, that Haetzni and others have suggested they may no longer qualify to be counted within the "camp of those faithful to the Land of Israel."[128]

Thus Jewish fundamentalists display a substantially broader range of attitudes toward Jews who are not within the movement than toward the international community. They appreciate expressions of support from some American ultraconservatives, retired American military officers, or Protestant fundamentalist groups, but in general are wary of the outside world. To a certain extent this even includes Diaspora Jewish communities. Although the movement views them as important potential sources of immigration, their political influence is not deemed to be great. Their responsibility, shamefully ignored to this point, is to bring an end to their own existence through mass emigration to Israel before assimilation drastically reduces their size. In this regard, manifestations of anti-Semitism are seen positively, as spurs to the emigration of Diaspora Jews.

Europe is seen as spinelessly responsive to Arab oil interests and Palestinian terrorism. Israel's economic and military dependence on the United States is characterized as likely to facilitate dangerous pressure on Israeli governments to accept some sort of territorial compromise. Virtually all Gush Emunim members support lowering the Israeli standard of living in order to reduce dependence on the United States. Significantly, both Haetzni and Ben-Nun, representing, as I have indicated, diametrically opposed viewpoints within the movement, agree that linking Israel's fate with gentile political actors—be they Lebanese Christians, Americans, or Russians—should be avoided except for reasons of short-term expediency. Thus, in direct reaction to the Reagan initiative, Haetzni suggested that Israel consider joining the Soviet bloc. In 1984 Ben-Nun argued for Israeli withdrawal from the "western world democratic front," against the continued purchase of sophisticated and expensive American arms, and in support of renewed ties with the Soviet Union.[129] In the aftermath of the Lebanon War, Eleazar Waldman answered a question about the location of "evil" in the modern world. He acknowledged the Communist bloc's moral inferiority to the West, but emphasized that Israel is standing alone in a wicked world.

> Today evil is exhibited by the entire world. I refer to the western world . . . mainly the *political* leadership of the western world, though of course there is a connection between culture and political behavior. Today these leaders admit openly that they calculate their policies and adopt political positions, not on the basis of justice and righteousness, but in view of their economic and political interests.
>
> . . . The State of Israel is not only the only state in the world fighting against evil, it is the only state that considers justice and righteousness in the determination of its policies.[130]

To be sure, appeals for increased American support for Israel on the basis of a joint struggle against the Soviet Union are not uncommon. In these appeals the United States is usually portrayed as blind to the threat that the grand geopolitical aspirations of Arab nationalism constitute for vital American interests. While American diplomats concentrate on the Arab–Israeli conflict, they ignore the inroads Moscow makes as a result of intra-Arab struggles. A key objective of Israeli foreign policy must be the reeducation of American leaders to the realities of Middle Eastern and international politics. These realities include the decisiveness of Israel's military power in the Middle East, its capacity to partici-pate in the region's political reorganization, and its central role in the fight against terrorism.[131]

But while such formulas may be used in communications di-rected toward the American government or sympathetic audiences outside of the fundamentalist movement, within its religious mainstream they are not taken seriously. The writings of Mor-dechai Nisan, a leading religious Gush intellectual, who teaches Middle Eastern politics at the Hebrew University's School for Overseas Students, provide an excellent example of this "double discourse," in which American audiences are provided with glow-ing tributes to America while militantly anti-American themes are stressed to supportive Jewish audiences. Nisan's 1982 book, *American Middle East Foreign Policy: A Political Reevaluation*, is addressed to U.S. policymakers. He argues there that "America and Israel represent the 'chosen' societies that carry the most noble dreams of civilization." The 1982 war in Lebanon, he asserts, "provided the most recent evidence for the identity of American and Israeli interests on global and regional issues."[132] But in an article directed to a supportive Jewish audience, Nisan charac-terized Israel's relationship to the United States as a colonial one, advocating Israeli policies of violence, extremism, and intransi-gence, instead of "surrender to America."[133]

A similar view of the United States, in which it is portrayed as an imperialist power committed to dismembering Israel for the bene-fit of sinister domestic interests, found expression in a February 1983 *Nekuda* editorial.

> The pressures the United States has placed on Israel to surrender the gains of the Peace for the Galilee War, and the American political offensive, designed in coop-eration with Hussein, Arafat, and their collaborators, are meant to return Israel to its "natural dimensions," that is, *to the lines of 1967*.
>
> The corporation that controls the President of the United States—the Bechtel Corporation—has personal and economic interests in Saudia Arabia, the Persian Gulf and in other Muslim countries. The American President, totally dependent on this clique, has been

converted to an antagonistic stand toward Israel's interests.[134]

In sum, Jewish fundamentalists are divided over how to relate to Jewish opposition, but except in terms of style and emphasis, virtually all display a distrustful antagonism toward gentiles. With respect to one group of gentiles, however, the local Arab population, Jewish fundamentalists are deeply divided.

Policy Toward and Eventual Status of Local Arabs. One of the most extensively and explicitly debated issues within Gush Emunim concerns the policies appropriate for dealing with the large Arab majority living in the West Bank and Gaza Strip, and the substantial Arab minority residing within the 1949 borders of Israel proper.

No evidence exists of concrete plans to carry out genocidal policies toward the "Arabs of the Land of Israel." Nevertheless, analysis of the range of disagreement within the Jewish fundamentalist movement over the Arab question must begin with the fact that a number of rabbis supportive of Gush Emunim have offered opinions that could provide the halachic basis for such policies. The substance of these opinions pertains to the identification of the Palestinian Arabs, or of Arabs in general, as Amalekites.

According to the biblical account, the Amalekites harassed the Israelites during their wandering in the desert, preying upon weak and helpless stragglers. As a consequence, God commanded the Jewish people not only to kill all Amalekites—men, women, and children—but to "blot out the memory of Amalek" from the face of the earth. Traditionally, great enemies of the Jews, such as Haman in ancient Persia (as described in the Book of Esther) and Torquemada during the Spanish Inquisition, have been identified as descendants of Amalek. Accordingly, the most extreme views within Gush Emunim on the Arab question, views quoted extensively by Israeli critics of the movement, speak of the Arabs as descendants of the Amalekites.[135] These critics reacted strongly when Haim Druckman greeted the crippling of two Arab mayors on the West Bank by quoting the Book of Deborah: "Thus may all Israel's enemies perish!" A Gush veteran, Haim Tsuria, defended Druckman: "In every generation there is an Amalek. In our generation, our Amalek are the Arabs who oppose the renewal of our national existence in the land of our fathers."[136]

But despite such rhetoric and occasional halachic disputations over whether an Arab can be killed in the absence of provocation (in view of the presumption of the need for self-defense), no important group within the movement publicly advocates genocide.[137] On the other hand, Meir Kahane's Kach party, which advocates the virtually complete expulsion of Arabs from the Land of Israel, received 22 percent of the vote in the 1985 local council elections in Kiryat Arba. Indeed, it appears that at least one-third of Gush Emunim believes that Jews should consider themselves to be "in a state of war with the whole Arab population of the country."[138] Their discussions focus on the merits of various techniques for bringing about the eventual departure of the all non-Jews from the Land of Israel. The following passages are representative of this viewpoint.

> Coexistence between a Jewish majority and an Arab minority in the Land of Israel, that does not endanger the historical objectives of the Jewish people, and the existence of Israel as a Jewish state, is problematic.
>
> . . . *If we want to avoid unremitting bloodshed, there is only one solution—the transfer of the Arab population of the Land of Israel to the Arab states. . . . This solution is a humane solution compared to the "final solution"* which the Arab world plans for us.[139]
>
> The goal of good neighborly relations with the Arabs of the Land of Israel is not only illusory, but it contradicts the meaning of the settlement enterprise in the Land of Israel. We have come to the land to inherit it because it is our land, and not the land of hundreds of thousands of Arabs living in it like a malignant and painful tumor—a cancer within the heart of the state.
>
> . . . we must settle within densely populated Arab areas, expropriating their land, and insulting their national feelings . . . constantly we must explain to ourselves and our people that Arabs or Jews can live in the Land of Israel—but not both peoples together.[140]
>
> Demographic research shows that within 40 years Arabs will be a majority in the state of Israel, and that

within 80 years they will be a majority within the borders of the 'Green Line.' Abandoning Judea, Samaria, and Gaza will not solve the problem, but only postpone it for a number of years. Clearly, if we do not bring about the departure of the Arabs, the day will come when they will be able, democratically, to destroy the state of Israel.[141]

I am more extreme than Kahane regarding encouragement of Arabs to leave the country. First of all, I favor paying the Arabs to leave the country. But that is just the carrot, not the stick. Gentlemen, this is a Jewish state and I favor negative means of encouragement as well . . . I know the difficulties involved in such policies, but it is the genuine solution and must be implemented completely and systematically.[142]

We must deal with the Land of Israel branch of the Arab people to make sure that it will lose every time something happens that hurts our life in the Land of Israel. We must induce them to leave here. They must be made to feel that the land is slipping away beneath their feet. . . . For the good of our peace, their peace, and the peace of all Israel, not only for the settlers of Judea, Samaria, and Gaza, and for our future in this land, for there to be any future at all, there is no place for Arabs with us here.

. . . We must find a new way, a new revolutionary way to deal with the Jewish–Arab conflict.[143]

Aside from Kach, no political party calls officially for the wholesale expulsion of Arabs. Yuval Neeman, however, at the 1986 Tehiya convention, in Kiryat Arba, declared that a half million Arab refugees presently living in the West Bank and the Gaza Strip would have to be relocated to Arab countries in any peace agreement.[144] More recently, Moshe Ben-Yosef sought to legitimize discussions of mass expulsions.

The fact that Eichmann spoke German does not mean that German cannot be the language of a normal human being, and it is kosher to discuss the idea of transfer, and even to put it into effect, despite the fact that Kahane speaks about it. It is kosher not only be-

cause it is an "actual solution," but also because it is
required for the vision of the whole Land of Israel.
. . . The idea of transfer has deep roots in the Zionist
movement.[145]

He goes on to quote respected leaders of Labor Zionism, such as
Berl Katznelson and Yitzhak Tabenkin, who favored the idea.

Although these sentiments gain ground within Gush Emunim
in periods of violent Arab attacks on Jews, commitment to the
expulsion of the Arab population as a radical solution to the
demographic problem is not a dominant view within Jewish fundamentalism.[146] Nevertheless, vigilantism and various other "iron
fist" techniques against "troublemakers" or in response to specific
Arab actions do have wide support. A poll of 455 settlers conducted in 1981 and 1982 showed that two-thirds of those questioned expressed agreement or strong agreement with the statement "It is necessary for settlers to respond quickly and
independently to Arab harassments of settlers and settlements."[147]
In the summer of 1985, Yesha called for a crackdown on the Arab
population, recommending closure of Arab newspapers and uni-
versities, dissolution of Arab cooperatives and youth organizations, loosening of restrictions on settler use of weapons, and
prosecution of all known PLO supporters.[148] Following a particularly brutal firebomb attack in April 1987, which killed a young
mother traveling to a West Bank settlement, hundreds of Jewish
settlers went on a rampage in the nearby Arab town of Kalkilia.
Daniella Weiss, general secretary of Gush Emunim, was reportedly among those who "threw bottles at shops in the town, rolled
barrels down the streets, and set fires to tires."[149] Gideon Altschuler, a founder of Tehiya and its general secretary until November 1987, has advocated issuing shoot-to-kill orders against
Arab stone throwers, including children.[150]

Beni Katzover expressed the "blood-boiling" response of most
Gush members to Arab attacks on settlers in his endorsement of
collective punishment as a policy for maintaining control over the
Arab population.

Our moderation, tolerance and care are the reasons
why the Arab public is dominated by the extremists.
Failure to retaliate against acts of terror is what con-
vinces the Arabs that it does not pay to cooperate with

the policy of coexistence. . . . What we need is collective punishment and harsh measures—so that they
learn to fear us.[151]

In a 1987 poll of rabbis living in the West Bank and Gaza, 86
percent of those responding judged that it was permissible to use
collective punishment against refugee camps or extended families.
The favored method (64 percent) was deportation.[152] But while
the majority of Gush Emunim members favor collective punishment as a law enforcement tactic, including the deportation of
hundreds or even thousands of Arab "agitators" and stone
throwers (along with their families), others warn against collective
punishment on the grounds that it implies, and may even help to
create, a Palestinian "collectivity" that does not exist naturally.[152]

Regardless of different opinions on the wisdom of collective
punishment as a law enforcement device, most fundamentalists do
not believe that policies of wholesale retribution or transfer can or
should be used to address the problem of the size of the Arab
population relative to that of the Jews. Mainstream opinion within
Gush Emunim toward the Arabs who live in the West Bank and
Gaza is that strict enforcement of security laws, effective bans on
Arab political and cultural activity, closure or direct Israeli supervision of Arab educational institutions, and minimal personal relations between Arabs and Jews can create an environment within
which settlement can flourish, annexation proceed, and the demographic problem be gradually alleviated. The general expectation,
sometimes stated and sometimes not, is that deprived of opportunities for political, cultural, and economic development, and
discovering the area to be ever more thoroughly "Judaized," Arabs
will emigrate in demographically meaningful numbers.[154]

While Arabs yet remain in the Land of Israel, Yaacov Ariel and
most other Gush rabbis stress that a clear distinction must be made
between attitudes toward and treatment of Arabs who meet the
conditions for living in peace with the Jews and those who do not.
There is much less agreement on what those conditions are, but
one that almost all the rabbis stipulate is that Arabs surrender any
claim to political influence in the country. Tzvi Yehuda wrote that
private meetings with Arab notables were to be encouraged for the
purpose of reducing levels of personal animosity, but only as long
as the Arabs involved abandoned all political demands.

First of all they must recognize that they have no arguments to make concerning political authority. How to behave toward minorities—that is something that can be clarified to avoid injustice. But with respect to politics and the state—it is impossible for us to disavow the truth that we owe them no part of the government! Only after they know this is there a place for discussions with them.[155]

This overall stance is expressed accurately, and unselfconsciously, in the photograph on the cover of the January 13, 1984, issue of *Nekuda,* an issue concerned particularly with the Arab question. (For a reproduction of this cover, see Appendix 4.) Above the caption "A Moment of Coexistence," a Gush settler, in military uniform, leads an elderly, blind Arab refugee across a road. The settler's machine gun is slung across his waist. He holds a club in one hand and the Arab's hand in the other. This is, in fact, what most Gush Emunim loyalists consider the proper relationship of Jews to Arabs in the Land of Israel—the Jews as young, dominant, strong, armed, in control, and fully alert; the Arabs as old, helpless, docile, dependent, grateful, but ultimately irrelevant.[156]

Within this mainstream perspective there are disagreements on specific points. An elaborate literature is developing pertaining to the halachic implications of the concept of *gar toshav* (resident alien). Most fundamentalist rabbis agree that, generally, observance of the seven Noachite commandments (including a ban on idol worship) and acceptance of Jewish sovereignty, in the form of tax payments to the Jewish government, should qualify a non-Jew for the protection of his person and property in a Jewish state. Others, however, argue that to attain gar toshav status, the non-Jew must not only observe the seven Noachite commandments, but also undergo a kind of conversion process and accept the holiness of the Torah. Still others insist that while non-Jews might be permitted to own land, the prohibition against transfer of land to non-Jews, known as *lo tehonem,* means that no real property not now in Arab hands may be allowed to come into their possession. Additional issues in this debate are whether the gar toshav can be allowed to live in Jerusalem and whether in the absence of the

Temple the status of gar toshav can be enforced de jure or only de facto.[157]

Stretching beyond the bounds of these halachic disputes are a broader set of policy concerns, including the important question of whether or not non-Jews can or should be granted some corporate minority status. Some fundamentalists argue that a separate, subordinate, but formal legal status should be imposed on Arabs to eliminate the ambiguity of their residence in Israel without citizenship.[158] Associated with this view is the model of Jewish life in the Muslim world, as a *dhimmi* community, meaning, in Muslim parlance, a monotheistic religious group deserving of protective subordination, and, more broadly, that of Jewish life in the Diaspora. Yaacov Ariel has put it this way:

> In the Galut [Exile] faithful Jews opposed both equal rights and equal responsibilities for Jews. We did not want to be in the army and fight the wars of others. We did not demand fully equal rights in education, social standing, or political action. We saw ourselves as guests and we wanted to be treated that way. . . . We never saw ourselves as citizens in the Galut. What we demand of the Arabs in our land is no different from what they demanded from us in Galut: be honored guests, who know how to acknowledge and honor the master of the house, or be citizens bearing the full yoke of responsibilities as well as rights. . . .[159]

Those who hold out the theoretical possibility of citizenship for West Bank and Gaza Arabs, such as Yaacov Ariel and the Tehiya party, do so by attaching conditions designed to make its acquisition virtually impossible (thorough security check, knowledge of Hebrew, three years' national service, declaration of loyalty to Israel as a Jewish-Zionist state, and so on).[160] Some fundamentalists argue that "cooperative" Arabs can be used as allies within the Arab population to help stabilize the situation; others condemn all attempts to forge political alliances with Arab elements.[161] Some would deprive Arabs of employment opportunities in Jewish settlements by hiring only Jews for construction and custodial work; others respond that Arab labor is still necessary, that such demands are impractical.[162] Some advocate reducing the political status of Arabs inside the green line to conform to that of Arabs in the West

Bank and Gaza and to prevent the crystallization of an effective political alliance between Israeli Arabs and left-wing Jews;[163] others believe that taking rights away from Arabs who are already Israeli citizens would be difficult and unnecessarily provocative.[164]

It is apparent even in the appeals made by fundamentalist authors who favor tough policies toward the Arabs that they judge most of their readers to have a visceral hatred of Arabs. Thus, while declaring that "humane" policies toward Arab political activists are not appropriate, Hanan Porat nonetheless quotes both Abraham Isaac Kook and Tzvi Yehuda to support his overall argument that the Arab problem must be addressed "not by denigrating Ishmael, but by elevating Israel."[165] But a small minority within Gush Emunim, whose contributions to Nekuda comprise some 10–15 percent of the articles published on the subject, are very critical of the negative attitudes toward Arabs that they say predominate within the mainstream of the movement.[166] In an article entitled "Do Not Hate!" Miriam Shiloh, for example, recounts violently anti-Arab songs and slogans popular among Gush Emunim youth. Such attitudes are wrong and dangerous, she warns. She gives an example of Arabs who helped her family during an auto accident and argues in favor of applying the Talmudic dictum "to love thy neighbor as thyself."[167] In a similar vein, arguments are occasionally made for greater efforts to establish "good neighborly relations with Arabs" or to teach Jewish children Arabic.[168]

Most authors who are solicitous of Arab rights and sensibilities are not leaders of the movement, though fluctuations in the editorial line of Nekuda suggest that key activists share some of their opinions.[169] On the individual level these writers stress the development of positive personal relations with Arab inhabitants. Politically they suggest that loyal Arabs should be extended formal rights to citizenship or, eventually, opportunities to participate within whatever political system is based in Amman. Most of them believe that the Jews must consider themselves strong enough to have "compassion" toward the Arabs, and must not be overtaken by a hatred that may lead to forsaking real Jewish values. "He who kills a gentile in anger," Yehuda Shabib has written, "is bound in the end to kill a Jew with premeditation."[170]

That this general approach toward the Arabs represents a minority view is clearly apparent in the apologetic tone its advocates often adopt.

On no account should I be mistaken for one of those "pretty souls" ready to "turn the other cheek." I support severe punishment for terrorists, stone-throwers, and trouble-makers. By severity I mean lengthy prison terms and also deporting Arabs involved in hostile activity.

. . . Yes we are nationalist Jews, believing in the right of the people of Israel to settle in its homeland, and that Judea and Samaria are central parts of that homeland . . . but we are also Jews whose tradition includes love and respect for every human being created in the image of God; who have been educated according to values of justice and morality as the basis for every human society.[171]

One response to internal questions about possible injustices committed against the Arabs is the argument that regardless of appearances, fulfillment of maximalist Zionism and completion of the redemption process will serve the true interests of the Arab people.[172] This idea was expressed concretely in a leaflet distributed to Jericho Arabs one week before a large Gush Emunim march was to be held in that city in 1987.

. . . see how settlement and Jewish neighbours have brought you livelihood, homes, television sets, cars and a standard of living you and your forefathers never dreamed of. . . . When we settle in Jericho, you will also enjoy blessings and prosperity.

[Having] Jews living in your city is the safest assurance that you and your children will continue living in this country.

. . . If the advice of the evil counsellors—your PLO and our Peace Now—is carried out, and Israel withdraws from the West Bank, you know that in a few years your extremists will take over and inflict another war on this country.

An Israeli army which will have to conquer Nablus, Hebron, and Jericho again and shed blood for them again—will it leave a single Arab in the West Bank?[173]

Among fundamentalists, however, solicitude for Arab well-being is not the predominant response to compassion toward

Arabs or to criticism of the movement's attitudes toward them. Much more characteristic is condemnation of the naivete that such sentiments reflect and outrage that such pro-Arab opinions should be expressed publicly in the pages of *Nekuda,* given past Arab terrorism and the damage that the expression of such views could do to Gush Emunim's image.[174] In 1985 many fundamentalist rabbis, including Yoel Ben-Nun, condemned government-sponsored programs to reduce tensions between Jews and Arabs in Israel by sponsoring social interaction between Jewish and Arab youth. Meetings between young people, Ben-Nun argued, would give the mistaken impression of equality and might interfere with the development of a strong national consciousness on the part of the Jewish participants.[175]

By contrast, some prominent personalities within the movement who represent diverse stands on other issues have argued that a less antagonistic relationship to the local Arab population is important for tactical political purposes. Haetzni has, from time to time, supported the idea of finding Arab elements willing to cooperate politically and administratively with the settlers.[176] Yisrael Harel, editor of *Nekuda,* has suggested that Arabs in the Gaza Strip, though not those in the West Bank, might be granted some form of cultural autonomy.[177] Ben-Nun and Yaacov Feitelson have contended that radical answers to the Arab problem are not available, and that unless arrangements can be created for a calm and normal life together with the Arabs in the West Bank and Gaza, Israeli opponents of annexation will be assisted in their struggle against it. Thus, Ben-Nun has warned repeatedly against complaining too vociferously about Arab stone throwing and against discussion of expulsion as a solution to the Arab problem. Such talk, he argues, encourages the belief that "no sort of co-existence between Jews and Arabs can occur," which in turn supports arguments for disengagement from populated Arab areas.

> *If it is true that no co-existence is possible, and if the public becomes convinced as well that there isn't any real possibility that a large portion of the Arab population will abandon the land, by one means or another, then the natural conclusion to be drawn will be a Jewish state within*

smaller borders—not an internal struggle with a large Arab population.[178]

As noted in chapter 4, despite substantial disagreements about what if any rights Arabs have or should have *in* the Land of Israel, there is complete agreement that Arabs have no rights *over* any part of it. But something more is implicit in Jewish fundamentalist disagreements over policies regarding local Arabs—an unquestioned assumption that the interests or aspirations of Arab inhabitants must not be allowed to affect the fulfillment of Jewish imperatives. If Arabs will not or cannot accommodate themselves to Jewish rule, they will, ultimately, have no place in the State or the Land of Israel.

Prospects for Peace. Jewish fundamentalists do not believe that a negotiated, comprehensive settlement of the Arab–Israeli conflict is possible, at least not without political or religious transformations that would make the Middle East something radically different from what it is today. On the other hand, many fundamentalists do fear that a deal could be struck between Israel and Jordan, though none believe it could serve as the basis for a lasting peace. Indeed, in practical terms, differences within the movement regarding peace prospects are narrower and less intense than those associated with any of the five areas already discussed. Still, various opinion clusters can be identified.

At one extreme, some religious leaders of Gush Emunim combining literal interpretation of the Bible and the halacha with a strong sense of messianic immediacy, argue that a state of war will continue until the reestablishment of the "Kingdom of Israel," the rebuilding of the Temple, and the arrival of the Messiah. For Eleazar Waldman, the wars to be fought against the evil that will press upon Israel until the completion of the redemption are mitzvahs which, like all mitzvahs, "must be done joyfully." Only with the completion of the redemption process, for which Israel is primarily responsible, can or will peace come.

What, in essence, is the Redemption to which we aspire? It is spiritual and moral completedness. "There will be neither evil nor corruption in all his holy mountain because the land will be filled with the knowledge of God," "My house is a house of prayer for all peoples." All shall worship the one God, and peace, tranquility, and love will prevail among all mankind. That is Redemption.[179]

According to Hanan Porat:

Tidings of peace will come to the world only from the Mountain of the Temple of God, and only when the Torah will go forth from Zion and the word of God from Jerusalem.[180]

From this perspective, peace is a messianic phenomenon. Since Jewish restoration of the *shlemut* (completeness) of the Land of Israel is a prerequisite for the redemption of the world, territorial compromise as a price of peace (*shalom*) is nonsensical. This linguistic linkage mirrors the close conceptual relationship between *shlemut* and *shalom* that is the basis for Porat's rejection of religious arguments for territorial compromise as a way to save Jewish lives. Just as God enjoined Joshua to fight wars and suffer Jewish casualties for the sake of the repair of the world, Porat writes, so too must present day Israel understand that

the value of the Land of Israel exceeds that of peace
. . . We are not commanded, at the outset, to make war upon and destroy the non-Jews living in the Land
. . . but if the peoples who control the Land at present do not accept the presence of the people of Israel and their sovereignty over the Land of Israel, then . . . we are commanded to conquer the Land by war, even at a high price.[181]

According to Gideon Aran, similar beliefs predominated among the leadership of the Movement to Halt the Retreat in Sinai:

The MHRS thinks that not only does the peace of its opponents conceal war within it but also that it is intertwined with collective humiliation and cultural assimilation. But even if it would preserve national honor, moral purity, and security for the state and its inhabitants, such a peace would still be unacceptable.[182]

Jews are not to see their responsibility for bringing peace as including direct efforts to bring about nonbelligerent relations with non-Jews, but as dragging a recalcitrant world toward redemption. Not only will hatred, anti-Semitism, and war continue until the redemption is complete, these manifestations of evil will intensify. Thus, Eleazar Waldman has written:

The period of struggles will accelerate, from the beginning of creation until the appearance of the Messiah, Son of David. The closer the world gets to the destruction of evil, the more determinedly evil clings to life, before its final elimination from the world.[183]

The Jewish contribution to peace is to fight to fulfill God's will and to achieve a pervasive sense of completedness, or harmony "within the Jewish people as a whole, between the people and its whole land, and between the Jews and their God."[184]

Closely related to this perspective, albeit framed in strictly secular terms, is the view that for all intents and purposes peace with the Arab world is impossible. The Arab–Israeli conflict is characterized as a contemporary version of the Hundred Years War. Its roots lie in Arab psychological and cultural fixations, Muslim religious imperatives to Jihad, anti-Semitism borrowed from Europe, and chronic instability encouraging irrational but politically necessary hatred of Israel.

The "House of Islam" lost Spain, parts of Europe ruled by the Ottoman Empire, and great areas of Asia today controlled by Soviet Russia. But what was true of territories on the margins of the Muslim world— non-Muslim political authority in areas previously ruled by non-Muslims—cannot be so in the very heart of the "House of Islam." For Muslims there is only one precedent—the Crusader state. What a deep wound this was in the heart of the "House of Islam." In the end it was wiped from the face of the earth, and thus also must (Israel) be obliterated by armed might in a Muslim holy war.[185]

... pan-Islamic doctrine incorporated in the ideology of Pan- Arabism; the dogma that Jews must be kept in inferior status to Islamic people, and the widespread adoption of Christian and Nazi anti-Semitism—constitute what must be recognized as nothing less than a virulent form of militant Islamic–Arab religious racism ... the prime instrument of Arab ideological unification. .... (Another) major factor in explaining the

Arabs rejection of any Jewish national rights in the Middle East lies in the complex web of internal (domestic) and inter-state Arab and Muslim conflicts, fears and jealousies which generally determine the policies and actions of the Arab world.[186]

In light of the overdetermined and intransigent nature of Arab enmity, no adjustments in Israeli policies can possibly advance the prospects for peace.

The concept of a "compromise" does not exist in the political lexicon of Islam, and the Arabs today envisage no other termination of their campaign than Zionism's complete uprooting.

. . . While Arab acquiescence today seems to be a dream . . . objectively, and notwithstanding the theoretical acrobatics indulged in by persons of good will and by various professors of political science—no solution looms on the horizon for the "problem," however it may be defined.[187]

It remains for Israel to avoid becoming entrapped in doomed attempts to find a compromise solution to the Palestinian problem. Israel must establish and preserve an overwhelming deterrent, waging preventive war when necessary, until, with the passage of several generations and following sweeping changes in the Arab world, a peace based on Israeli control of the whole land might perhaps be achieved. One of the best known and bluntest exponents of this point of view is Raphael Eitan.

If we are deemed weak, this would invite war. If we are thought of as strong and patient, this will remove the danger of war. . . . The Syrians want what all the Arabs want, to annihilate Israel. They do not want a small piece of Israel, nor do they want a large piece of it, or only some part. They do not want this and they do not want that. They simply want to liquidate Israel. (I) do not believe in any negotiations with the Arabs. . . . [188]

Eitan's theme within Tzomet, the political movement that he founded, has been the need for Israel to constitute itself as a modern day Sparta, prepared to fight wars for the foreseeable future.

The root of the problem is the extent of the readiness of the coming generation to fight. The solution must be to begin now, in the kindergartens. We must educate the children so that they will give on their own the spiritual-moral answer to our enemies, or, to the extent necessary, to strike with the fist. But we must begin to teach them in kindergarten. Once the youth reaches the army it is already too late.[189]

From this perspective, signs of Arab moderation, even if credible, should be ignored for the foreseeable future, until the complete fulfillment of Zionist objectives. This may entail war. According to Abraham Yoffe, a former Israeli army general, longtime head of Israel's Nature Reserve Authority, and a founder of the Movement for the Whole Land of Israel, "The will of the people is expressed in war. That is the whole Torah."[190] The necessity of war, no matter how moderate Arab negotiating positions may appear to be, flows from the uncompletedness of Zionism's mission.

We are here in the Land of Israel no more than as a "pioneer at the head of the entire Jewish people." The State of Israel, as presently constituted, does not represent the fulfillment of Zionism. This is a state on the way. . . . Our duty is not completed: . . . The state must provide a refuge for the Jewish people as a whole. The Arab people will never accept this idea![191]

A few fundamentalists—mainly, but not solely, secular ultranationalists—have described conditions under which a comprehensive Middle East peace could be achieved without the miraculous culmination of the redemption process. They often envision a cultural and political transformation of the area in which the predominantly but, in their view, superficially Arab character of the region would disappear. In the nonreligious version of this conception, the non-Arab peoples of the Middle East would, with Israeli assistance, break the artificial domination of the area by Arab imperialism.

We speak of the "Arab world," but there is no Arab world. There exists perhaps an Arab Empire, but even that is only taking shape. The Arab world is a dream. . . .

The Arab imperialist movement is still described by propagandists in both the East and the West, as a progressive and positive liberation movement. That is far from the truth. The Arabs have fourteen absolutely independent states. If Arabs are to be liberated it is from Arab rule. . . .

. . . In most of the territories they rule the Arabs are no more than one of the *minorities* and not even in each case are they the largest minority, the most vigorous, and certainly not the most cultured.[192]

On the basis of this vision of the Middle East, Tzvi Shiloach has described a true peace that would be based on two federations, built out of ethnic mini-states into which Iraq, Syria, and Lebanon are eventually destined to dissolve. The northern federation would include most of what is now the central and northern parts of Lebanon and Syria, and northern and eastern Iraq. The southern federation, led by Israel, would include what is now Israel and Jordan plus southern Lebanon and Syria, western and southern Iraq, and Kuwait; it would become the "United States of the Middle East," and emerge as a technological, scientific, industrial, and military power of international proportions. Together with Turkey and Iran, it would form the "geo-strategic axis of the entire area."[193]

Ezra Zohar has argued that both culturally and geographically, Egypt must be considered outside of the Middle East. In his view, the region gets its overall character from the non-Arab countries of Israel, Turkey, and Iran, and from the Kurds, Maronites, Greeks, Cypriots, Druse, Beduin, and Alawites. "No one people or group has a majority, or even a large enough portion of the population, to insure its hegemony." On this basis, Zohar argues that a reorganized Middle East, with many more states joined together in a common market, is possible. The most important factor in bringing this transformation about, he suggests, is a vigorous Israeli foreign policy designed to encourage the establishment of autonomous ethnoreligious entities in place of large Arab or Pan-Arab states.[194]

Yuval Neeman has also described the requirements of a comprehensive and lasting peace in the area. With Shiloach and Zohar, he rejects negotiations or internationally imposed or brokered solutions. "A Jewish–Arab peace is not to be sought in the realm of subtle diplomacy; it is an historical process."[195] However, Neeman not only accepts the existence of the Arab nation, he emphasizes its unity and size, stretching from "the Atlantic Ocean to the Persian Gulf," as justifying in Arab eyes the acceptance of Jewish rule over the whole Land of Israel. But such an historic compromise between the Arab and Jewish nations will require a social and psychocultural revolution in the Arab world. Arabs will have to appreciate the "deep reasons" that they suffer from frustration and behave with aggression and out of hatred. The revolution must include "the reconstruction of Arab society, the productivization of its mentality, and the realization of its potential."[196]

Religious fundamentalists rarely articulate visions of a Middle East at peace before the completion of the redemption process. Two who have presented such images of peace are Yoel Ben-Nun and Yaacov Ariel. Ben-Nun's conception of the redemption process as essentially indistinguishable from human political and cultural struggles permits him to consider long-term changes toward peace that might be brought about by what would appear to be purely human effort. He rejects "current policies which try to achieve understanding based on secular politics and using western-Christian legal concepts." Neither "feeble western-Christian humanism . . . nor wild Khomeinism," he argues, can serve as a basis for a stable peace, but only "the Torah of Israel which was designed, first for the peoples of this area, and then for the rest of the world." Thus he not only delineates a vision of eventual peace, but suggests negotiations as a route to achieve it. The parties to the negotiations, however, will be neither politicians nor diplomats, but Jewish and Muslim religious leaders, whose political authority would reflect a cultural transformation of both peoples. Such leaders

> might develop in the coming generation and be capable of getting to the root of the conflict. . . . This leadership would be able to achieve a deep and honest understanding between the two sides, based on their ancient faith, on their mutual opposition to idol-worship, and their faith in the oneness of God, thereby

moderating the savagery and cruelty still deeply embedded in the Arab world.[197]

Ariel's ideas about a stable peace that might be achieved in the absence of a Messiah, while less developed than Ben-Nun's, are more explicit in regard to the application of Jewish religious law to relations between Jews and their Arab enemies. The Torah, he argues, "does not endorse peace sought by unsound compromise. The Torah values genuine peace and reprehends any loss of opportunity in the search for a true and lasting peace." A Torah-sanctioned peace, however, requires deep changes in both Jewish and Arab modes of thinking. Jews must begin the peace process by "investing all our energies into bringing about a spiritual and moral change in our own society." Given such a cultural revolution at home, it will then be possible to effect even more comprehensive change among Israel's neighbors.

> Our enemies are expected to accept the values of the Torah, to undergo an actual revolution in their way of thinking and living. Such is the only way to a true and lasting peace . . . entailing acceptance of the Divine Revelation of the Torah at Sinai.

While admitting these suggestions may sound like "utopian hankering," Ariel warns that such transformations are the only route to peace.[198]

Within the fundamentalist camp, another approach to peace focuses on the possibility of ameliorating belligerency in the short run, rather than on comprehensive settlement. This comparatively sanguine view of Israel's short- and medium-term political, as opposed to strictly military, options is based on an assumption that at least some Arabs and Muslims are rational enemies with differentiated, identifiable, finite interests. Several Gush Emunim figures, although committed to an overwhelming Israeli military deterrent as the sine quo non for peace in the area, have suggested that a carrot-and-stick policy toward selected Arab and non-Arab groups could produce informal arrangements to serve Israeli interests while preventing war. Thus, in 1976 Tzvi Shiloach suggested establishing territorial continuity between Israel and an independent Maronite enclave in Lebanon.[199] Supporters of Ariel Sharon's view of Jordan as a Palestinian state reflect this kind of thinking in their presumption that creation of a Palestinian target for Israeli retaliation in Amman will result in good behavior by rational Palestinian leaders. In 1982 Eliyakim Haetzni argued for a comprehensive set of informal alliances with various groups in Lebanon, including Palestinians south of the Awalli River, to keep that country fragmented, weak, and effectively dependent on Israel.[200]

The disastrous outcome of the Christian–Israeli alliance during the Lebanon War, however, did much to undermine the credibility of this approach within the fundamentalist movement. Haetzni's view, for example, appears to have changed. In January 1985, he sharply attacked military and political echelons for not having conducted a scorched earth policy in Lebanon, including the utter destruction of Beirut and the expulsion of hundreds of thousands of Shiites from the country's southern region.[201] In April 1986 he warned that Israeli weakness in Lebanon and signs of indecisiveness on the Golan Heights would mean war with Syria in the near future.[202]

Nevertheless, some fundamentalists have continued to suggest that various avenues of political opportunity do exist in the Arab world. The best known proposal, which originated within Herut circles but is also supported by influential personalities in Tehiya, is the idea of Transjordan as a Palestinian homeland, if not a state. But although this proposal is used extensively for polemical purposes, most fundamentalists, as noted earlier, have abiding ideological aversions to formally surrendering Jewish sovereignty claims over large portions of the East Bank. Nor, in view of the apparent stability of the Hashemite kingdom, have advocates of this idea come up with specific measures Israel might take to implement it.

On the other hand, Yoel Ben-Nun and Moshe Levinger have both suggested that Israeli diplomatic initiatives focus on achieving de facto agreements with Syria to bring some order to Lebanon and stabilize Israel's northern front.[203] Whereas most fundamentalist commentary on Egyptian–Israeli relations emphasizes the outrageousness of Egyptian behavior in light of formal treaty commitments to normalize relations with Israel, Meir Har-Noi argued in 1986 that Israel should accept the "cold peace" with Egypt as a justification for not moving toward negotiations on other issues and as a means of protecting the domestic political position of Egyptian President Hosni Mubarak.[204]

Ultimately, however, voices within Gush Emunim calling for useful opportunities for Israeli political or diplomatic activity in the Arab world are lost within the unremitting chorus of declaration, warning, and debate over how best to prevent or sabotage initiatives that might lead to peace negotiations. Insofar as Gush Emunim adherents concern themselves with Israeli policy toward Arabs outside the Land of Israel, this is their concern and the focus of their analysis. Such analyses pour forth in great volume and intensity whenever negotiating initiatives appear to be moving forward. As these initiatives fade, so does discussion of Israeli foreign policy toward the Arab world. Haetzni is the most prolific of Gush authors regarding what he has repeatedly seen as the great and imminent danger that various Israeli, Jordanian, Egyptian, European, or American attempts to move the peace process ahead might be successful. In April 1985, for example, he condemned the Likud for letting Prime Minister Peres and other dovish ministers hijack Israeli foreign policy.

It has become clear that the architect of the Hussein-Arafat agreement was Mubarak the Egyptian, and that the agreement is only the first stage in a well constructed plan whose culmination will be an Egyptian-Jordanian-PLO-Israeli meeting to discuss surrender of the Land ("Camp David" having been thrown into the waste basket because it was deemed, God save us, too pro-Israeli).[205]

Whoever does not want to live in a "Peace Now" state, the plans for which are here and now being implemented, had better well organize to dam up the flood, and do it *now*—or they will wake up one day, in Judea, Samaria, and Gaza and in Golan, and perhaps also in Jerusalem, as we did in Sinai: too late.[206]

Somewhat more representative of this dominant frame of mind than the typically panicky Haetzni is Amiel Unger, who systematically presents an uncompromising, but polemically attractive, negotiating position. Unger suggests a set of demands that Gush Emunim can formally endorse in order to rally public opinion against negotiations, should they appear likely, and ensure their failure, should they begin.

Unger explicitly rejects Ben-Nun's and Levinger's suggestions that a de facto agreement with the Syrians is possible. Discussions about Assad the "godfather of Lebanese terrorism," weaken Israel's rejection of negotiations with the PLO. Those who believe that there are some Arabs more willing and able to come to terms with Israel than others are suffering from dangerous delusions. "There is no difference in this regard between Amman, el-Bireh, and Iksal in the Galilee." By including Israeli Arabs as part of the Arab enemy, Unger is able to suggest a negotiating position that can sound reasonable to many Israelis, while being so far from the Arab position as to prevent the "Sadatization" of Arafat.

> If Israel is pressured to speak with a "joint" delegation of Arabs, it should include Meari and Toufik Ziad [Israeli Arab members of Knesset]. And if they speak of borders, the borders that we should speak about are from 1921, before 2/3 of the Land of Israel was given to Abdullah.
>
> . . . If the Arabs demand areas free of Jews, we will make symmetrical demands—areas free of Arabs. Whoever demands evacuation of Susia will have to submit to the demand to evacuate Sakhnin and whoever wants Tekoa to be free of Jews will be pressured to agree to pay in Um El Fahm [Jewish settlements on the West Bank and Arab villages in the Galilee].[207]

Implicit within the fundamentalist debate on the prospects for peace is the conviction that compromise is simply not a route to that objective. Some accommodate themselves to the continuing state of war by seeing it as an increasingly bloody but increasingly promising harbinger of redemption, or by shifting the focus of their attention to the necessity for religious and cultural change. Others, whether they anticipate a divinely defined redemption or not, steel themselves for a belligerent relationship with the Arab/Muslim world that will extend as far into the future as they can imagine. Within this realm of discourse, political negotiations for peace, under whatever guise and however structured, cannot be an opportunity. The episodic emergence of initiatives designed to bring about such negotiations is important, however. Jewish fundamentalists understand negotiating opportunities, which are tempting to many Israelis, as times of testing, for themselves and for the Jewish people as a whole. Will or will not the Jewish people become trapped in a process whose very assumptions contradict the imperatives which God and Jewish history have established?

VI

Present Trends and Future Implications

The worldview of Jewish fundamentalism is based on myths of Jewish chosenness, mission, and territorial sovereignty similar to those that shaped Jewish politics before the Roman expulsion. Now, as then, establishment of Jewish political sovereignty over the Land of Israel constitutes the vital focus of zealous action; now, as then, the territorial issue is but the most concrete expression of a highly parochial brand of Jewish redemptionism—a worldview that stands in as sharp a contradiction to Western liberal/democratic values today as it did to Greco-Roman civilization in ancient times. In contemporary Israel the new role of these particular motifs and values, drawn out of the vast mythic repertoire of Jewish religion, Jewish history, and Jewish culture, is explained by a combination of several factors. First, and most basic, was the historic success of Zionism in recreating a dynamic Jewish political presence in the Land of Israel. Second were the manifold consequences of the Six Day War and the Yom Kippur War, which reawakened irredentist sentiments and set the stage for the effective mobilization of new political and social forces inside of Israel. Third was the dedication of well-placed and ambitious elites. By linking ultimate Jewish and redemptive values to traditionally Zionist political objectives of settlement and sovereignty, these elites were able to attract a substantial number of enthusiastic activists; to draw upon the political, administrative, and economic support of leading political parties; and to capture the imagination of wide sectors of Israeli society.

In the first chapters of this study I presented some evidence for the influence that Jewish fundamentalism has had on the attitudes, commitments, and votes of large numbers of Israelis. Since the rise of Gush Emunim in the mid-1970s, thousands of Israelis have been involved in militant political activity on behalf of fundamentalist objectives. The movement has repeatedly proven its capacity to generate well organized political action simultaneously over a variety of issues, sustained in terms consistent with, if not corresponding to, consensual Israeli political opinions. An actively messianic interpretation of Jewish imperatives remains dominant within the national religious sector, from which Gush Emunim continues to attract settlers, and among youthful cadre.[1] Israel's chief rabbinate, the basis and limits of whose authority have never been clearly delineated, has virtually embraced the fundamentalist credo.[2] In the 1984 elections Tehiya, the party most closely associated with Gush Emunim, attracted the third-largest number of votes (after Labor and the Likud). In 1987 most polls showed that Tehiya/Tzomet, Kach, and the National Religious Party can expect to command from thirteen to sixteen seats in the next Knesset in 1988.[3]

Given the extent to which fundamentalist activists and supporters staff educational institutions in the religious sector, and the extraordinarily high birthrate among key fundamentalist groups, such as Gush Emunim settlers, it is fairly certain that the number of Israelis whose thinking is governed by these myths, and whose lives are dedicated to the achievement of fundamentalist objectives, will slowly increase.[4] But to anticipate the eventual impact of any revolutionary doctrine, the key question is how saliently and with what effect the images, goals, symbols, and attitudes its adherents have legitimized percolate through the wider society. From this perspective, how Jewish fundamentalism affects the trajectory of Israeli politics will depend largely on how relevant and useful Israelis find its messages in the context of the predicaments they are likely to face. Will fundamentalist ideas—and the assumptions, categories, attitudes, and slogans associated with them—appear irrelevant and dangerous to increasing numbers of Israelis? Or, having been injected into the mainstream of Israeli politics, will they provide a convenient, authenticated vocabulary for competing elites and groups in need of inspiring formulas to advance or consolidate their own interests? It is, of course, impossible to provide a definitive answer to this question, but it is worthwhile considering the different directions of current trends.

Settlement Issues. While settlement of the West Bank and Gaza Strip has been the main vehicle of fundamentalist political success, it has also presented the movement with problems and disappointments. Since 1984 Israel's severely straitened economic circumstances have led to sharp reductions in expenditures on settlement and infrastructure. For both economic and psychological reasons, this has hampered the achievement of Gush objectives regarding the number and distribution of new settlements and settlers. In response to what it regards as a freeze on settlement-related expenditures, Gush Emunim has sponsored the formation of a parliamentary lobby. As noted in chapter 1, the lobby is composed of members of parliament with strong political and ideological connections to the fundamentalist movement. Its purpose is to act as advocate and watchdog for the interests of the settlers. As several Gush leaders have noted, however, this effort contradicts the larger purpose of the movement to be accepted in the eyes of the Israeli public not as a separate interest group like any other, but as the self-sacrificing representative of the nation as a whole.[5] This difficulty is accentuated by the highly focused program of the movement, stressing territorial, political, and spiritual–ideological issues above all others. As Charles Liebman, a leading analyst of Israeli culture, has pointed out, the fundamentalist movement has not yet offered Israeli Jews convincing responses to problems of economic inequality and social injustice.[6] To the extent, then, and as long as such issues are prominent on the Israeli political agenda, the movement's competitive position suffers.

Another practical problem to which Gush Emunim has not responded effectively, which is aggravated by economic crisis, is the task of increasing the proportion of Jewish settlers employed inside the West Bank. Only 21 percent of employed settlers work inside their settlements.[7] Of the commuters, the decisive majority travel to metropolitan areas inside the green line. Of those settlers who do work inside their own locality, the vast majority are employed, directly or indirectly, in public service (schools, administration, religious councils, zoning boards, and so forth). While this pattern gives strong impetus and plentiful resources for sustained settler political activity, it also means that the livelihood of many Gush activists is dangerously dependent on government generosity.

An additional difficulty pertains to relations between religious and nonreligious settlers. As I have stressed, the fundamentalist movement is composed of a religious majority and an important nonreligious minority. In general, Gush Emunim settlements have been established either as religious or as nonreligious. Although one mixed Gush settlement earned national recognition for its success in achieving mutual cooperation and tolerance among its religious and nonreligious members, other attempts have mostly failed.[8] Along with differences over the extent to which veteran settlers should be allowed to screen newcomers for social, cultural, and economic compatibility, conflicts in the educational and recreational spheres over religious issues have interfered with Gush efforts to attract and absorb additional settlers.[9]

One problem that has proven far more serious than most fundamentalists originally anticipated has been that of attracting large numbers of settlers to the West Bank and Gaza Strip. The expectation that the Yeshivot Hesder located in the West Bank would produce steady streams of dedicated young settlers has not been fulfilled. Since 1982 the majority of these graduates have left the West Bank to pursue educational and career opportunities inside the green line.[10] In 1983 both Gush Emunim and the Likud adopted a new strategy to accelerate the settlement of the occupied territories. According to this plan, heavily subsidized settlement of the West Bank and Gaza by scores of thousands of upwardly mobile suburbanites was intended to make up for the shortage of pioneering, self-sacrificing ideologues. The campaign was based on the notion that new ideas are absorbed more readily after circumstances have been created to make them appear appropriate. Put another way, this was and is the view that the West Bank and Gaza can be turned into a kind of hothouse for the cultivation of sentiments supportive of Likud or fundamentalist perspectives. Meron Benvenisti, Israel's most prominent analyst of the de facto annexation process, has laid bare the theory behind this expensive and ambitious policy more effectively than anyone else. Writing in 1984, Benvenisti stated:

> The aggressive Gush-Drobles plan [to settle 100,000 Jews in the West Bank by the end of 1986] . . . has not been a spectacular success. The planners were the first to realize that it had failed and to identify the rea-

son: the shortage of ideologically motivated settlers . . .

consequently a new strategy was developed.[11]
According to Benvenisti, the first objective of this new strategy,
initiated by the Likud government and implemented in close
cooperation with Gush Emunim, was

rapid creation of a strong constituency of Israelis who,
while they may not necessarily hold with Likud ideology, can be relied upon to fight any scheme involving
territorial compromise in order to protect their newly-
acquired "quality of life" in the territories.[12]

Once established in the occupied territories, Benvenisti continues, these non-ideological Israelis would be thrust into circumstances that would strongly encourage them to adopt perceptions,
attitudes, and beliefs espoused by both the Likud and the fundamentalist movement.

The spread of Jewish localities will expand points of
friction and will make alienation more noticeable to increasing numbers of Jews and Arabs. Interaction will
be tenuous. The deep-seated animosity and mutual
sense of insecurity will create a very high level of perceived threat, resulting in total dichotomization. Encounters . . . will be characterized by the clear hierarchy
that prevails where the Jews are dominant and the
Arabs subservient. . . . Imbued with nationalistic pa-
thos, (the new Jewish settlers) will monopolize the environment.[13]

At the beginning of the subsidized settlement campaign, fundamentalist leaders' admonitions to make welcome the new settlers
despite their apolitical stance reflected a clear-eyed understanding
of the role to be played by the non-ideological settlers.

We must shake off the image that settlement in Judea,
Samaria, and Gaza is intended for certain chosen individuals and that it is not so desirable for "the people"
to live among us. We must remember, and constantly
remind ourselves, that our future is dependent on the
identification of wide strata of ordinary people with
our enterprise. This identification, which exists potentially, must find channels for its activation—that is, in

settlement among us. Otherwise, what identification exists will not be deep-rooted and will be liable, God forbid, to evaporate with time or during a period of stress such as the state is likely to experience in the future.[14] Eventually, with the intransigent hostility of the Arabs increasingly apparent, with the repeated failure of efforts by dovishly inclined groups to move the country toward territorial compromise, and with de facto annexation turned into a network of "routine" processes, the overwhelming majority of Israelis will accept the new contours of the state as both unchangeable and, finally, correct. This is the logic of facts creating interests that then require ideas to enshrine and protect those interests. If most Israelis cannot be convinced, intellectually, to act on behalf of redemption or the whole Land of Israel as driving forces in their lives, fundamentalists believe, many can be placed in circumstances under which their own interests and fears will lead them, if not force them, in the right direction.

The lures of massive public subsidies and luxury housing had increased the number of Jews living in the West Bank, outside of expanded East Jerusalem, to nearly 70,000 by the end of 1987. On the other hand, even this increase did not correspond to that anticipated by Gush Emunim and government planners in 1983.[15] Still, these new settlers now outnumber the Gush veterans, who live primarily in the "rural" settlements established in the 1970s and in 1980 and 1981. More than 70 percent of Jewish residents of the West Bank now live in "urban" areas.[16] Consequently, for example, Yesha, which was founded as an association of local councils of rural settlements and often functions as a formal arm of Gush Emunim, finds itself unable to speak with confidence on behalf of the majority of West Bank settlers. Although the bulk of their votes did go to annexationist parties in 1984, a significant proportion of the inhabitants of the new townships neither share the worldview of Jewish fundamentalism as outlined in this study nor automatically follow Gush Emunim's lead in political disputes. This was particularly evident during the controversy over Yesha's 1985 resolution characterizing any Israeli government ready to compromise on the West Bank issue as traitorous.[17]

If current trends do not warrant a prediction that fundamentalist sentiments will eventually prevail among many or most of the new settlers, available evidence can demonstrate the plausibility of this long term strategy. According to one study of settler opinion, 63 percent of those interviewed moved across the green line for social and economic reasons, but many of these developed "ex post facto ideologies once they (had) made the move."[18] Support for this judgment can also be drawn from a poll comparing the opinions of residents of Maale Adumim, the largest suburban settlement in the West Bank, with those of residents of Kiryat Arba, the largest Gush Emunim town. Although the attitudes of Maale Adumim residents were found to differ from those registered in Kiryat Arba, they were much closer to fundamentalist attitudes than to those shared by the cross section of Israelis from which the Maale Adumim population is often said to be drawn. In Kiryat Arba, for example, 99 percent of respondents answered no to the question "Do you believe a real peace can be achieved through territorial compromise?" In Maale Adumim, 80 percent answered likewise. Responding to a question about their reaction to a government decision to evacuate the settlement in the context of a peace agreement, 65 percent of those polled in Kiryat Arba said they would resist (nonviolently) until forcibly evacuated, while 30 percent indicated they would take up arms. In Maale Adumim, the proportions were 60 percent and 10 percent, respectively.[19]

The voting record of Israelis living in the territories at the time of the 1981 and 1984 elections is also instructive. Elections held in the spring of 1981 preceded the 1983–1984 rush of subsidized settlers into the West Bank and Gaza (during which the number of settlers in these areas doubled). In the 1981 elections, the voice of the ideologically motivated Gush Emunim settlers predominated. Together, the Likud, Tehiya, and the National Religious Party, all of which favored permanent absorption of the occupied areas into Israel, received 78 percent of the votes cast in the West Bank, though only 44 percent of the total Israeli vote.[20] In 1984, despite the influx of so many new settlers, political support for the annexationist camp appeared, if anything, to have increased. In that election, 86 percent of West Bank and Gaza Strip settlers voted for the Likud, Tehiya, the National Religious Party, or Morasha; by contrast, 41 percent of the total Israeli vote went to these parties.[21] Even in the large, urban-style settlements, in 1984 residents voted for parties supportive of key fundamentalist objectives in much larger proportions than did voters within Israel itself. According to Benvenisti, what he calls "the Likud bloc" received 77 percent of the vote in Maale Adumim, whereas "the Labor bloc," received 23 percent; in Ariel support for the annexationist parties reached 98 percent.[22]

Ariel's development is instructive in this context in one other respect. Its current mayor, Ron Nahman, is an active and articulate booster of his city, both in Israel and to groups of potential Jewish immigrants abroad. In personal presentations, and in a specially prepared slide presentation about Ariel, Nahman explicitly describes it as Israel's "yuppie" community par excellence, complete with aerobic exercise classes, fashionably designed homes, high-technology industries, and state-of-the-art recreational facilities. He makes no political or ideological appeals. Nahman himself would appear to epitomize the young, upwardly mobile, non-religious, suburban Israeli whom subsidized settlement was designed to attract to the territories. In fact, however, he was active in Gush Emunim circles before the massive subsidization campaign began. In a Gush symposium before the 1981 elections he suggested that Yesha organize a list for the Knesset. When this suggestion was not accepted, he endorsed the strategy of creating circumstances in which each party would find enough of its members living in the West Bank and Gaza to force it to support the annexation process.[23]

Political Competition. The interaction between the positive symbols of settlement, pioneering, and dedication to the Land of Israel that fundamentalist action has revitalized, and the new interests the process of de facto annexation has created, has been apparent in vigorous competition for the political support of both new and old settlers. Even during the 1984 campaign, according to Benvenisti, the Labor party "emphasized that it was a Labor government that decided in 1974–76 on the establishment of the two largest West Bank urban centers, namely Ariel and Maale Adumim." Benvenisti has characterized the Labor party as stung by its failure to attract votes in the new suburban settlements during the 1984 elections. Since then, he says, it has gone further, "bowing to the inevitable."

Labor activists have launched a political campaign to lure the suburban settlers to their banner. Central to their political message is the Likud-Labor coalition agreement of September 1984 which stipulates that "existing settlements will be developed without interruption." . . . The United Kibbutzim Movement decided in mid-1985 to settle the southern Mount Hebron area, claiming it was part of the Allon Plan. Histadrut firms, controlled by Labor, are actively engaged in construction on the West Bank. One company, Even Vasid, has formed a partnership with a settlers' "development corporation."[24]

At a November 1987 meeting of what is known as the Labor party mainstream, held in Maale Ephraim, a large township on the West Bank, most speakers condemned Shimon Peres for moving too far toward a generous territorial compromise and accommodation with the Palestinian Arabs.[25] Similar sentiments expressed by the chief of the Labor Party branch in Maale Adumim elicited a declaration from Defense Minister Yitzhak Rabin that "there is no controversy with regard to the fact that Jerusalem and its environs, as well as Maale Adumim, will remain under Israeli sovereignty."[26]

On the right, the competition is even more intense—not so much for settler votes as for the favor and implicit endorsement of leading Gush Emunim personalities. Ambitious politicians who had previously shown little ideological commitment to the whole Land of Israel or interest in the settlement of the territories have taken every possible opportunity to portray themselves as dedicated above all else to the settlement and permanent absorption of the West Bank and Gaza. Among these is Housing and Construction Minister David Levy, who regularly attends the inauguration of new settlements. Through speeches, rush projects, unprecedentedly large resource allocations, and close consultation with Gush Emunim activists, he has sought to strengthen his claim to lead the Likud in the post-Begin era by associating himself with Jewish fundamentalism's primary objective. In June 1987 he reacted furiously to the inclusion in the official *Israel Atlas* of a passage he considered critical of Gush Emunim. He suspended the book's publication and its editorial staff, and commissioned a substitute chapter from a well-known Gush sympathizer.[27]

Levy's efforts in this area have been matched by those of other ambitious Likud leaders, including, before his elevation to the premiership, Foreign Minister Yitzhak Shamir (mainly through his loyal supporter, former Deputy Minister of Agriculture Mikhael Dekel) and Ariel Sharon, who at various times since 1977 has headed the agriculture, defense, and trade and industry ministries.[28] In November 1987, Yigal Cohen-Orgad, a resident of Ariel who served as finance minister in the second Likud government, published a detailed article in *Nekuda* defending himself against Gush Emunim charges that he was unsupportive of settlement in the West Bank. Regretting that in "our camp" insufficient attention is paid to facts in the course of public debate, he provides comprehensive statistical data to prove that the settlement of the West Bank proceeded at a faster pace while he was finance minister than during any other period.[29]

Essentially the same dynamic is apparent in the recent history of the National Religious Party. Many observers have traced its relatively dismal showing in the 1984 elections to indications after the Lebanon War that some of its key leaders—Zevulon Hammer and Yehuda Ben-Meir—were having second thoughts about the wisdom of de facto annexation. A storm of protest erupted within the fundamentalist movement. Hammer himself was banned from visiting Gush settlements, but his successful intraparty maneuvering in 1986 suggests that whatever his private feelings, he feels compelled to honor the movement's efforts. Chosen to lead the National Religious Party at its convention in the summer of 1986, Hammer developed a position that relied upon an alliance between his Young Guard faction, Druckman's Matzad movement, and another Gush-associated group from Merkaz HaRav. He rejected talk of an effective "takeover" of the party by Matzad, emphasizing the party's tolerance of many religious points of view. But party moderates were repeatedly defeated in their bid for high position by Matzad and hawkish Young Guard candidates. In a personal interview, Hammer declared his opposition to the evacuation of any settlements and his support for new ones. Citing "all the beautiful things it represents," he welcomed Matzad "back to the fold" as "flesh of our flesh, separated from us only very briefly."[30]

Among the personalities prominent in Gush Emunim who had left the National Religious Party but have since returned to take important positions within it are Druckman himself, Hanan Porat, Uri Elitzur, and Yosef Shapira. Shapira, who has long been identified with the Bnei Akiva movement and with Gush Emunim, joined Hammer as the party's second cabinet minister.[31]

From a broader political perspective, the continuation of the national unity government has tended to obscure the vitality of the fundamentalist movement and the leverage it is in a position to exercise over the Likud. The 1984 elections produced a virtual dead heat between the Likud and its religious and ultranationalist allies on one side and the Labor Party and its liberal/dovish allies on the other. Indeed, the total votes received by the parties most closely associated with the Likud and with Labor are nearly equal. Likud, Tehiya, the National Religious Party, Morasha, and Ometz together received 875,001 votes. The Labor Party, Yahad, Shinui, and the Civil Rights Movement together received 874,821. Only 180 votes separated these two blocs, so radically opposed on so many issues.[32] It is not surprising, then, that neither party could manage to form a government and that to avoid new elections from which neither side was confident it would emerge in a stronger position, the Likud and Labor were forced into the uncomfortable but convenient arrangement of a national unity government. Under the terms of the coalition, each bloc agreed to defer decisive action toward resolution of the main problem facing the country, in regard to which they are in such fundamental disagreement—the ultimate disposition of the West Bank and Gaza Strip.

Once political maneuvering or new elections (which must be held by the end of 1988) bring an end to this state of affairs, the visibility and influence of Gush Emunim and its allies is almost certain to increase. If the Labor Party manages to form a government, the fundamentalists, in common cause with the Likud, will spearhead a vigorous parliamentary and extraparliamentary opposition. If, on the other hand, the Likud organizes the new government, it will once again turn to Gush Emunim to legitimize and help implement the rapid changes it will deem necessary to suppress both Arab and Jewish dissent and effectively to annex the West Bank and Gaza. Indeed, if it does not do this, the Likud is unlikely to be able to form a government and maintain itself in power. With the society as evenly and deeply divided as it is on the very issue of greatest importance to the fundamentalist movement, the Likud would have nowhere to go for allies but to the right, and the fundamentalists would have no reason to avoid exacting the strongest commitments possible. A presentiment of this alliance was available in the World Zionist Organization elections held in the spring of 1987. Herut and Tehiya appeared in those elections on a joint list that featured Eleazar Waldman in the fifth position. Geula Cohen of Tehiya, a fervent admirer of the movement, was eighth. Ariel Sharon and David Levy, ministerial patrons who, as noted, have vied with one another for the approval of Gush Emunim settlers, occupied the second and third places.[33]

The Implications of Palestinian Violence. Among the most important circumstances associated with settlement in the West Bank are the threat of Arab violence against the inhabitants of large bedroom communities and harassment of Jewish commuters. As explained in chapter 5, some fundamentalists fear that overemphasizing the threat that local Arab hostility poses to the lives and equanimity of Jewish settlers undermines the effort to incorporate the occupied territories into what Israelis consider their country. They can point to substantial reductions in the price of building plots on the West Bank and the wariness with which increasing numbers of Israelis treat travel to or through the territories as evidence of the negative impact of Palestinian violence. On the other hand, many fundamentalists believe that the fear and hostility that waves of Arab rioting, as well as firebombing attacks and stone throwing, engender among the new settlers can dramatically enhance the appeal of their tough anti-Arab rhetoric and of their insistence that the full power of the state be used to make Judea, Samaria, and Gaza as safe for Jews as any other part of Israel.

On April 11, 1987, a molotov cocktail was thrown at the car of a Jewish family as they passed a small Arab village on their way home to Alfei Menashe, a suburban settlement located just over the green line northeast of Tel Aviv. The wife, five months pregnant, was burned to death. Her husband and four children escaped with burns, though one of the children subsequently died of his injuries. The incident triggered a riot by 300 enraged settlers in the nearby Arab town of Kalkilia. Scores of shops and cars were destroyed, and orchards and fields burned. Though some of the rioters were from Alfei Menashe, most appear to have come from nearby settlements more closely associated with Gush Emunim. The next day Gush Emunim convened a meeting of its secretariat in the sports arena at Alfei Menashe. Moshe Levinger, Daniella Weiss, and Eliyakim Haetzni were among those who accused the government of apathy and ineffectiveness in dealing with the personal security issue. Calling for strict and comprehensive steps to be taken against local Arabs, they blamed the violence on the leniency of the authorities and on Foreign Minister Peres's attempts to bring about an international peace conference. Ministers closely associated with Gush Emunim, such as Haim Corfu and Ariel Sharon, visited Alfei Menashe to make similar points. Although many residents reacted with fear rather than hostility to the incident, and others appeared to resent the political use to which their personal tragedy was being put, one prominent member of the settlement, a lieutenant colonel in the army, did speak at the Gush meeting. He declared that he and all the people of the settlement would act in the surrounding villages "with the means at our disposal." "We will act in those places in the tradition of Unit 101, of Deir Yasin, Kibya, and Kfar Kassem."[34]

On balance, although Arab unrest in the occupied territories will reduce the number of Israelis moving into them and even encourage some to leave, it will also provide the fundamentalist movement with specific opportunities to increase its base of support.

Relations Between Jewish Fundamentalists and the Haredim. As noted, the Yeshivot Hesder, inspired and largely staffed by Gush Emunim rabbis, have not recently been a source of large numbers of pioneering settlers. This is just one aspect of a more general recruitment problem that has surfaced for the movement in precisely that sector within which its greatest successes have been registered, religious youth. There is increasing evidence that within Merkaz HaRav, and other yeshivas that have served as channels for the development of Gush elites and cadre, a trend toward ultrareligiosity and otherworldly concerns has replaced the national religious ethos associated with Gush Emunim. Alluding to the black garb worn by ultra-Orthodox Jews, fundamentalists refer to this trend as "blackening." It seems associated, in part, with the natural thrust toward increasing rigidity and purity of observance entailed in the religious fundamentalists' acceptance of the absolute authority of Jewish law. The trend is reflected in increasing opposition among rabbis in these yeshivas to the participation of their students in the armed forces or in any other activity that reduces the time and energy they can devote to ritual observance and the study of sacred texts.[35]

Within Bnei Akiva, the national religious youth movement that has been the largest recruitment pool for Gush Emunim leaders and activists, increasing sensitivity to criticism by ultra-Orthodox Jews is apparent. Compromises with secularists, contends Agudat Yisrael, contradict Jewish law and lead to sin. Gush Emunim also comes under attack in these circles for cultivating a form of idolatry in its attitude toward the special sanctity of the Land of Israel. Although the struggle for the permanent absorption of Judea, Samaria, and Gaza was still the top-priority item at the most recent national convention of Bnei Akiva, the range of viewpoints on other issues was unprecedentedly wide. And a distinct shift was also noted toward an emphasis within the youth movement on social, cultural, and religious issues not directly connected to annexation and settlement of the territories. This shift was interpreted as a response partly to the outcome of the Lebanon War, in which for the first time significant numbers of yeshiva graduates and students were killed in combat, and partly to the shock of the arrest and trial of the Jewish terrorist underground for acts that many religious leaders condemned as directly contrary to Jewish law.[36]

In the future, segments of the ultra-Orthodox population may prove to be another important source of support for the fundamentalist movement. As explained in chapter 1, Agudat Yisrael and the various groups that make up the Haredi community have tended to act politically only on issues that involve maintaining or enhancing the economic resources at the disposal of their educational, religious, and social institutions, or to protect their isolation from the mainstream of secular and sinful Israeli society. As I have noted above, the attraction that the extreme, nonpolitical pietism espoused by these groups holds for many yeshiva students in the national religious sector poses a significant challenge to the recruitment efforts of the Jewish fundamentalist movement. Nevertheless, past patterns and these rivalries should not obscure the real potential for an alliance, should key rabbis within the Haredi subcultures decide that wars or struggles over the Land of Israel or the Temple Mount do herald the approaching climax of the redemption process.[37] According to one study of 375 *baalei tshuvah* (repentants) who have entered the Haredi community, 70 percent "said th~v felt they were living in the beginning of a messianic process."[38] In institutions such as the Ateret Cohanim (Crown of the Priests) Yeshiva in the Old City of Jerusalem, sacred texts dealing with sacrifices and other details of Temple service are studied. Members of one Hasidic sect are weaving vestments to be worn by the priests. Such activity is undertaken in explicit anticipation of the rebuilding of the Temple.[39] The single-mindedness and discipline with which ultra-Orthodox leaders can mobilize their followers, the demographic weight of these communities in Jerusalem, and the six Knesset seats they usually control could make significant contributions to both legal and extralegal fundamentalist efforts.

Aside from widely cited trends within this community toward militant forms of political action on issues deemed important by their leaders, evidence exists for the plausibility of an alliance between fundamentalist and pietistic Jews. This includes the attempt, implemented so far with mixed success because of the financial scandals associated with it, to build a large ultra-Orthodox city—Immanuel—in the middle of the West Bank.[40] In addition, as explained in chapter 3, Morasha presented itself in the 1984 elections as a list led by a prominent ultra-Orthodox politician—Abraham Verdiger—and a leader of Gush Emunim, Haim Druckman. The Shas (Sephardi Torah Guardians Association) party, which split from Agudat Yisrael in an effort to increase parliamentary representation for Sephardic ultra-Orthodox Jews, gained four seats in the 1984 elections. Although some of its representatives have been relatively dovish in regard to foreign policy, most have echoed the ultranationalist and extreme anti-Arab sentiments commonly heard in Gush Emunim circles. Nor is it likely that even the nonreligious elements within the fundamentalist movement would balk at satisfying demands by the ultra-

Orthodox for state enforcement of many religious laws, if such an alliance could establish their own political supremacy.

In this context, disputes over key aspects of the religious status quo, which isolates the Haredim from the contaminating influences of modern Israeli society, could trigger an alliance between these groups and the fundamentalists. Such a development is partly implicit in the warning offered by Member of Knesset Menachem Porush of Agudat Yisrael. If the exemption of yeshiva students from army service is rescinded, he declared, "we will go underground, and in the underground (*machteret*) we shall continue to study."[41] Ariel Sharon's energetic solicitousness of ultra-Orthodox demands with respect to the exemption of yeshiva students suggests that he, at least, perceives the possibility of such an alliance.

There are sufficient reasons, in short, to warrant expectations that Jewish fundamentalism will remain a vital force in Israeli politics and enjoy new opportunities to move toward its ultimate objectives. But despite the factors and trends upon which this judgment is based, other evidence suggests that the future success of the movement is not guaranteed. Certainly Jewish fundamentalism cannot be viewed as a political juggernaut gathering strength from year to year and threatening soon to achieve a dominant position in Israeli society. The very success of the movement in expanding settlement in the occupied territories, attracting different types of Israelis to those settlements, and moving its agenda toward the center of Israeli politics has created a variety of serious practical problems. Nor, in facing those problems, can the movement be seen as ideologically and programmatically united. To be sure, the differences I analyzed in chapter 5 exist within the framework of a distinct, coherent, and potent worldview. But they are substantial enough to have complicated efforts to build a united organizational framework for political action.

The Leadership Problem and the Struggle for Jewish Control of the Temple Mount. The most substantial threat to the accomplishment of fundamentalist objectives is the difficulty that a large proportion of Gush Emunim activists have in modulating their actions and the expression of their beliefs, and especially accepting and implementing a consensus-building strategy toward the wider

Israeli public. Actions are liable to be taken and positions articulated that, though tactically unwise, cannot be fully renounced. The movement as a whole is made vulnerable because the excesses, or "purity," of some can be used by its opponents to portray Gush Emunim not as "authentic," but as "insane."

In this respect, Jewish fundamentalism in Israel illustrates a broader problem that must confront any such movement. The element that gives fundamentalism its vitality—the unshakable belief that a supreme authority requires immediate and sustained action toward political goals—contains within it a dangerous tendency toward extremism. Since the world can never reproduce the pure form of a utopian vision, the ambitions of fundamentalists must be compromised in order to be consolidated. But compromise of transcendental imperatives can be legitimized only by the decisions of charismatic leaders who can impose their own interpretation of the practical meaning of those imperatives. In the absence of such leadership it is to be expected that severe tensions will arise between fundamentalists willing to compromise in order to consolidate political gains and those for whom pure and absolute imperatives permit no compromise.

In this context it is possible to appreciate just how serious a blow Rav Tzvi Yehuda Kook's death was to the political development of Gush Emunim. No leader with his charisma or moral authority, acceptable to both the religious majority and the secular ultranationalist minority of the movement, has emerged to replace him. Moshe Levinger has neither the temperament, the scholarly reputation, nor the broad following necessary to play this role. And no candidates for such a leadership position appear to be on the horizon.

The implications of Rav Tzvi Yehuda's absence are apparent in Jewish fundamentalist efforts since 1983 to assert Jewish rights over the Temple Mount in Jerusalem as a prelude to the removal of the Muslim shrines and the reconstruction of the Temple. While he lived, Tzvi Yehuda's opposition to activity related to the Temple Mount evidently was enough to keep it off Gush Emunim's agenda. But in terms of the fundamentalist worldview, the logic of doing something to express Jewish attachment to and aspirations for the Temple Mount is impossible to ignore. This is all the more true given the site's location in "united Jerusalem," its centrality in

Jewish history and Jewish law, and its current status as a zone of virtual Arab/Muslim autonomy. In recent years discussion of the tactical advantages of creating an Israeli consensus for rejecting the status quo on the Temple Mount, as a way to foil various proposals to advance negotiations by including the formula "Muslim rule over Muslim holy places," has helped increase the intensity of fundamentalist demands for change. Others argue that redemptionist Zionism requires a dramatic change in the status of the Temple Mount and wish to prepare the way for the building of the Third Temple. Those who make the most radical demands, for the destruction of the Muslim shrines and the immediate construction of the Temple, openly reject what they consider the mistaken inclination of Tzvi Yehuda to wait for a mass spiritual revival or miraculous divine intervention before acting to rebuild the Temple.[42]

Some leading rabbis have used recent archeological finds to eliminate religious restrictions against Jewish entry onto the Temple Mount. The most influential of these has been former Army Chief Rabbi and Ashkenazic Chief Rabbi Shlomo Goren. He has been supported in his efforts by Eleazar Waldman, Sephardic Chief Rabbi Mordechai Eliyahu, and the chief rabbis of Tel Aviv, Netanya, and Haifa.[43] Thus has ended a situation in which fundamentalists eager to avoid the political explosiveness of the Temple Mount issue could unchallengeably do so by referring to universally recognized halachic restrictions against Jews' entering the area (see chapter 3). Partly as a result of these developments, partly as a result of the desire by many in Gush Emunim to do something so decisively repugnant to the Arab world that peace negotiations would forever be prevented, and partly as a result of the very logic of fundamentalist ideology, the Temple Mount issue has emerged from the realm of crackpot utopianism to occupy a central place in the political activity of the mainstream of Gush Emunim. Although until the early 1980s very few articles, letters, and editorials in *Nekuda* even mentioned the Temple Mount, from 1983 to 1986 dozens of such items, virtually all advocating Judaization of the area in one way or another, were published.[44] Early in 1986 a series of demonstrative visits to the Temple Mount by sympathetic members of Knesset (including prayers, photographers, and challenges to the Muslim authorities) ignited furious Arab reaction. In June 1986, on the anniversary of the Israeli occupation of East Jerusalem, 12,000 fundamentalists marched in protest from Merkaz HaRav to the Mount of Olives to view a sound-and-light show entitled "The Temple Mount is the Heart of the People." Amid violent clashes, a detachment of soldiers and policemen succeeded in preventing 100 of these demonstrators from forcing their way onto the Temple Mount itself.[45]

Within a Jewish fundamentalist frame of reference, the argument of those demanding a change in the status quo is difficult to refute. Why, they ask, should Jews consider the Western Wall, which was nothing but a retaining wall for Herod's Temple, a particularly holy place? What sort of authentic redemptionist Zionism is it whose adherents stand at the very edge of the Temple Mount itself and hypocritically commemorate the Temple's destruction by fasting and bemoaning the plight of Jews "unable" to "return to the Mountain of the Lord and rebuild the Temple?" If Jerusalem is truly the united sovereign capital of Israel, then why in the very holy center of Jerusalem, on the Temple Mount, do Arab Muslims hold sway, preventing Jews from raising their flag, building a synagogue, or even praying publicly?[46]

Yesha and the mainstream of Gush Emunim do indeed appear to have responded positively to such criticism. While Israel Eldad, Moshe Levinger, and Shlomo Aviner have warned of the dangers of moving too far and too fast toward these objectives,[47] *Nekuda* published two editorials in late 1985 and early 1986 warning of radical and violent steps likely to be taken by Jewish fundamentalists if the government did not act swiftly to change the status quo.

Today only a relatively small number are active in the struggle to implement Jewish rights on the dearest and holiest place of all. It is clear, however, that the people will be unable to tolerate the anomaly and that the struggle will unavoidably expand. It is the responsibility of the government of Israel, with the help of the Chief Rabbinate, to give special attention to dealing with this holy and emotion laden matter before it explodes.[48]

Those in the Government and the Chief Rabbinate who pay only lip service to the basic rights of the people of Israel to the Temple Mount' . . . must bear re-

sponsibility for the fire liable to erupt from the burning fuse and which, God forbid, may ignite a terrible
religious war, whose echoes would reverberate from
one end of the earth to the other.

*. . . The public in Judea, Samaria, and Gaza has spoken
of these matters for two years. . . . We warn those whose errors determine, even if unintentionally, that day after day
the Temple Mount remains in Muslim hands. We warn
them that Jewish eyes and souls yearn for the Temple
Mount and that they, with their own hands, are stoking
the fires which will erupt to solve the problem, and not by
normal, natural, or legal means.*

*We issue this warning to all the organs of the Government
of Israel and also to the Chief Rabbinate of the Land of Israel.*[49]

These editorials evince what had become, by the mid-1980s, an
escalating commitment by the mainstream of the fundamentalist
movement to alter the status quo on the Temple Mount in some
dramatic fashion—by either replacing Muslim guards with Israeli
police, organizing public Jewish prayer services on the site, building a large synagogue there, treating it as a settlement area, or
preparing it for the reconstruction of the Temple. A September
1986 *Nekuda* editorial read as follows:

What is proper regarding the whole Land of Israel
must also be proper regarding the Temple Mount . . .
if for returning to the whole Land of Israel, and for
the establishment of the state, we have pushed the end,
by the same token we must now build the Temple.[50]

The sensitivity of the site is accented every Friday by the 50,000
Muslim worshipers who gather there for prayer. In October 1987,
fearful that Jewish fundamentalists would attempt to demonstrate
on the site during Succoth, one of Judaism's three pilgrimage
holidays, 2,000 Muslims waged a three-hour battle with police
using tear gas and live ammunition to drive them from the compound.[51] Nonetheless, according to prominent Israeli newspaper
columnist Doron Rosenblum, the destruction of the Muslim
shrines on the Temple Mount is "only a matter of time." The
aftermath, he predicts, will be horrible:

. . . the immediate cancellation of the peace agreement with Egypt; . . . spontaneous demonstrations in every Arab country; news bulletins on American networks announcing declarations of war by the entire Arab world; . . . mobilization of the reserves amidst . . . reports of tensions on all four fronts; the flow of Egyptian forces into Sinai; firing in the Golan and the Jordan Valley; dogfights with Iranian, Saudi, Libyan, Iraqi, and Syrian planes; . . . rumors of the massacre of Syrian Jews; . . . guerrilla war in the occupied territories between Arabs and settlers; "massacres" that will be called total anarchy; intervention by the superpowers and war that will go on for months or even years.[52]

In May 1987 one army reserve general called for the immediate implementation of a plan to defend the Muslim shrines:

I personally know of fighters from elite [army] units, graduates of the finest yeshivas in Jerusalem and Judea, who are imbued with messianic fervor: "May the Temple be rebuilt speedily in our own days." These irresponsible people could get hold of a ton of explosives, and, under cover of a foggy dawn, approach the Temple Mount in a couple of armored personnel carriers . . . and plant the explosives at the Dome of the Rock. If they managed to plant a few hundred kilos, they could bring the dome crashing down onto the rock, thereby visiting disaster on themselves and on us.[53]

The Temple Mount issue represents a terrible dilemma for Gush Emunim as a fundamentalist movement lacking effective and charismatic leadership. On the one hand, no single trend within the movement contains more potential for effecting rapid and radical change consistent with its overall worldview. No event is more likely than a government-supported fundamentalist initiative aimed at Judaizing the Temple Mount to achieve a profound realignment of public attitudes within Israel, to precipitate an eminently crushable armed revolt in the occupied territories, to disrupt the Egyptian–Israeli relationship, and to distance Israel, politically and culturally, from the entire gentile world. And no single issue contains greater potential than the strong and growing fundamentalist commitment toward the Judaization of the Temple Mount to destroy the unity of the movement, to deflect it from politically productive activities vis-à-vis the majority of Israelis, or to provide its enemies with the means to isolate, discredit, and defeat it. In the absence of a charismatic source of legitimacy for decisions to postpone action on this issue, the danger is very great that "purist" vanguardist elements within the movement will regularly expose it to political attacks of "mysticism," "apocalypticism," and "insanity"—attacks that at the very least interrupt consensus-building efforts, but that also can support more devastating legal and political attacks against it.

With Yitzhak Shamir's assumption of the premiership in 1985, and the disappearance of concrete negotiating opportunities with Jordan, the impetus toward changing the status quo on the *Haram el-Sharif,* and even toward "cleansing the Temple Mount of the abominations" (the Dome of the Rock and el-Aksa Mosque) slowed. Relying heavily on quotations from Tzvi Yehuda, Shlomo Aviner has constructed a tortured argument for continuing the halachic ban on entry into the Temple Mount area and "achieving closeness to it by keeping distance from it." Only when the whole Jewish people is united in its dedication to rebuilding the Temple, he contends, should anything be done to Judaize the site.[54]

Should a Labor Party victory appear imminent, or even possible, however, the vanguardists within Gush Emunim will again seek to preempt the political process by raising the banner of the Temple Mount. Such developments will be very dangerous. But they may also provide adroit politicians with opportunities to divide Gush Emunim, portray its leadership as either insincere or terrifying, dramatize the risks run by Israelis who entertain the visions of glory advanced by Gush, and sharply reduce, if not destroy, the movement's near-term political potential.

The Temple Mount issue is one of several that gave rise to the most serious internal crisis in the history of contemporary Jewish fundamentalism. In late 1986, Daniella Weiss became a focus of bitter dispute within the movement. Her vigorous activities on behalf of amnesty for participants in the terrorist underground, her televised attacks on the historical contribution of Labor kibbutzim to the Zionist enterprise, and her intensely vanguardist sentiments have led many veterans of the movement to call for her dismissal as Gush Emunim's general secretary. Some leading rabbis, including Yoel Ben-Nun and Menachem Frumin, publicly separated themselves from Gush Emunim as led and organized in late 1986 and early 1987. This split precipitated harsh rebukes by vanguardists who insist that Gush Emunim must be true to the immediacy of its redemptive mission. These attacks, in turn, led some fundamentalists to suggest that the time of Gush Emunim as a relatively informal, pioneering organization, reliant on a spontaneously generated internal consensus and noncalculated political programs, had passed. They advocated creation of a new organization with an elected leadership, able to mobilize wider sectors of Israeli society around a new consensus.[55] In May 1987, following a threat by Ben-Nun to stage a sit-down strike in front of Gush offices in Jerusalem, a meeting was held between representatives of the different points of view. The result was an agreement under which Moshe Levinger was identified as the overall ideological guide of the movement, Weiss was permitted to remain as general secretary, Ben-Nun agreed to resume active participation in Gush Emunim's secretariat, Hanan Porat was given responsibility for propaganda, and Beni Katzover was named to head the political committee.[56] As of this writing, it is still too early to know how effective these arrangements will be, but they are unlikely to provide a permanent solution to the problems raised by the combination of Tzvi Yehuda's death and the choices and opportunities faced by the fundamentalist movement as a result of its partial success.

The divisions within Gush Emunim, especially between vanguardists and consensus builders and between religious and nonreligious fundamentalists, can help explain much about the dynamics of the movement, the problems it faces, and the mix of political strategies it is likely to pursue. It is a commonplace of Israeli affairs that without the Arab–Israeli conflict, the cleavages within Jewish society would present substantially graver threats to the country's political fabric than they have until now. The same basic point applies with even greater force to Gush Emunim. Rav Abraham Isaac Kook's formula for merging the devotion and authenticity of religious Jews with the energy, technical skills, and political savvy of secular ultranationalist and activist secular Zionists requires an ongoing, increasingly "luminous" and challenging redemption process. As long as that process is moving forward, difficulties that religious Jews cannot help having in working side by side secular Jews can be put aside. But Rav Kook's dialectical and mystical rationalizations for cooperation are far less satisfying for ordering the routines of daily life and of institutionalized political, social, educational, and economic activity. Thus, to pre- serve the unity of the movement, both religious and nonreligious fundamentalists have a strong interest in maintaining a sense of crisis, of the need for extraordinary effort, and of the imminence of great danger or great opportunity.[57]

These structural requirements of the movement, combined with the absence of charismatic leadership, may make Jewish fundamentalism in Israel a less effective political player in the long run, but a more explosive and dangerous element in Israeli and Middle Eastern affairs in the short and medium term. Despite the political caution and consolidation that many of Gush Emunim's most sophisticated personalities advocate, it is far more likely that contemporary Jewish fundamentalism will imitate the self- destructive extremism of the first-century Zealots and the second- century followers of Bar Kochba than that it will be able to build a new and stable consensus. For Israelis, and indeed for the rest of the world, a larger question is whether the catastrophic conse- quences of the fundamentalist politics of the Second Temple's time will also be recapitulated.

VII

Conclusion

Assessing Jewish Fundamentalism's Long Term Potential

At the beginning of this book, I used Amos Elon's descriptions of Israeli Independence Day celebrations in 1968 and 1987 to suggest how drastically Israel changed in the twenty years following the Six Day War. Built to reflect the voluntarist spirit and social democratic nationalism of the Labor Zionist movement, Israel developed into a deeply divided and highly politicized society. Right-wing Zionism, marginalized for generations by the Labor Zionist founders of the country, rose to power. Exploiting the resentments and anti-Arab attitudes of Sephardic Jews, who previously had been excluded from key institutions, the Likud used its irredentist program to capitalize on the romance and enthusiasm stimulated by the Six Day War and the fears generated by the Yom Kippur War. From this setting arose a redemptionist Jewish fundamentalist movement that provided devoted settlers, inspiring leadership, and an exciting and coherent worldview, and thereby acted both as an instrument of the Likud and as a powerful influence on it.

No one can tell what Israel, or the Middle East, will be like twenty years from now. Nor can one chart, with confidence, the future of Jewish fundamentalism. But one can be sure that the two will be linked. Virtually no serious observers believe a negotiated solution to the Arab–Israeli conflict is possible unless Jewish fundamentalism's key goal—establishment of permanent Jewish rule of the whole Land of Israel—is thwarted. Yet, for the foreseeable future, the political leverage this movement and its allies can exert will prevent the Israeli political system from responding

177

positively, by normal, peaceful parliamentary means, to opportunities to achieve such an agreement, no matter how attractive its
terms. Nor can Israel stably incorporate the territories within its
sovereign domain—partly because of international opposition,
partly because of sharp divisions within Israel itself over the wisdom of doing so, but also because the entrenched interests and
extremist proclivities of Gush Emunim settlers make it unlikely
that any arrangement even minimally satisfactory for Palestinians
in the West Bank and Gaza could be agreed upon and implemented.[1]

The overheated political climate that results from Israel's inability to disengage from or absorb these areas, and the cycles of
violence, international obloquy, and threats of war that maintain
it, create conditions that enhance the attractiveness of fundamentalist ideas. For however "authentic" is the fundamentalist message, it is but one authentic expression of what Jewish political
culture has been and can be. To thrive, Jewish fundamentalism
must rely not simply on authenticity, but on conditions that
encourage hundreds of thousands of Jews to see in its radically
parochial and expansionist message a relevant and even compelling
interpretation of their predicament. For its adherents, and indirectly for much wider strata whose thinking is shaped by the
categories, myths, and assumptions it promotes, Jewish fundamentalism makes sense of the contradictions between what mainstream Zionism promised to Jews (security and respect in their
own land) and what it has been able to deliver. Gush Emunim, in
other words, relies not only on the absence of movement toward
peace, but also on the inability of any other political force to
convey to a majority of Israelis an alternative formula, equally
authentic, equally reassuring, but grounded in accommodation
and cooperation, rather than in isolation and confrontation.

Nowhere is this more evident than in the Labor Party's emphasis on the "demographic problem"—the concern that absorption of the West Bank and Gaza Strip will give Israel either an Arab
majority or too large an Arab minority to satisfy the minimal
conditions of Zionism. The point of this argument was, and is, to
frighten Israelis out of their attachment to the occupied territories
by creating images of the impossibility of living in the same
country with so many Arabs. But given a rapidly growing Arab

population of nearly 700,000 inside the green line, and the lack of a plan for territorial compromise acceptable to Arab representatives (Palestinian or otherwise), this argument has done little but convince many Israelis of the need to get rid of the Arabs, not the territories. Such thinking nourishes the kind of radical Jewish exclusivism cultivated so assiduously by the fundamentalist movement.

At the end of October 1987, Minister without Portfolio Yosef Shapira, an influential figure within Gush Emunim, publicly suggested that the transfer of Arabs from both Israel and the territories be accomplished by paying $20,000 to each Arab willing to leave permanently. In defense of his proposition, Shapira cited a survey his party conducted among rabbis in the West Bank and Gaza Strip to gauge preelection sentiments. In answer to the question "What is your opinion regarding the emigration of gentiles from the country?" 62 percent responded that "We must force them to do so by any means at our disposal and see in it an exchange of populations," 13 percent favored the encouragement of voluntary emigration, and 10 percent said "this is not the time to discuss the question."[2]

Other politicians and respected personalities—including retired General Rehavam Ze'evi, former head of the Central Command, now curator of Tel Aviv's Land of Israel Museum; Herut's Mikhael Dekel, deputy minister of defense; Ariel Sharon, minister of trade and industry; Gideon Altschuler, Geula Cohen, and Yuval Neeman of Tehiya; and several of Shapira's colleagues in the National Religious Party—joined in a lively and sustained debate over what sort of voluntary, semivoluntary, or forcible transfer schemes might be implemented.[3] This debate emerged against a background of bloody clashes in the West Bank and Gaza Strip, and of new demographic statistics showing that in 1988 a majority of the children under the age of fifteen living within the area ruled by Israel will be Arabs.[4]

The importance of the debate is not in the likelihood that any of these proposals will soon be implemented, but in the unmistakable widening of the parameters of acceptable political discourse to include the mass transfer or "repatriation" of Arabs as a discussable option. It is also evidence of the kind of long term influence fundamentalist ideas can have, given the right circumstances, on the direction of Israeli political life. Gush Emunim, according to Doron Rosenblum, has often succeeded in transforming "the criminal to the crazy, the crazy to the odd, the odd to the mistaken, the mistaken to the good, the good to the excellent, the excellent to the accomplished reality, and the accomplished reality to the consensus view."[5]

Just how much success could Jewish fundamentalism have in Israel? To begin with, Israel is not Iran. The kind of social revolution that swept Khomeini to power is virtually inconceivable in the Israeli context. Nor should the Likud be underestimated with regard to its autonomy or its potential to develop in much more pragmatic directions than it has under the leadership of Begin, Shamir, and Sharon. Indeed, late in 1987, Likud politicians clashed directly with Gush Emunim in an effort to take control of the Yesha Council.[6] Clearly, Shimon Peres was exaggerating when he told 2,000 retired Labor party workers in June 1987 that the Likud has "ceased to exist. [It] has become an appendage of Gush Emunim and Tehiya and religious parties. There is no longer a Likud—only a Rabbi Levinger and Daniella Weiss."[7]

Those who hold that the organizational difficulties have drained self-confidence and vitality from Gush Emunim since 1984 are correct. But it must not be forgotten just how unusual is the national unity government arrangement that has prevailed since the 1984 elections, and how severe the constraints it places on the movement as an effective interest group. The fact is that fundamentalist ideas and elites are now part of the Israeli political landscape. While the nonfundamentalist hawkish right appears incapable of differentiating itself clearly from its fundamentalist allies, the dovish/liberal left still lacks coherent, compelling visions of the country to which a majority of Israelis might turn for guidance and reassurance. New elections, the polarization of political sentiments, the Likud's need for coalition partners, continued unrest in the territories, and heightened regional tensions all contribute to an environment in which Jewish fundamentalism can flourish.

Jewish Fundamentalism and American Foreign Policy. The question posed for both liberal democratic Israelis and American policymakers is therefore not how to respond to the prospect of a fundamentalist Israel. It is, rather, how to shape circumstances and interpret them in ways that would undermine the attractiveness of the fundamentalist message. For Israelis the stakes are high and obvious. But important American interests are also involved. A peace agreement that would eliminate the pattern of costly and dangerous wars between American and Soviet proxies—Israel and the Arab states, respectively—is a central foreign policy objective of the United States. For this reason, given the intimacy of the American–Israeli relationship, and because the United States must be concerned with the consequences of an Israel torn between radically opposed conceptions of itself, Washington must seek ways to prevent the explosiveness that surrounds Jewish fundamentalism from being unleashed on the region and the world.

The internal strain associated with its influence and with dramatic swings of the Israeli political pendulum is likely to be reflected in a spasmodic pattern of Israeli behavior, including extreme oscillation in official policies toward peace negotiations and toward the Arab inhabitants of the West Bank and Gaza. These stresses have been apparent even within the national unity government, in the desperate fighting between Shamir and Peres over the prospect of negotiations under some sort of international aegis. With the passing of this awkward coalition, the intensity of political conflict within Israel will increase dramatically. Government annexationist efforts to sabotage processes leading toward politically uncomfortable negotiations may follow, or precede, rather daring attempts by dovish governments to create diplomatic or political facts before the opposition can mobilize the fears and emotions of the electorate. In this context vanguardist arguments within Gush Emunim will attract increasing support. Pressure will build for actions able to irrevocably alienate gentile opinion toward Israel, and Arab opinion in particular.

Even if a governing coalition could be formed of parties willing to accept an agreement based on the principle of territory for peace, the implementation of that policy would trigger intense and widespread opposition and pose real challenges to the parliamentary regime's ability to sustain itself. Such events would be reminiscent of those that led to the collapse of the Fourth Republic in France in 1958, when uprisings by Algerian settlers and units of the French army on behalf of *Algérie française* attracted wide support from right-wing and clerical parties in metropolitan France. In Israel such a crisis would almost certainly involve repeated demonstrations by hundreds of thousands of Jews, violence against both Jews and Arabs, challenges to the authority and legitimacy of the government, a host of rabbinical decrees opposing the government's intentions, the creation of scores of new illegal settlements, threats of civil war, a sudden influx of militantly ultranationalist Diaspora Jews, and, as suggested above, attempts at spectacular actions such as the destruction of the Muslim shrines in Jerusalem.[8] It is quite conceivable that such opposition could be overcome by skillful and determined Israeli leaders—especially leaders able to characterize their willingness to compromise as the inescapable result of a superpower diktat. But even against the background of vigorous American and Soviet pressure, and even assuming the government's willingness to use tough, possibly ruthless measures against its opponents, success would not be guaranteed.

Should such a genuine attempt to implement a territorial compromise fail, the fundamentalist movement might well find it possible to exploit a breakdown of parliamentary democracy and the ensuing confusion for its own purposes. In a poll taken of Israeli Jews in January 1987, 34 percent either agreed or definitely agreed that "in Israel's current condition it is preferable to have a strong leadership which can set the house in order without being dependent on elections or voting for the Knesset." Another 21 percent chose the response "do not quite agree," and 38 percent selected "definitely disagree."[9] Israel is, indeed, so deeply divided on key territorial and ideological issues, and has such a short and essentially untested tradition of constitutional democracy, that successful challenges to the regime cannot be ruled out. The most often discussed scenario of this sort is that of popular but unscrupulous right-wing politicians joining with ambitious military commanders to "restore order and sanity" amid chronic, polarized, and increasingly violent intra-Jewish struggles. Gush Emunim could provide these elements with necessary political support and ideological legitimacy.[10]

The emergence of an Israeli regime dependent on, if not actually led by, fundamentalist elites would destroy the special relationship with the United States, based as it has been on perceptions of common moral, political, and cultural purposes. An Israel decoupled from the United States, opposed in principle to a negotiated peace, unfettered by the norms of liberal democracy, animated by redemptionist imperatives, and disposing of a large and sophisticated nuclear arsenal would pose challenges to American foreign policy and security interests at least as profound as those resulting from the Islamic Revolution in Iran. The United States thus has a strong interest in finding effective ways to support those inside Israel who are struggling against the fundamentalists and their allies. It is neither too early nor too late to prepare the ground for management of the crises that are bound to come. Washington should stress, much more strongly than it has in the past, how central to America's special relationship with Israel is the cluster of democratic, libertarian, and universalistic values our two countries have always shared. We should make crystal clear the extent to which our friendship and support ultimately depend on these shared values—values we can directly portray as unrealizable in the "greater Israel" to which the fundamentalists aspire.[11]

Jewish Nationalism and Jewish Fundamentalism. If Jewish nationalism and sovereignty mean anything, they mean that the largest measure of responsibility for the neutralization of Jewish fundamentalism rests with Jews, both in Israel and in the Diaspora. In a Jewish historical context, contemporary fundamentalism is an example of *dheikat haketz,* a struggle to push, force, or press for the end—for the final redemption—by achieving, at any cost, Jewish rule over the whole Land of Israel. The question it raises is new as it relates specifically to the West Bank, the Gaza Strip, and the Palestinian Arabs; but in another sense, for Jews it is very old. No one has posed it more effectively or presciently than Gershom Scholem.

In 1959, well before the rise of Gush Emunim, Scholem observed that the messianic idea has held an extraordinary attraction for Jews. He therefore found it unsurprising that "overtones of Messianism" and a "readiness for irrevocable action in the concrete realm" accompanied the success of Zionism. On the other hand, recalling the catastrophic revolts against Rome and the Sabbatian episode, he warned that "the blazing landscape of redemption" is a hazardous field for political ambition. Zionism may have drawn strength from Jewish messianism, but in the past, he notes, Jews have had to pay a price for acting on these beliefs—an exceedingly high price.

> Whether or not Jewish history will be able to endure this entry into the concrete realm without perishing in the crisis of the Messianic claim which has virtually been conjured up—that is the question which out of his great and dangerous past the Jew of this age poses to his present and to his future.[12]

The Jewish people is still reeling from its most recent experience of near annihilation—the Holocaust. In their search for a way out of the current political impasse, Israeli Jews are confronted with another type of historically familiar challenge—the seductive but perilous temptations of redemption. Meeting this challenge will require the political maturity to avoid succumbing to these temptations and to find instead the earthly, and imperfect, alternatives.

APPENDIX 1

Glossary

Achdut Haavodah—Socialist-Zionist party that split from the dominant Mapai party in 1944; emphasized activism toward national and territorial objectives; merged with other socialist-Zionist parties in 1968.

Agudat Yisrael—Ultra-Orthodox political organization founded in 1912; members' attitudes range from anti-Zionist to non-Zionist.

Akiva—Leading rabbi of the early second century C.E.; is believed to have declared Simon Bar Kochba the Messiah.

Amana—(Covenant) the settlement-building arm of Gush Emunim.

Ariel, Yisrael—Rabbi; number two on Rabbi Kahane's Kach list in 1981 elections; known for his extreme views.

Artzi—Scholarly/polemical fundamentalist journal published irregularly since 1982.

Aviner, Shlomo—Rabbi of the Beit-El settlement near Ramallah; editor of the journal *Aturei Kahanim*, published by the Crown of the Priests Yeshiva in the Old City of Jerusalem.

Bar Kochba, Simon—Leader of the second great Judean revolt against the Romans, 132–135 C.E.

Ben-Nun, Yoel—Rabbi; leading activist within Gush Emunim; veteran of Ofra settlement near Ramallah; regular contributor to *Nekuda*; consensus builder; an editor of *Artzi*. See appendix 3 for biography.

Ben-Yosef (Hagar), Moshe—Passionate polemicist; regular contributor to *Nekuda*; secularist; lives in Tel-Aviv; advocates imposition of a reformed halacha on all Israelis.

Bnei Akiva—(Sons of Akiva) youth movement of the National Religious party.

Cohen, Geula—A Herut firebrand; veteran of Irgun and Lehi; bolted from Herut to help found Tehiya; member of Knesset; nonreligious, ultranationalist.

Druckman, Haim—Rabbi; member of Knesset; a founder of and leading activist within Gush Emunim; organizer of Matzad; now returned to National Religious Party from Morasha.

Eldad, Israel—Leading ideologue in Lehi before 1948; writer, teacher, journalist; well known for his advocacy, in 1950s and 1960s, of Jewish sovereignty from "the Nile to the Euphrates"; Gush Emunim and Tehiya activist; nonreligious.

185

Elon Moreh—Jewish settlement site in Nablus area of West Bank evacuated by court order in 1979.

Eretz Yisrael—Land of Israel.

Fisch, Harold—Author, former rector of Bar-Ilan University; associated with founding of Movement for the Whole Land of Israel.

Garin—Settlement nucleus.

Geulah—Redemption.

Green line—1949 armistice line separating Israel from Egypt, Lebanon, Syria, and Jordan.

Haetzni, Eliyakim—Lawyer; veteran settler in Kiryat Arba; Gush Emunim activist; polemicist; regular contributor to *Nekuda*; secular, vanguardist in orientation.

Hakibbutz Hameuchad—Socialist Zionist settlement movement with activist (expansionist, nationalist) emphasis; affiliated with the political party Achdut Haavodah.

Halacha—The entire corpus of Jewish religious law.

Har Habayit—(Temple Mount); biblical Mount Moriah; southeastern corner of the Old City of Jerusalem; Jewish term for the Haram el-Sharif.

Haram el-Sharif—(Noble Sanctuary); Muslim Arab term for the Temple Mount; site of the Dome of the Rock and the el-Aksa Mosque.

Haredim—Ultra-Orthodox Jews; non-Zionist or anti-Zionist.

Irgun—Also known as Etzel (the National Military Organization), underground military/terrorist arm of the Revisionist movement during the British mandate; commanded by Menachem Begin.

Jabotinsky, Vladimir (Ze'ev)—Founder of Revisionist Zionism; mentor of Menachem Begin.

Kach—Fundamentalist political organization headed by Rabbi Meir Kahane, emphasizes the expulsion of Arabs from the entire Land of Israel.

Kasher, Menachem—Rabbi; religious scholar; author of *The Great Period*; known in fundamentalist circles for his identification and detailed analysis of contemporary period as that of the redemption.

Katzover, Beni—Founding member of Gush Emunim; participant in Sebastia settlement; leader of the Nablus area settlers; Tehiya activist; religious.

Kiryat Arba—Largest Jewish settlement in the West Bank; overlooks Hebron.

Knesset—Israel's Parliament.

Kook, Abraham Isaac—First chief rabbi of Palestine (1921–1935); originator of theories of religious Zionism that form the ideological basis of contemporary Jewish fundamentalism.

Kook, Tzvi Yehuda—Rabbi; son of Abraham Isaac Kook; leader and charismatic guide of Gush Emunim activists; director of Merkaz HaRav until his death in 1982.

Lehi—Freedom Fighters for Israel; also known as the Stern Gang, for its leader, Abraham (Yair) Stern; terrorist underground group specializing in assassination during the British mandate; split from the Irgun.

Levinger, Moshe—Rabbi; a founder of Gush Emunim and, along with his wife, Miriam, of Jewish settlement in Hebron.

Machteret—Underground; Jewish terrorist groups associated with fundamentalist movement uncovered in 1984.

Matzad—Religious Zionist movement; founded by Haim Druckman after his departure in 1982 from the National Religious Party; formerly a component of Morasha; now a faction of the National Religious Party.

Merkaz HaRav—The Rabbi's Center; the Jerusalem yeshiva founded by Rav Abraham Isaac Kook; subsequently led by his son, Rav Tzvi Yehuda Kook; center for the development of Jewish fundamentalist thinking.

Mitzvah—A religious commandment within the halacha.

Morasha—Political party founded in 1984 by Haim Druckman combining religiosity with ultranationalism; composed of Matzad and the ultra-Orthodox party Poalei Agudat Yisrael (Pagi).

Neeman, Yuval—Israel's leading nuclear physicist; secular ultranationalist; a founder and the leader of Tehiya; former cabinet minister; presently a member of Knesset.

Nekuda—(Point); the monthly journal of Yesha; internal ideological journal and news magazine of Gush Emunim; began publishing in 1979.

Orot—Lights; multivolume work of Rav Abraham Isaac Kook; mystical presentation of his religious Zionism; also the name of a short-lived political movement established by Hanan Porat in 1984.

Pikuach nefesh—Principle of preserving life rather than observing the halacha.

Porat, Hanan—Rabbi; Charismatic founding member of Gush Emunim; veteran settler of Kibbutz Gush Etzion; religious, mystical orientation.

Sabbatianism—Reckless faith in a false messiah; derived from belief in seventeenth century of messiahship of Shabbatai Zevi.

Sebastia—Biblical site near Nablus; location of the first successful attempt by Gush Emunim to establish an illegal settlement (1974).

Shechem—Biblical name of Nablus, largest city on the West Bank after East Jerusalem.

Tehiya—Political party founded in 1979 by Gush Emunim activists; composed of secular and religious fundamentalists; led by Yuval Neeman.

Torah—The Pentateuch; more broadly, Jewish religious law.

Tzomet—Movement for Zionist Renewal; founded after the Lebanon War by former Chief of Staff Rafael Eitan; merged with Tehiya in 1984; left Tehiya in 1987.

Waldman, Eleazar—Rabbi; head of yeshiva in Kiryat Arba; elected to the Knesset on the Tehiya list.

Yamit—District of northeastern Sinai, including a city of the same name; before its evacuation by Israel in April 1982, inhabited by 5,000 Israeli settlers.

Yesha—Hebrew acronym for Judea, Samaria, and Gaza; also the name of the Association for Jewish Local Councils in Judea, Samaria, and the Gaza District; the Hebrew *yeshua* means "salvation."

Yishuv—The portion of the Jewish people residing, at any one time, in the Land of Israel.

APPENDIX 2

Polling Data Illustrative of Israeli Attitudes on Selected Questions

Territorial Compromise

Regarding the West Bank (held by Israel since the Six Day War in 1967), what is the biggest concession you would be willing to make in order to arrive at a *peace agreement* with the Arab countries?

Of Israeli Jews, 30 percent said no concessions. January 1975[1]

If Israel had to choose between peace and annexation of the territories held since the 1967 war which would you choose?

Of Israeli Jews, 54 percent chose annexation. July 1984[2]

In peace negotiations with the Arabs, Israel should suggest territorial compromise against suitable security guarantees.

Of Israeli Jews, 54 percent disagreed. September 1986[3]

Are you in favor of a peace agreement with Jordan according to which Israel will give up territory in Judea and Samaria?

Of Israeli Jews, the proportions against any concession were as follows:

   48.9 percent November 1985
   43.6 percent February 1986
   44.9 percent March 1986
   47.7 percent October 1986
   46.4 percent April 1987[4]

Which of the following proposals on the future of Judea and Samaria is closer to your own position?

Of Israeli Jews, 66.8 percent cited either annexation or permanent control without annexation. July 1987[5]

188

Are you in favor of a peace agreement with Jordan according to which Israel will give up territory in Judea and Samaria?

Of Israeli Jews aged 22–29, 56 percent said no; of those aged 18–29, 73 percent said no. March 1986[6]

Settlement of the West Bank

Should Jewish settlement be allowed in Hebron?

Of Israeli Jews, 46.3 percent said yes. March 1980[7]

Should we continue with Jewish settlements in all of Judea and Samaria?

Of Israeli Jews, 31.2 percent said yes. March 1981[8]

Do you support or oppose relinquishing any settlements in the West Bank?

Of Israeli Jews, 50 percent were opposed. September 1984[9]

Do you favor or oppose the internal organization of settlers in Judea and Samaria to assure their safety?

Of Israeli Jews, 37.9 percent were in favor. December 1984[10]

Are you willing for Jewish settlements in Judea and Samaria to be evacuated in exchange for a peace agreement with Jordan?

Of Israeli Jews, 62 percent said no. April 1987[11]

Are you willing to freeze new settlements in Judea and Samaria?

Of Israeli Jews, the proportions against such a freeze were as follows:

35.4 percent November 1985
35.9 percent February 1986
35.5 percent March 1986
36.6 percent October 1986
37.9 percent April 1987[12]

Arabs

Do you support the use of terror to confront Arab terror?

Of Israeli Jews, 36.6 percent said yes. May 1980[13]

Of Israeli Oriental Jews, 46 percent said yes. May 1980[14]

There cannot be peace between us and between all the Arab countries.

Of Israeli Jews, 37.3 percent agreed. 1981[15]

A Jewish group to fight terror with terror should be created.

Of Israeli Jews, 18.7 percent agreed. December 1983[16]

The Arab population across the green line should be deported.

Of Israeli Jews, 15 percent agreed. July 1984[17]

Can justify or relate with understanding to the Jewish terrorist underground.

Of Israeli Jews, 62 percent agreed. June 1984[18]

Arabs in Israel should not be permitted to criticize the government.

Of Israeli Jews aged 15–18, 55.1 percent agreed. August 1984[19]

Deny Israeli Arab citizens the right to vote in Knesset elections.

Of Israeli Jews, 24 percent agreed. 1985[20]

Agree with the 600 ideas of the Kach movement of Meir Kahane regarding the Arab minority.

Of 600 Israeli Jewish high school students, 42.1 percent agreed. 1985[21]

I support those working to make the Arabs leave Judea and Samaria.

Of Israeli Jews, the proportions agreeing were as follows:

> 22 percent 1983
> 35 percent August 1985
> 29 percent February 1986
> 34 percent May 1986
> 38 percent September 1986[22]

Miscellaneous

Believe in the coming of the Messiah.

Of Israeli Jews, 36 percent said yes. 1974[23]

The Jewish people is a Chosen People.

Of Israeli Jews, 57 percent agreed. 1974[24]

Willing to sharply reduce standard of living in order to end Israeli dependence on America.

Of Israeli Jews, 38.2 percent said yes. June 1980[25]

The idea of rebuilding the Temple before the coming of the Messiah.

Of Israeli Jews, 18.3 percent supported it. May 1983[26]

The idea of razing the Muslim shrines to rebuild the Third Temple.

Of Israeli Oriental Jews, 25 percent supported it. May 1982[27]

Given the labels "rightist," "moderate rightist," "moderate leftist," and "leftist," how would you describe yourself?

Of Israeli Jews, 20 percent answered "rightist." January 1982[28]

The Committee for Solidarity with Beir Zeit [a left-wing Jewish group with ties to West Bank Arabs] should be outlawed.

Of Israeli Jews, 60 percent agreed. March 1983[29]

The political system should be changed radically and a strong regime of leaders who are not dependent on parties should be instituted.

Of Israeli Jews, 20 percent agreed. March 1983[30]

Do you prefer an undemocratic government whose positions and actions you approve to a democratic one whose views and actions you oppose?

Of Israeli Jews, 17 percent said yes. March 1983[31]

A *cohen* [descendant of the priestly caste] must not marry a divorced woman.

Of Israeli Jews, 32 percent agreed. March 1986[32]

Jews known to be PLO supporters should definitely not have the right to vote for Knesset.

Of Israeli Jews, 61.4 percent agreed. January 1987[33]

Known Kahane supporters should definitely not have the right to vote for Knesset.

Of Israeli Jews, 33.4 percent agreed. January 1987[34]

The right of dissent is of no importance.

Of Israeli Jewish youth, 30 percent agree. April 1987[35]

NOTES TO APPENDIX 2

1. Poll conducted by the Israel Institute of Applied Social Research, reported in Russel Stone, *Social Change in Israel: Attitudes and Events, 1967–1979* (New York: Praeger, 1982) p. 41.
2. Asher Arian, "What the Israeli Election Portends," *Public Opinion*, August/September 1984, p. 55.
3. Poll conducted by Hanoch Smith, reported in *Jerusalem Post*, October 2, 1986.
4. Polls conducted by Modi'in Ezrahi, reported in *Maariv*, April 20, 1986 (translated in Foreign Broadcast Information Service, April 24, 1986, p. I6); and *Maariv*, July 15, 1987 (translated in FBIS, July 16, 1987, p. L6).
5. Poll conducted by Modi'in Ezrahi, reported in *Maariv*, July 15, 1987 (translated in FBIS, July 16, 1987, p. L6).
6. Poll conducted by Modi'in Ezrahi, reported in *Maariv*, April 20, 1986 (translated in FBIS, April 24, 1986, p. I6).
7. Poll conducted by Modi'in Ezrahi, reported in *Jerusalem Post*, March 26, 1980.
8. Poll conducted by Modi'in Ezrahi, reported in *Jerusalem Post*, March 31, 1981.
9. Poll conducted by Public Opinion Research of Israel (PORI), reported by Gloria Falk "Israeli Public Opinion: Looking toward a Palestinian Solution" in *Middle East Journal*, vol. 39, no. 3 (Summer 1985) p. 252.
10. Poll conducted by Modi'in Ezrahi, reported in *Jerusalem Post*, January 13, 1984.
11. Poll conducted by Modi'in Ezrahi, reported in *Maariv*, May 12, 1987 (translated in FBIS, May 15, 1987, p. I8).
12. Poll conducted by Modi'in Ezrahi, reported in *Maariv*, April 20, 1986 (translated in FBIS, April 24, 1986, p. I6); and *Maariv*, May 12, 1987 (translated in FBIS, May 15, 1987, p. I8).
13. Results of a poll taken shortly after bombing attack on West Bank mayors, reported in *Haaretz* as cited in *Nekuda*, "The Fourth Explosion," June 6, 1980.
14. *Ibid.*
15. *Haaretz*, April 8, 1981.

16. Poll conducted by Modi'in Ezrahi, reported in *Jerusalem Post,* January 13, 1984.

17. Poll conducted by Dahaf, reported by Yoram Peri in *Davar,* August 3, 1984.

18. Poll conducted by Dahaf, reported in Charles S. Liebman, "The Religious Component in Israeli Ultra-Nationalism," *Jerusalem Quarterly,* no. 41 (Winter 1987) p. 128.

19. *Ibid.*

20. Sammy Smooha, "Political Intolerance: Threatening Israel's Democracy," *New Outlook,* vol. 29, no 7, July 1986, p. 29.

21. Poll conducted by the Van Leer Institute, reported in *Israleft Biweekly News Service,* no. 266, July 10, 1985, p. 6.

22. Poll conducted by Hanoch Smith, reported in *Davar,* October 2, 1986.

23. Poll conducted by U. Farago, *Stability and Change in the Jewish Identity of Working Youth in Israel: 1965–1974* (in Hebrew) (Jerusalem: Levi Eshkol Institute for Economic, Social and Political Research, Hebrew University). Reported by Baruch Kimmerling in "Between the Primordial and Civil Definition of the Collective Identity," n.d., p. 16.

24. *Ibid.*

25. Poll conducted by Modi'in Ezrahi, reported in *Jerusalem Post,* June 10, 1980.

26. Poll conducted by PORI, reported in *Haaretz,* May 12, 1983; cited by Ofira Seliktar, *New Zionism and the Foreign Policy System of Israel* (Carbondale, Illinois: Southern Illinois University Press, 1986) p. 212.

27. Poll conducted by PORI, reported in Middle East Research Institute, *MERI Special Report,* vol. 2, no. 1 (May 2, 1984).

28. Polls conducted by Modi'in Ezrahi, reported in *Jerusalem Post,* February 2, 1982.

29. Poll conducted by Dahaf, reported in *Koteret Rashit,* March 9, 1983 (translated in JPRS no. NEA-83179, April 1, 1983, p. 73).

30. Polling data reported in *Al-Hamishmar,* March 20, 1983.

31. *Ibid.*

32. Poll conducted by Hanoch Smith, reported in American Jewish Committee, *News from the Committee,* April 17, 1986.

33. Poll conducted by Modi'in Ezrachi, reported in Yochanan Peres, "Most Israelis are Committed to Democracy," *Israeli Democracy,* February 1987, p. 17.

34. *Ibid.*

35. Polling results reported by Aryeh Naor in *Yediot Acharonot,* April 21, 1987 (translated in *Israel Press Briefs,* no. 53, May/June 1987, p. 8).

APPENDIX 3

Biographies of Selected Gush Emunim Activists

Uri Elitzur. Raised in a religious household in Jerusalem and educated in the state religious school system, Uri Elitzur is the son of Professor Yehuda Elitzur, whose field is Jewish history and the history of the Land of Israel. His mother was a well-known author of Israeli children's books.

Active in the Bnei Akiva youth movement, he studied for three years in the Merkaz HaRav yeshiva in the mid-1960s, but interrupted his studies there to serve in a Nahal army unit (combining paratrooper training and agricultural settlement work). After obtaining a university degree in mathematics, he began work as a teacher. Resentment against what he had perceived during his tour of army service as discrimination against religious soldiers, the trauma of the Yom Kippur War, and shock at seeing pictures of West Bank settlers being manhandled by soldiers led him and his wife to join Gush Emunim in the summer of 1974 and move to Ofra, near Ramallah in the West Bank.

With Gush leader Haim Druckman in the number two position on the National Religious Party list in the 1977 elections, Elitzur worked hard on its behalf. He was bitterly disappointed in the party's support of the Camp David accords. With Hanan Porat, his former roommate at Merkaz HaRav, Elitzur was one of the religious activists who helped form Tehiya. While working in Amana, the Gush-affiliated settlement organization, he appeared in the number-11 place on the Tehiya list in 1981. Discouraged by Tehiya's performance, and concerned about the precedent Israeli withdrawal from the Yamit district would create, he was a major force in the organization of the Movement to Halt the Retreat in Sinai. After the evacuation of Yamit in April 1982 he returned to Ofra and spent the next year in meditative study in a Gush Emunim yeshiva. At the end of the year he resumed work in Amana and became one of its two general secretaries. Having left Tehiya with Porat, he joined Druckman's Morasha party, but he was disappointed with its performance and rejoined the National Religious Party, where he is in charge of information and propaganda.
(Source: Hagai Segel, "A Man For All Seasons," *Nekuda*, no. 110, May 27, 1987, pp. 26–29, 55.)

Rabbi Yoel Ben-Nun. As a child in a religious household in Israel of the 1950s, Yoel Ben-Nun received a state-religious education, was active in the Bnei Akiva youth movement, and developed a sense of being part of a religious minority excluded from status and power by what he has termed "the aristocracy and oligarchy of Mapai (the Labor party)." He studied in the Merkaz HaRav yeshiva, and after the Six Day War studied and taught in Yeshiva Har Etzion in the Gush Etzion area of the West Bank (south of Jerusalem). Active in the establishment of Alon Shvut, a veteran settlement in that area, Ben-Nun was one of the founders of Gush Emunim in 1974.

Subsequently, he moved to Ofra, near Ramallah, where the administrative headquarters of Yesha and the editorial offices of *Nekuda* are located. A regular contributor to *Nekuda*, Ben-Nun played a leading role in the editing and publication of *Artzi*, a scholarly and polemical fundamentalist journal that began to appear in 1982, and of *Megadim*, a scholarly and religious journal published in Gush Etzion by the Yaacov Herzog Institute of Yeshiva Har Etzion, whose first issue appeared in 1986.

In his vigorous criticism of efforts by some Gush Emunim leaders to gain the release of all convicted Jewish terrorists, Ben-Nun threatened to lead a public sit-down strike in front of the movement's Jerusalem offices. He withdrew his threat in anticipation of the leadership shake-up that occurred in May 1987. (Sources: Yoel Ben-Nun, "Why in Koteret Rashit?" *Koteret Rashit*, no. 114B, February 6, 1985, pp. 36-37; and Aviva Shabi, "Cracks in the Gush," *Yediot Acharonot,* May 15, 1987.

Tzvi Shiloach. Born in southern Poland in 1911, Tzvi Shiloach came to Palestine in 1931. A nonreligious Jew, Shiloach became a high-ranking Labor party politician and publicist. In the early 1950s, under Ben-Gurion's tutelage, he edited a party newspaper, *Hador*. Subsequently he was appointed to head the Information Department of the Israel Institute of Productivity, became a member of the Labor Party Central Committee, and served as editor of another party publication, *Hamifal*. After the Six Day War, Shiloach left the Labor party to join the Movement for the Whole Land of Israel, serving as an editor of its newspaper, *Zot Haaretz*. In 1979 he participated in the establishment of Tehiya and briefly served in the Knesset as a representative of that party. Residing now in a West Bank settlement, Shiloach is a regular contributor of articles to *Yediot Acharonot*, Israel's largest mass circulation daily. (Sources: Rael Jean Isaac, *Israel Divided: Ideological Politics in the Jewish State* [Baltimore: Johns Hopkins University Press, 1976] p. 169; and *Nekuda*, no. 100, July 11, 1986, p. 66.)

Daniella Weiss. Born in the mid-1940s in Palestine to American- and Polish-born parents, Daniella Weiss grew up in an Orthodox Jewish environment. She received a degree in English literature and political science at Bar-Ilan University, but was uninvolved in politics until the early 1970s.

After the Six Day War she was inspired by the success of Moshe Levinger and others in establishing a Jewish presence in the territories occupied during that war. After the Yom Kippur War of 1973, Weiss joined the Elon Moreh settlement nucleus, led by Beni Katzover, which tried unsuccessfully seven times to establish itself near Nablus, in opposition to government policy, and succeeded on its eighth attempt. Although her husband, a successful businessman, commutes to work in Tel Aviv, she has lived since that time in Kedumim, a settlement that grew out of the original nucleus. Weiss has divided her time between raising her four children and political work. In 1979 she affiliated herself with Tehiya and was active in the Movement to Halt the Retreat in Sinai. Known for her close relationship with Rabbi Moshe Levinger, Weiss was chosen, in 1985, by Gush Emunim to be its general secretary.

Two years later she was the focus of intense criticism by many in the movement for her strident style. Weiss has been called "the queen of the Knesset cafeteria," because of her close and regular informal contacts with members of Knesset.
(Sources: Malka Eisenberg, "Women on the Frontier," *Counterpoint*, vol., May 1985, pp. 6–7; David Shipler, "Jewish Settlers Power Grows," *New York Times*, June 5, 1980; and personal interview, *Jerusalem Post International Edition*, February 15–21, 1987.)

Aharon Ben-Ami. Born in Palestine in the mid-1920s to second aliyah immigrant agricultural workers, Aharon Ben-Ami grew up in an activist Zionist environment. Afforded a religious education by his parents, unusual in that context, Ben-Ami is nevertheless not religiously observant. In the 1940s he joined the socialist Zionist Palmach, the strike force of the mainstream Zionist underground army, composed mostly of recruits from Achdut Haavoda and its affiliated kibbutzim. Later he joined the military wing of Revisionist Zionism, the Irgun. He fought in the 1948 war and appeared on the Herut list for the Knesset in the 1949 elections, but was not elected. He left for the United States, where he eventually earned his Ph.D. in sociology. In the mid-1960s he taught sociology at Tel Aviv University and Haifa University while participating with activist laborites in Rafi, Ben-Gurion's 1965 breakaway faction from the Mapai (Labor) party.

After the Six Day War Ben-Ami helped organize the Movement for the Whole Land of Israel, and wrote articles for its newspaper, *Zot Haaretz*, and for the Revisionist journal *Herut*. Ben-Ami was greatly impressed by the vigor and idealism displayed by the religious settlers of Gush Emunim in the aftermath of the Yom Kippur War. He became one of the first residents of Ariel, a large settlement in the northern bulge of the West Bank, where he served on the local council. He also became an active supporter of Tehiya. Since 1986 he has served as the editor of the newspaper *Hayarden*, which is designed to bring Gush Emunim's message to a wider Israeli audience.
(Source: Uri Orbach, "One Bank to the Jordan," *Nekuda*, no. 95, January 21, 1986, pp. 16–18.)

Romem Aldubi. *Nekuda* describes Romem Aldubi as an outstanding example of the new generation of Gush Emunim. Born in 1963, he was raised in Tel Aviv in a nonreligious home. His father, Tzvi Aldubi, is a well-known Israeli sculptor. Both of his parents hold dovish political views that are diametrically opposed to Aldubi's own.

In the early 1980s Aldubi attended a yeshiva in Jerusalem, where he heard of efforts to form a garin to establish itself in the city of Shechem (Nablus). While at the yeshiva he also heard Rav Tzvi Yehuda Kook say that it was more important to build a yeshiva in Shechem than in Hebron. When Yamit was evacuated he recognized one of the organizers of the Shechem garin resisting the evacuation and was inspired to devote his life to the reestablishment of Jewish life in Shechem. He has since explained that he felt "Abraham knocking on my door."

Aldubi sought advice from, and subsequently modeled himself after, Beni Katzover, well known for his success in opening the area around the city of Shechem to Jewish settlement in the mid-1970s. Following Katzover's advice, he began by studying alone in Shechem, near the grave of Joseph. Gradually others joined him, and there now (1987) are fifteen in the Joseph Still Lives Yeshiva. Although offered temporary housing in nearby settlements while he waits for government approval to settle in the city, Aldubi refuses to live anywhere until he can be at home in Shechem. (He reportedly sleeps mostly in his car.) In addition to the yeshiva, he has organized a garin that now includes thirty families from Jerusalem, Tel Aviv, and various settlements. Aldubi spends his days studying, meeting with prospective candidates for the garin, lobbying Knesset members and government officials, and consulting with Amana and Gush Emunim leaders, in an effort to generate movement on the issue to which he has chosen to devote his life. (Source: Bembi Erlich, "Master of that Dream," *Nekuda,* no. 106, January 9, 1987, pp. 22–25.)

Abraham Bar-Ilan. Abraham Bar-Ilan was raised in a religious household, from whose traditions he has strayed. In 1975 the Ministry of Housing and Construction, for whom he worked as an engineer, sent him to the city of Yamit for several months' work on design and construction projects. The death of his father in that same year affected him deeply, and he came under the influence of Rabbi Yisrael Ariel, director of the Yamit Yeshiva Hesder. His study in the yeshiva turned him from a nonideological technician to an observant Jew convinced of the decisive importance of settlement in the Land of Israel as a means of eventually transforming the entire Jewish people.

Bar-Ilan left his job and became head of the building board of Yamit. During the struggle to prevent the evacuation of the Yamit area, he served as administrative director of the Yamit Yeshiva Hesder and as the logistical expert in charge of providing supplies and other services to the Movement to Halt the Retreat in Sinai. Even as plans for the evacuation of the area proceeded, he supervised the construction of shelters, gardens, and over 200 apartments. Bar-Ilan also created Amichai, a marketing company for Yamit products of all kinds, whose profits helped finance the movement to stop the retreat. Utterly distraught when Yamit was finally evacuated and destroyed, with his family Bar-Ilan moved to the Gaza Strip in 1982. A founder of the large Gush settlement of Neve Dekalim, he now serves as the chief engineer for the regional council of the Gaza Coast district.(Source: Bembi Erlich, "The Tzaddik of Yamit," *Nekuda,* no. 110, May 25, 1987, pp. 16–17.)

The caption on the Nekuda cover reads "A Moment of Coexistence." For a discussion of the significance of this particular photograph, see page 136.

APPENDIX 5: The "Rebuilt" Temple

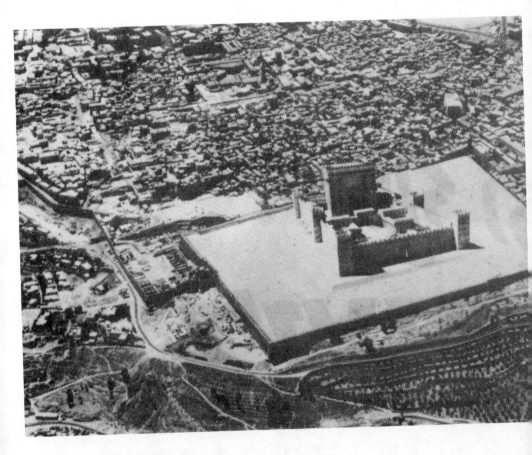

The caption on this widely known photomontage of the Temple Mount reads, "Naturally, when the peoples of the world come to learn from us, they are attracted not just by Holiness—the Land of Israel—but by the holy of holies." See note # 44 to chapter 6 for a discussion of this photograph.

Notes

Notes to Chapter 1

1. Amos Elon, *The Israelis: Founders and Sons* (New York: Holt, Rinehart and Winston, 1971) p. 3.
2. Amos Elon, "Letter from Israel," *New Yorker*, July 27, 1987, p. 33.
3. See George M. Marsden, *Fundamentalism and American Culture* (Oxford, England: Oxford University Press, 1980) for a discussion of the origins of the term *fundamentalism* in relationship to the insistence by American Christian Evangelicals in the late nineteenth and early twentieth centuries that true Christians adhere in an undeviating fashion to the five fundamentals.
4. From the publisher's description of Lionel Caplan, ed., *Studies in Religious Fundamentalism* (Albany: State University of New York Press, 1987). On the fundamentalist potential of nonreligious ideologies, see, in particular, Richard Tapper and Nancy Tapper, "'Thank God We're Secular!' Aspects of Fundamentalism in a Turkish Town," pp. 51–78.
5. For applications of the concept of "fundamentalist" in the Israeli context that correspond closely to my own, see Janet Aviad, "The Contemporary Israeli Pursuit of the Millennium," *Religion*, vol. 14 (1984) pp. 199–222; David Newman, "Gush Emunim Between Fundamentalism and Pragmatism," *Jerusalem Quarterly*, no. 39 (1986) pp. 33–43; Ehud Sprinzak, *Gush Emunim: The Politics of Zionist Fundamentalism in Israel* (New York: American Jewish Committee, 1986); Baruch Kimmerling, *Zionism and Territory* (Berkeley, California: University of California Institute of International Studies, 1983) p. 182; Jacob Katz, "Is Messianism Good for the Jews?" *Commentary*, vol. 83, no. 4 (April 1987) pp. 35–36; and Jonathan Webber, "Rethinking Fundamentalism: the Readjustment of Jewish Society in the Modern World," in Caplan, *Studies*, p. 116.
6. Concerning the organizational and ideological merger between the secular ultranationalist Movement for the Whole Land of Israel and Gush Emunim, see below, pp. 61–63, Lilly Weissbrod, "Core Values and Revolutionary Change," in David Newman, ed., *The Impact of Gush Emunim* (London: Croom Helm, 1985) pp. 79–80; and Julien Bauer, "A New Approach to Religious-Secular Relationships?" in Newman, pp. 91–110.
7. See Danny Rubinstein, *On the Lord's Side: Gush Emunim* (in Hebrew) (Tel Aviv: Hakibbutz Hameuchad, 1982) p. 179; Ilan Peleg, *Begin's Foreign Policy, 1977–1983: Israel's Move to the Right* (New York: Greenwood Press, 1987) pp. 117–122; Gershon Shafir, "Changing Nationalism and Israel's 'Open Frontier'

on the West Bank," *Theory and Society,* vol. 13, no. 6 (November 1984) pp. 818–819; Giora Goldberg and Efraim Ben-Zadok, "Gush Emunim in the West Bank," *Middle Eastern Studies,* vol. 22, no. 1 (January 1986) pp. 69–72; and Amnon Sella, "Custodians and Redeemers: Israeli Leaders' Perceptions of Peace, 1967–1979," *Middle Eastern Studies,* vol. 22, no. 2 (April 1986) pp. 236–251.

8. See Amnon Rubinstein, *The Zionist Dream Revisited: From Herzl to Gush Emunim and Back* (New York: Schocken Books, 1984) pp. 108–109. See also Lilly Weissbrod, "Gush Emunim Ideology—From Religious Doctrine to Political Action," *Middle Eastern Studies,* vol. 18, no. 3 (July 1982) p. 273; and preface to Newman, *Impact.*

9. See "Blessings to the Lobby," *Nekuda,* no. 85, April 5, 1985 p. 7; and an interview with the chairman of the lobby, Herut veteran Uzi Landau, *Nekuda,* no. 85, April 5, 1985, pp. 8–9. Estimates for the increased size of the group are from an unpublished paper by Rick Hasen, "The Strength of the *Gush Emunim* Infrastructure," 1986.

10. Yehuda Hazani, "The Lobby for the Sake of Heaven," *Nekuda,* no. 84, March 1, 1985 pp. 24–25.

11. Polls conducted by Modi'in Ezrahi reported in *Maariv,* January 27, 1987, and April 21, 1987; and polls conducted by Dahaf, reported in *Yediot Acharonot,* June 19, 1987.

12. Jerusalem Domestic Service, July 8, 1987 (transcribed in the Foreign Broadcast Information Service [FBIS], July 8, 1987, P. L2). FBIS material from 1980 to June 1987 is found in *Daily Report: Near East and Africa;* subsequent material is in *Daily Report: Near East and South Asia.*

13. Moshe Hurvitz, "How They Are Pressuring the President," *Koteret Rashit,* no. 199, September 24, 1986 pp. 13–15, 47; Danny Kipper, "President Reconsidering Pardon for Jewish Underground Detainees," *Yediot Acharonot,* February 19, 1987; and Judy Siegel, "The President Defends His Move on Lifers," *Jerusalem Post International Edition,* week ending April 11, 1987.

14. Israel Eldad, "Before the Fire: Gush Emunim's First Decade," *Nekuda,* no. 69, February 3, 1984, p. 17.

15. Tsvi Raanan, *Gush Emunim* (in Hebrew) (Tel Aviv: Sifriat Poalim, 1980) p. 46.

16. For an explicit comparison along these lines by a Gush activist who faults the fundamentalist movement for not yet living up to the standards of the pre-1948 kibbutz movement, see Ezra Zohar, "Where are the Secularists and the People of the Slum Neighborhoods?" *Nekuda,* no. 92, October 23, 1985 pp. 10–11. On the comparison of Gush Emunim to the pre-1948 kibbutz movement, see Ehud Sprinzak, *Gush Emunim,* p. 23.

17. See Thomas L. Friedman, "History's Favorite Israelis," *New York Times,* June 11, 1987, p. A4.

18. Sprinzak, *Gush Emunim,* p. 2.

19. David Schnall, "An Impact Assessment," in Newman, *Impact,* p. 15. See also Gideon Aran, "From Religious Zionism to Zionist Religion: The Roots of Gush Emunim," in Peter Medding, ed., *Studies in Contemporary Jewry,* Vol. 2, (1986) p. 116; Myron J. Aronoff, "The Institutionalisation and Cooptation of a Charismatic, Messianic, Religious-Political Revitalisation Movement," in Newman, *Impact,* pp. 46, 60; Ofira Seliktar, *New Zionism and the Foreign Policy System of Israel* (Carbondale, Illinois: Southern Illinois University Press, 1986) pp. 95,

159–160, 271; and Leon Wieseltier, "The Demons of the Jews," *New Republic* November 11, 1985 p. 19, 271.

20. Eliezer Don-Yehiya, "Jewish Messianism, Religious Zionism and Israeli Politics: The Impact and Origins of Gush Emunim," *Middle Eastern Studies*, vol. 23, no. 2 (April 1987) p. 225. For a particularly negative assessment of Gush Emunim's future prospects, see Avram Schweitzer, *Israel: The Changing National Agenda* (London: Croom Helm, 1986) pp. 88–91.

21. See, in particular, Seliktar, *New Zionism*, p. 263; and Goldberg and Ben-Zadok, "Gush Emunim," pp. 69–72.

22. Poll conducted by Dahaf for *Koteret Rashit* (March 9, 1983). See also polling data in appendix 2, dealing with attitudes toward the voting rights of Jews supportive of the PLO compared to those supportive of Meir Kahane.

23. See polling data in appendix 2.

24. See polling data in appendix 2.

25. See polling data in appendix 2.

Notes to Chapter 2

1. On the concept of a "revitalization movement," see Myron J. Aronoff, "Gush Emunim: The Institutionalization of a Charismatic, Messianic, Religious-Political Revitalization Movement in Israel," in *Religion and Politics, Political Anthropology*, vol. 3 (New Brunswick, New Jersey: Transaction Press, 1984).

2. In a book about Jews and the Jewish state, use of C.E. (Common Era) and B.C.E. (Before the Common Era) instead of A.D. (Year of Our Lord) and B.C. (Before Christ) is preferable. Concerning the messianic axis of intra-Jewish politics in second through fifth-century Persia, see Jacob Neusner, "Power," in Leo Landman, ed. *Messianism in the Talmudic Era* (New York: Ktav Publishing House, 1979) pp. 397–424.

3. Joseph Klausner, *The Messianic Idea in Israel: From Its Beginning to the Completion of the Mishnah* (New York: Macmillan, 1955) pp. 259–261.

4. Benyamin Z. Kedar "Masada: The Myth and the Complex," *Jerusalem Quarterly*, no. 24 (Summer 1982) pp. 57–63 and Yehoshaphat Harkabi, *The Bar Kochba Syndrome* (Chappaqua, New York: Rossel Books, 1983). See also the speech Josephus puts in the mouth of the king, Aggrippa, as he seeks to dissuade the Jews from their intention to revolt, in Josephus *The Jewish War* (Suffolk: Penguin, 1985) pp. 159–162.

5. In 115 C.E. a series of violent Jewish uprisings against local populations and Roman rule broke out in several major centers of the Diaspora, including Egypt, Cyrenicia, Cyprus, and Mesopotamia. These were fueled by intense messianic yearnings and fresh memories of the Roman destruction of the Temple and Jerusalem. Although quickly crushed, these small wars resulted in heavy casualties on both sides and banishment of all Jews from Cyprus. See Michael Grant, *Jews in the Roman World* (U.S.A.: Dorset Press, 1973) pp. 236–241.

6. For an excellent treatment of recent controversies and scholarship concerning the Bar Kochba Rebellion, see Benjamin Isaac and Aharon Oppenheimer, "The Revolt of Bar Kokhba: Ideology and Modern Scholarship," *Journal of Jewish Social Studies*, vol. 36, no. 1 (Spring 1985) pp. 33–60.

7. Jacob Neusner, *First Century Judaism in Crisis: Yohanan ben Zakkai and the Renaissance of Torah* (Nashville: Abingdon Press, 1975) p. 165.

8. See Arie Morgenstern, "Messianic Concepts and Settlement in the Land of Israel," in Richard I. Cohen, ed., *Vision and Conflict in the Holy Land,* (New York: St. Martin's Press, 1985) pp. 141–162; and Harkabi, *Bar Kochba.*

9. Richard Gordon Marks, "The Image of Bar Kokhba in Jewish Literature Up to the Seventeenth Century: False Messiah and National Hero," unpublished Ph.D. dissertation (Los Angeles: University of California, 1980) p. 36.

10. *Ibid.,* p. 80.

11. Nahum Glatzer, *Essays in Jewish Thought* (University of Alabama Press, 1978, p. 3, as quoted by Marks in *Image,* p. 81.

12. Gershom Scholem, "The Messianic Idea in Judaism," in *The Messianic Idea in Judaism and Other Essays on Jewish Spirituality* (New York: Schocken Books, 1971) pp. 11–16.

13. Klausner, *Messianic Idea,* p. 33.

14. Gershom Scholem, "Toward an Understanding of the Messianic Idea in Judaism," in *Messianic Idea,* p. 19.

15. Moses Maimonides, "Kings and Wars," chapter 12, section 2, in Isadore Twersky, ed., *A Maimonides Reader* (New York: Behrman House, 1972) pp. 224–225. My interpretation of Maimonides intention is based on Scholem, "Toward an Understanding," pp. 24–33.

16. Gershom Scholem, *Sabbatai Sevi: The Mystical Messiah* (Princeton, New Jersey: Princeton University Press, 1973) chapters 5 and 6.

17. Gershom Scholem, "Redemption through Sin," in *Messianic Idea,* pp. 78–141.

18. David Vital, *Zionism: The Formative Years* (Oxford, England: Clarendon Press, 1982) p. 209.

19. *Ibid.,* pp. 209–210.

20. Quoted in Vital, *Zionism,* p. 212.

21. *Ibid.*

22. Ben Halpern, *The Idea of the Jewish State* (Cambridge, Massachusetts: Harvard University Press, 1969) p. 88.

23. Charles Liebman and Eliezer Don-Yehiya, *Religion and Politics in Israel* (Bloomington, Indiana: University of Indiana Press, 1984) p. 62.

24. This perspective on Zionism is most closely associated with Rabbi Isaac Jacob Reines (1839–1915), a founder of Mizrahi. It is referred to derogatorily in Jewish fundamentalist circles as *kupat holim* (sick fund) Zionism—that is, Zionism as merely a refugee aid society or health insurance organization.

25. The text of the declaration and the list of rabbis who signed it are reproduced in Menachem Kasher *The Great Era* (in Hebrew) (Jerusalem: Torah Shlema, 1968) pp. 374–78.

26. See, especially, Amnon Rubinstein, *The Zionist Dream Revisited: From Herzl to Gush Emunim and Back* (New York: Schocken Books, 1985).

27. See, for example, Rael Jean Isaac, *Israel Divided: Ideological Politics in the Jewish State* (Baltimore: Johns Hopkins University Press, 1976) pp. 20–44; A. B. Yehoshua, *Between Right and Right* (Garden City, New York: Doubleday, 1981) pp. 76–78; Baruch Kimmerling, *Zionism and Territory: The Socio-Territorial Dimensions of Zionist Politics* (Berkeley, California: University of California, Institute of International Studies, 1983) pp. 147–182; Eliezer Livneh, *Israel and the Crisis of Western Civilization* (in Hebrew) (Tel Aviv: Schocken Books, 1972) pp. 68–93; Charles Liebman and Eliezer Don-Yehiya, *Civil Religion in Israel* (Berkeley, California: University of California Press, 1983) pp. 200–205.

28. Abraham Isaac Kook, "The Road to Renewal," *Hanir* (1909), reprinted in *Tradition*, vol. 13, no. 3 (Winter 1973) p. 144.
29. *Ibid.* p. 140.
30. *Ibid.* p. 141.
31. *Ibid.*
32. *Ibid.*, p. 151.
33. *Ibid.*, p. 150.
34. Abraham Isaac Kook, "Souls of Chaos" (1914), reprinted in Ben Zion Bokser, ed., *Abraham Isaac Kook: The Lights of Penitence, Lights of Holiness, the Moral Principles, Essays, Letters, and Poems* (New York: Paulist Press, 1978) pp. 257–258.
35. Letter to Rabbi Duber Milstein from Abraham Isaac Kook (1908), reprinted in Bokser, *Kook* pp. 344–345. Concerning Jewish atheism, "cleansed of its defilement," as the return "to the highest realms of pure religion," see "The Pangs of Cleansing" (1914), in Bokser, *Kook*, p. 267.
36. Kook, "Road to Renewal," pp. 150–151.
37. Abraham Isaac Kook, *Orot*, quoted in Arthur Hertzberg, *The Zionist Idea* (New York: Harper and Row, 1959) pp. 419–420.
38. Abraham Isaac Kook, from *Orot*, quoted in Eliezer Schweid, *The Land of Israel: National Home or Land of Destiny* (Rutherford, New Jersey: Herzl Press, 1985) p. 184.
39. Kook, "Road to Renewal," pp. 151–152.
40. This discussion of Gahelet is based on the ground-breaking study of Gideon Aran, "From Religious Zionism to Zionist Religion: The Roots of Gush Emunim," in Peter Medding, ed., *Studies in Contemporary Jewry*, vol. 2, (Bloomington, Indiana: Indiana University Press, 1986) pp. 117–143.
41. Tzvi Yehuda Kook, "Zionism and Biblical Prophecy," in Yosef Tirosh, ed., *Religious Zionism: An Anthology,* (Jerusalem: World Zionist Organization, 1975) p. 176.
42. Tzvi Yehuda Kook, "On the Genuine Significance of the State of Israel," homily delivered in March 1978, published in *Artzi*, vol. I (1982) p. 5.
43. Tzvi Yehuda Kook, "Zionism and Biblical Prophecy," in Tirosh, *Religious Zionism* p. 177.
44. *Ibid.* p. 169.
45. Ehud Sprinzak, "The Iceberg Model of Political Extremism," in David Newman, ed., *The Impact of Gush Emunim: Politics and Settlement in the West Bank* (London: Croom Helm, 1985) p. 37.
46. From the text of notes to the address of Tzvi Yehuda Kook, published as "This Is the State of which the Prophets Dreamed," *Nekuda*, no. 86, April 26, 1985, pp. 6–7.
47. Rabbi Yohanan Fried, quoted in Daniel Ben-Simon, "Merkaz HaRav: Here Developed Gush Emunim," *Haaretz*, April 4, 1986, p. 8.
48. Aran, "From Religious Zionism" p. 135. See also Ben-Simon, "Merkaz HaRav."
49. Ben-Simon, "Merkaz HaRav."
50. For a representative sample of Tabenkin's writings, see "The Danger of Destruction and the Chances for Jewish Activism," in Aharon Ben-Ami, ed., *The Book of the Whole Land of Israel* (in Hebrew) (Tel-Aviv: Freedman, 1977) pp. 159–168. See also Yosef Tabenkin (son of Yitzhak Tabenkin), "Between the Wilderness and the Sea: The Land is One," *Artzi*, vol. 2 (1982) pp. 51–52.

51. For example, the Agriculture Ministry, the Inter-Ministerial Committee on Settlement, and the Land Settlement Department of the Jewish Agency (an arm of the World Zionist Organization).

Notes to Chapter 3

1. Much of the planning and financing of the Hebron—Kiryat Arba operation was actually provided by the Movement for the Whole Land of Israel. See Amnon Rubinstein, *The Zionist Dream Revisited: From Herzl to Gush Emunim and Back* (New York: Schocker Books, 1985) pp. 99–100.
2. "Manifesto of the Land of Israel Movement, August 1967," translated in Rael Jean Isaac, *Israel Divided: Ideological Politics in the Jewish State* (Baltimore: Johns Hopkins University Press, 1976) p. 171.
3. The origins of the Democratic Movement for Change, led by Yigal Yadin, can be found in this milieu. Although the movement managed to garner nearly 12 percent of the vote in the 1977 parliamentary elections, internal divisions destroyed it.
4. Judea and Samaria are the biblical names for the general areas south and north of Jerusalem (respectively). Historically, they include substantial portions of pre-1967 Israel, but not the Jordan Valley or the Benyamina district (both within the West Bank). For political purposes, and despite the geographical imprecision involved, the annexationist camp in Israel prefers to refer to the area between the green line and the Jordan River not as the West Bank, but as Judea and Samaria.
5. Gush Etzion is an area south of Bethlehem that was one of the only areas containing Jewish settlements captured and held by the Arabs in the 1948 war. Former residents made a dramatic return to the area soon after the Six Day War, and the Labor party declared its support for settlement there.
6. See Gershon Shafir, "Changing Nationalism and Israel's 'Open Frontier' on the West Bank," *Theory and Society,* vol. 13, no. 6 (November 1984) pp. 818–819.
7. At the same time (November 1979), Moshe Dayan resigned as foreign minister to protest what he perceived as the Begin government's commitment to annexing the West Bank.
8. Beni Katzover, interview broadcast on November 13, 1979, by Jerusalem Domestic Service, (translated in FBIS, November 14, 1979, p. N2).
9. *Haaretz,* October 23, 1979.
10. *Haaretz,* October 15, 1979 (translated in FBIS, October 26, 1979, pp. N4–N5); and *Jerusalem Post,* October 16, 1979.
11. Jerusalem Domestic Service, November 1, 1979 (translated in FBIS, November 2, 1979, pp. N1–3).
12. Jerusalem Domestic Service, November 11, 1979 (translated in FBIS, November 13, 1979, pp. N2–4).
13. Jerusalem Domestic Service, November 13, 1979 (translated in FBIS, November 13, 1979, pp. N2–N4).
14. *Davar,* November 14, 1979 (translated in FBIS, November 15, 1979, pp. N9–10).
15. *Jerusalem Post,* December 25, 1979.
16. Jerusalem Domestic Service, November 15, 1979 (translated in FBIS, November 16, 1979, pp. N4–6, 8); and Israel Defense Forces Radio, November 15, 1979 (translated in FBIS, November 16, 1979, pp. N6–7).

17. *Yediot Acharonot,* January 17, 1980 (translated in FBIS, January 18, 1980, p. N7).

18. Jerusalem Domestic Television Service, March 26, 1980 (translated in FBIS, March 28, 1980, P. N7).

19. Jerusalem Domestic Service, May 2, 1980 (translated in FBIS, May 5, 1980, p. N1).

20. For details on how this was accomplished, see Ian Lustick, "Israel and the West Bank after Elon Moreh: The Mechanics of De Facto Annexation," *Middle East Journal,* vol. 35, no. 4 (Autumn 1980) pp. 557–577.

21. Tsvi Raanan, *Gush Emunim* (Tel Aviv: Sirfriat Poalim 1980) p. 47.

22. The interrelationships among the above-mentioned groups and institutions, their importance as sources of leadership for the fundamentalist movement, and the opportunities to pursue common objectives provided by the various Gush Emunim-linked organizations discussed below are illustrated in the biographies of several key activists included in appendix 3. For discussion of the ideological links among Kookist thinking, former Lehi members, and activist laborites, see Gideon Aran, *The Land of Israel Between Politics and Religion: The Movement to Halt the Retreat in Sinai* (in Hebrew) (Jerusalem: Jerusalem Institute for Israeli Studies, 1985) pp. 3–4, 25.

23. The extent to which fundamentalist activists view *Nekuda* as an in-house forum, where genuine concerns, doubts, and aspirations can be shared, is reflected in letters to the editor that occasionally scold leaders of the movement who criticize one another "publicly" (that is, in Israeli daily newspapers or in the electronic media), rather than keeping such matters "within the family" by discussion them in the pages of *Nekuda. Nekuda* is available only by subscription.

24. *Haaretz,* September 16, 1979 (translated in Joint Publications Research Service, [JPRS], *Near East and North Africa Report,* no. 74485, October 31, 1979, p. 83.

25. Jerusalem Domestic service radio broadcast, September 5, 1980 (transcribed in JPRS, No. NEA-76442, September 17, 1980, pp. 62–63).

26. Indeed, the financial compensation offered to the Yamit settlers was very generous, amounting, according to one early estimate, to approximately $530 million. See Jerusalem Domestic Service, January 11, 1982, (translated in FBIS, January 12, 1982, p. 19).

27. Yechiel Orio, "Talmi Yosef: The Stubborness of a Few," *Nekuda,* no. 34, September 28, 1981, p. 13; Aran, *Land of Israel,* p. 89.

28. Aran, *Land of Israel,* p. 12.

29. The word generally used is *hurban,* meaning "destruction." It is the term traditionally used to refer to the greatest of all catastrophes in Jewish history—the destruction of the First and Second Temples. More recently it has been used, as well, to refer to the Holocaust.

30. The purpose and relative success of the new subsidized settlement effort has been discussed extensively elsewhere. See Ian S. Lustick, "Israeli State-Building in the West Bank and the Gaza Strip: Theory and Practice," *International Organization,* vol. 41, no. 1 (Winter 1987) pp. 151–171.

31. In 1984 the Likud received 48 percent of Gush Emunim settler votes, Tehiya 23 percent, and Morasha 21 percent. The National Religious Party placed only four deputies in the Knesset, receiving a mere 4 percent of Gush Emunim settler votes. This dismal performance reflects the extent to which the party was hurt by the defection of Porat and Druckman, and the doubts raised about maximalist Gush

Emunim demands by Zevulon Hammer and Yehuda Ben Meir (former Young Guard leaders who have remained inside the party. See *Nekuda,* no. 77, August 31, 1984, p. 4.

32. Mainly as a result of a personal feud with Tehiya' Geula Cohen, Eitan separated from Tehiya in November 1987 to form his own Knesset faction. His call to Tzomet supporters to reconstitute the movement is likely to attract many of his early supporters whose attitudes on certain issues, such as treatment of the local Arab population, are more extreme than those officially espoused by Tehiya.

33. *Nekuda,* no. 77, August 31, 1984, pp. 34–35.

34. "Gush Emunim Arises," *Nekuda,* no. 84, March 1, 1985, p. 4. See also Noam Arnon, "Neither Destroy nor Split," *Nekuda,* no. 89, July 26, 1985, pp. 18–19.

35. Arnon, "Neither Destroy nor Split," p. 19.

36. See Aran, *Land of Israel,* pp. 1–4; and Ehud Sprinzak, *op. cit.,* pp. 6–7.

37. Jan Demarest Abu Shakra, *Israeli Settler Violence in the Occupied Territories: 1980–1984* (Chicago: Palestine Human Rights Campaign, 1985) p. 15. See also Dedi Zucker, *Report on Human Rights in the Occupied Territories* (Tel Aviv: International Center for Peace in the Middle East, 1983).

38. Yoav Peled and Gershon Shafir, "Thorns in Your Eyes: The Socio-Economic Basis of the Kach Vote," 1986.

39. See pages 169–176, for a discussion of the Temple Mount issue itself.

40. It is ironic but instructive that Etzion was pictured engaging in apparently friendly conversation with an Arab on the cover of a special issue of *Nekuda* in June 1980 dedicated to friendly relations with the Arabs. The caption reads "Who is hurting coexistence?" In fact, the issue appeared very close to the day of the attack on the Arab mayors that Etzion, five years later, would be convicted of having helped to organized.

41. *Nekuda,* no. 88, June 24, 1985, p. 24.

42. *Nekuda,* no. 73, May 25, 1984, p. 6, and the resolutions of Yesha concerning the affair, p. 7; and *Nekuda,* no. 75, July 6, 1987, p. 7.

43. *Nekuda,* no. 77, August 31, 1984, p. 4.

Notes to Chapter 4

1. Shmuel Eisenstadt, in *The Transformation of Israeli Society* (London: Weidenfeld and Nicolson, 1986), offers no more than a capsule summary of Gush thinking. On the "loathing" of Israeli intellectuals for Gush Emunim and their ignorance of its thinking, see Aharon Meged "The Gush Emunim Phenomenon," *Davar,* December 12, 1980. For creditable summaries of the fundamentalist worldview, see Giora Goldberg and Efraim Ben-Zadok, "Gush Emunim in the West Bank," *Middle Eastern Studies,* vol. 22, no. 1 (January 1986) pp. 57–61; and Janet Aviad, "The Contemporary Israeli Pursuit of the Millennium," *Religion,* vol. 14 (1984) pp. 199–222.

2. Shlomo Aviner, "Messianic Realism," in Avner Tomaschoff, ed., *Whose Homeland* (Jerusalem: World Zionist Organization, 1978) p. 117.

3. Haim Sredler Feller, "Religious Terror and Messianic Fever," *Newsletter of the Citizens Rights and Peace Movement,* vol. 3 (May 1986) p. 7. On the importance of Kasher's work for the Jewish fundamentalist movement as a whole, see also David Biale, "The Messianic Connection: Zionism, Politics, and Settlement in Israel,"

The Center Magazine, vol. 18, no. 5 (September/October 1985) pp. 36-39; and Janet Aviad, "Contemporary Israeli Pursuit," pp. 202-203.

4. Fisch, *op. cit.,* p. 134.

5. *Genesis* 17:7,8 quoted in Fisch, *Zionist Revolution,* p. 20.

6. Jacob J. Ross, *A Chosen People* (in English and Hebrew) (Jerusalem n.d.).

7. Shlomo Aviner, "Messianic Realism," pp. 115-116

8. Shlomo Aviner, "The Moral Problem of Possessing the Land," *Artzi,* vol. 2 (1982) p. 11. *Artzi* is a scholarly and ideologically oriented fundamentalist journal, edited by Yoel Ben-Nun, that has appeared irregularly since 1982.

9. Eleazar Waldman, "Struggle on the Road to Peace," *Artzi,* vol. 3 (1983) p. 20.

10. *Ibid.*

11. See Menachem Kasher, *The Great Era* (in Hebrew) (Jerusalem: Torah Shlema, 1968) pp. 53ff. The prophecy is from Ezekiel 36:8, interpreted in the Talmud (Sanhedrin 98a) as the "most manifest sign of redemption."

12. For these and for representative Gush Emunim arguments that the existence of the Palestinian people is "fictitious," see Yaakov Ariel, "The Return of the Regained Territories: The Halakhic Aspect," in Aviner, *Whose Homeland,* p. 151; and Mordechai Nisan, "The Nature of Palestinian Identity without the PLO," *Artzi,* vol. 4 (Spring 1986) pp. 52-63.

13. *Ibid.,* pp. 157, 159.

14. Tzvi Yehuda Kook, "Between the People and Its Land," *Artzi,* Vol. 2 (Spring 1982) p. 19. See also Shlomo Aviner, "The Completeness of the Land," *Artzi,* vol. 1 (1982) p. 26; as do so many others, Aviner refers to Tzvi Yehuda's use of this model for policy toward the Arabs.

15. Hanan Porat, "Policies toward the Arabs of the Land of Israel," *Artzi,* vol. 4 (Spring 1986) p. 10 (emphasis in original).

16. *Ibid.,* p. 9. Prepared in the wake of the trials of the members of the Jewish terrorist underground, this special volume of *Artzi* features many articles warning against individualist and indiscriminate violence against Arabs, while stressing, without exception, the need for uncompromising policies toward any Arabs actively opposing Jewish rule. On page 11 of this *Artzi,* special prominence is given to a circular written by Tzvi Yehuda and distributed to religious school principals, in which Tzvi Yehuda criticizes Jewish children he has seen harassing Arabs and calls for decent treatment of Arabs as individual human beings.

17. *Ibid.,* p. 101.

18. *Ibid.,* p. 114.

19. Shlomo Aviner, "Our Attachment to the Land of Israel," *Artzi,* vol. 1 (1982) pp. 16-17.

20. Menachem M. Kasher, *The Yom Kippur War* (Jerusalem: House of the Whole Torah, 1974) p. 7 (emphasis added). For the fundamentalists radical distrust of all gentile nations, including the United States, see "Festival of Fools," *Nekuda,* no. 87, May 24, 1987, p. 4, an editorial concerning President Reagan's visit to the Bitburg cemetery.

21. Fisch, p. 96.

22. *Artzi,* vol. 1 (1982) p. 2, citing Tzvi Yehuda Kook, February 1978.

23. *Artzi,* vol. 1 (1982) p. 3, citing Tzvi Yehuda Kook, December 1978.

24. Eleazar Waldman, "Struggle," p. 20.

25. Eleazar Waldman, "Questions and Answers Regarding the Struggle Against Evil," *Artzi,* vol. 3 (1983) p. 27.

26. Fisch, *Zionist Revolution*, p. 20.
27. Tzvi Yehuda Kook, "Between the People," pp. 15–16 (emphasis in original).
28. Fisch, *Zionist Revolution*, p. 21.
29. Hanan Porat, "Policies toward the Arabs," pp. 5–6.
30. Harold Fisch, *The Zionism of Zion*, (in Hebrew) (Tel Aviv: Zmora, Bitan, 1982) p. 179.
31. Hanan Porat, "Policies toward the Arabs," p. 6.
32. Haim Druckman, "The Cry of the Land of Israel," *Artzi*, vol. 1 (1982) p. 37.
33. Eliezer Schweid, "The Machteret and the Ideology of Gush Emunim," *Nekuda*, no. 75, July 6, 1984 p. 20.
34. Fisch, *Zionist Revolution*, p. 85.
35. *Ibid.*, pp. 18, 86–87.
36. Fisch, "The Land of Israel and the Question of Preserving Life," in *The Zionism of Zion*, p. 169.
37. Menachem Kasher, *The Great Era*, p. 32.
38. Menachem M. Kasher, *Yom Kippur War*, pp. 8, 12–37.
39. *Ibid.*, p. 127.
40. *Ibid.*, pp. 9–11.
41. Fisch, *Zionist Revolution*, p. 77.
42. *Ibid.*, pp. 77, 87.
43. *Ibid.*, p. 87.
44. *Ibid.*, p. 95.
45. *Ibid.*, p. 94.
46. Kook, "Between the People," p. 21.
47. Fisch, *Zionist Revolution*, p. 166.
48. *Ibid.*, p. 169.
49. *Ibid.*, pp. 165, 169.
50. Kook, "Between the People," p. 23.
51. Tzvi Yehuda Kook, "And Again to Break the Yoke of the Gentiles from Our Neck," *Artzi*, vol. 1 (1982) p. 3.
52. Fisch, *Zionist Revolution*, p. 166.

Notes to Chapter 5

1. Gideon Aran, *The Land of Israel Between Religion and Politics: The Movement to Stop the Retreat in Sinai* (in Hebrew) (Jerusalem: Jerusalem Institute for Israel Studies, 1985) p. 23.
2. *Nekuda*, no. 59, June 10, 1983, p. 16.
3. Shlomo Aviner, "Messianic Realism," in Avner Tomaschoff, ed., *Whose Homeland* (Jerusalem: World Zionist Organization, 1978) p. 117.
4. For this debate, see Yehoshua Zuckerman (then director of Merkaz HaRav), "Implementing the Ambush of Faith," *Nekuda*, no. 43, May 21, 1982, pp. 18–22; Shlomo Aviner, "The Way of Rav Tzvi Yehuda, May He Rest in Peace, and Our Struggle for the Land of Israel," *Nekuda*, no. 50, November 11, 1982, pp. 16–17; and Isser Klansky and Haim Steiner, "Courage and Strength in the Struggle for the Completeness of the Land," *Nekuda*, no. 56, March 28, 1983, pp. 20–23.
5. Illustrative of this debate are Yisrael Ariel, "Was There Indeed a Revolt against Heaven?" *Nekuda*, no. 73, May 1984, pp. 16–17; Yehuda Zoldan, "Patience of

Redemption," *Nekuda*, no. 76, August 10, 1984, pp. 22–23; David Hanshke, "What Has Happened to the Lights of Rabbi Abraham Isaac Kook?" *Nekuda*, no. 79, October 1984, pp. 12–13, 28; David Stiu, "The Lights Are Not Out!" *Nekuda*, no. 84, March 1, 1985, pp.18–20; and long, angry letters from David Hanshke in *Nekuda*, no. 85, April 5, 1985, p. 4, and David Stiu in *Nekuda*, no. 87, May 24, 1985, p. 3.

6. Eleazar Waldman, "The Struggle on the Road to Peace," *Artzi*, vol. 3 (1983) pp. 18, 20.

7. Yisrael Yaakov Yuval, "Religious-Zionist Messianism: Prospects and Perils," in Tomaschoff, *Whose Homeland*, pp. 104–105. Yuval's particular interpretation of Rav Kook would appear to place him outside the boundaries of the fundamentalist worldview; but by basing his argument on Abraham Isaac Kook's writings, he does illustrate the authoritative nature of Kookist ideas within the fundamentalist camp.

8. For an excellent summary of the halachic debate over a variety of disputes on issues such as status of non-Jews in the Jewish state, non-Jews' property rights, definition of idolatry, and applicability of pikuach nefesh to territorial issues, see J. David Bleich, "Judea and Samaria: Settlement and Return," *Tradition*, vol. 18, no. 1 (Summer 1979) pp. 44–78. Bleich's summary judgments tend to fall on the "dovish-moderate" side of the interpretive spectrum.

9. See Aryeh Newman, "The Centrality of Eretz Yisrael in Nachmanides," *Tradition*, vol. 10, no. 1 (Summer 1968) pp. 21–30.

10. Shlomo Aviner, "Nor Have We Been False to Thy Covenant," *Artzi*, vol. 1 (1982) pp. 43–44.

11. Shlomo Aviner, "Dialogues between Shaltiel and the Sage," *Artzi*, vol. 1 (1982) p. 32.

12. Interview with Yehoshua Zuckerman, *Nekuda*, no. 73, May 25, 1984, p. 8.

13. Yaakov Ariel, "Return of the Regained Territories—The Halakhic Aspect," *Whose Homeland*, pp. 127–155; and Yaakov Ariel, "Our Relations with the Arabs: The Halakhic Moral Dimension," *Artzi*, vol. 4 (Spring 1986) p. 12.

14. These and other fundamentalist rabbis who take this halachic position express the view that it is, of course, inconceivable, that the territories acquired by Israel in 1967 could be considered a security liability and not a security asset. See Avraham Elkana Kahana-Shapira, "Eretz Israel's Integrity in Halakhah and Agadah," in Tomaschoff, *Whose Homeland*, pp. 160–175; and Yehoshuah Menachem Ehrenberg, "Territories, War, and Danger to Life," in Tomaschoff, *Whose Homeland*, pp. 176–181.

15. Yisrael Ariel, "Was There Indeed a Revolt," p. 16.

16. Zoldan, "Patience of Redemption," pp. 22–23.

17. Yitzhak Shilat, "Useless Messianism and False Messianism," *Nekuda*, no. 76, August 10, 1984, pp. 16–17.

18. Yoel Ben-Nun, "The Way of the Lights and the War of the Perversion," *Nekuda*, no. 91, September 15, 1985, p. 11.

19. *Nekuda*, no. 88, June 24, 1985, p. 24.

20. Yehuda Etzion, "From the Laws of Existence to the Law of Destiny" *Nekuda*, no. 75, July 6, 1984, p. 23; and Yehuda Etzion, "Finally to Raise the Banner of Jerusalem," *Nekuda*, no. 93, November 22, 1985, p. 22.

21. Yehuda Etzion, "Finally to Raise the Banner of Jerusalem," p. 23.

22. Yehuda Etzion, "From the Banner of Jerusalem to a Movement of Redemption," *Nekuda,* no. 94, December 20, 1985, p. 28.

23. In certain of his articles Etzion strongly criticizes Tzvi Yehuda, and it is reliably reported that he considers the Kookist approach to redemption to be superseded by his own, adapted largely from the work of an obscure religious member of Lehi, Shabbatai Ben-Dov. See Ben-Nun, "The Way of the Lights," p. 11; Ehud Sprinzak, *Each Man Right in His Own Eyes: Illegalism in Israeli Society* (in Hebrew) (Tel Aviv: Sifriat Poalim, 1986) p. 140; and Yehuda Etzion, "From the Laws of Existence to the Law of Destiny," *Nekuda,* no. 75, July 6, 1984, pp. 22–23, 26–27.

24. Aviva Segal, "If It is Forbidden for Yehuda Etzion to Be a Prophet, Then It Is Forbidden for You Too, Yedidya," *Nekuda,* no. 92, October 23, 1985, p. 24. For a major defense of Etzion's views by the editor of Shabbatai Ben-Dov's writings, see Dan Tor, "To Continue to Push the End," *Nekuda,* no. 96, February 21, 1986, pp. 12–13.

25. While some nonreligious fundamentalists—including Eldad and Haetzni—consider themselves members of Gush Emunim and are fully accepted as such, others—including Neeman, Cohen, and Eitan—while active partners or benefactors of Gush Emunim, should not formally be seen as part of it.

26. From an interview with Geula Cohen, quoted in Julien Bauer "A New Approach to Religious-Secular Relationships?" in David Newman, ed., *The Impact of Gush Emunim: Politics and Settlement in the West Bank,* (London: Croom Helm, 1985) p. 101. Not coincidentally, the Hebrew meaning of her first name, Geula, is "redemption."

27. *Haaretz,* September 16, 1979. See JPRS, no. 74485, October 31, 1979, p. 85. For detailed comment by a secularist founder of the Movement for the Whole Land of Israel concerning the dissipation of will among Labor Zionist youth and the significance of Gush Emunim as the spiritually exhausted Labor movement's true successor, see an interview with Professor Rivka Shatz-Oppenheimer, "The True Messianism of Gush Emunim," *Nekuda,* no. 69, February 3, 1984, pp. 12–13. See also Eliezer Schweid, *The Land of Israel: National Home or Land of Destiny* (Rutherford, New Jersey: Herzl Press, 1985) pp. 198, 212.

28. Uri Zvi Greenberg, "Ode to the Nation" (1933) translated in Israel Eldad, *The Jewish Revolution: Jewish Statehood* (New York: Shengold Publishers, 1971) pp. 52–53.

29. Eldad, pp. 85–86.

30. David Weisburd, "Deviance as Social Reaction: A Study of the Gush Emunim Settlements in Israel," unpublished Ph.D. dissertation (New Haven, Connecticut: Yale University, 1985) p. 224.

31. In addition to the sources cited in this chapter, excellent examples of this approach are available in Eliezer Livneh, *Israel and the Crisis of Western Civilization* (in Hebrew) (Tel Aviv: Schocken Books, 1972); and Aharon Ben-Ami, ed., *The Book of the Whole Land of Israel,* (in Hebrew) (Tel Aviv: Freedman, 1977).

32. Eldad, *Jewish Revolution,* p. 56.

33. Fisch, *Zionist Revolution,* p. 78.

34. Eldad, *Jewish Revolution,* p. 56.

35. *Ibid.,* pp. 55–56.

36. Tsvi Raanan, *Gush Emunim* (Tel Aviv: Sifriat Poalim, 1980) pp. 216–217.

37. Eldad, *Jewish Revolution,* pp. 134–135.
38. *Koteret Rashit,* no. 102, November 14, 1984, p. 23. For similar suggestions of Israel's proper geopolitical ambitions, set in nonreligious fundamentalist terms, see Ora Shem-Ur, *The Challenges of Israel* (New York: Shengold Publishers, 1980) especially pp. 69–70, 74.
39. Yuval Neeman, "National Goals," in Alouph Hareven, ed., *On the Difficulty of Being an Israeli* (in Hebrew) (Jerusalem: Van Leer, 1983) p. 268.
40. Yehuda Elitzur, "The Borders of Eretz Israel in Jewish Tradition," in Tomaschoff, *Whose Homeland,* pp. 42–53.
41. Yoel Elitzur, "Is Lebanon also the Land of Israel?: The Northern Borders of the Land of Israel in the Sources and According to the Halacha," *Nekuda,* no. 48, n.d., pp. 10–13.
42. Shlomo Aviner, "Nor Have We Been False," p. 38.
43. Tzvi Yehuda Kook, "Between the People and Its Land," *Artzi,* vol. 2 (1982) p. 19.
44. Uzi Kelcheim, "Our Moral Title to the Land of Israel—in the Writings of Ramban (Nachmanides)," in Tomaschoff, *Whose Homeland,* p. 69.
45. Hanan Porat, "In Sinai the Brigade of Fighters Was Established," *Nekuda,* no. 43, May 21, 1982, p. 17.
46. Personal interview with Eleazar Waldman, Kiryat Arba, April 30, 1984. See *Jerusalem Post Supplement,* March 25, 1983, pp. 4–5. This was also Menachem Begin's position, maintaining loyalty to the traditional slogan of the Revisionist movement, still officially valid, "Both banks of the Jordan—this one is ours and that one is also!"
47. Elitzur, "Is Lebanon also the Land of Israel?" pp. 10–13.
48. *Maariv,* March 18, 1983.
49. *Nekuda,* no. 50, November 12, 1982, p. 23.
50. Yoel Ben-Nun, "The State of Israel vs. the Land of Israel?" *Nekuda,* no. 72, April 16, 1984, p. 31.
51. For most purposes the expanded East Jerusalem area was annexed in June 1967. Israeli law was applied to the Golan Heights in December 1982, but discussions disturbing to Gush Emunim continued within the Labor party over the possibility of a territorial compromise with Syria.
52. See, for example, Dan Margalit, "Zevulon Hammer's Turnabout," *Haaretz,* October 4, 1982 (translated in FBIS October 6, 1982, pp. 114–170; interview with Hammer broadcast on Israel Defense Forces radio, October 10, 1982 (transcribed in FBIS, October 12, 1982, pp. 18–9); interview with Yehuda Ben-Meir, *Nekuda,* no. 54, February 4, 1983, pp. 10–13; and Yehuda Amital, "In the Trap of Perfection," *Nekuda,* no. 52, December 24, 1982, pp. 8–11.
53. Amital, "In the Trap," p. 10.
54. See *Nekuda,* no. 53, January 15, 1983, p. 3; interview with Yehoshua Zuckerman, "Merkaz Harav as a Propaganda Center," *Nekuda,* no. 54, February 4, 1983, p. 5; Yisrael Ariel, "Agudah with a Knitted Skullcap," *Nekuda,* no. 55, February 22, 1983, pp. 28–29; Yoel Ben-Nun, Moshe Levinger, and Moshe Simon, "Responses to Rav Amital," *Nekuda,* no. 53, January 15, 1983, pp. 4–7; and Hanan Porat, "The Controversy with Rav Amital over the Land of Israel," *Nekuda,* no. 56, March 28, 1983, pp. 26–29, 36.
55. Eldad, *Jewish Revolution,* pp. 171–172.

56. A very similar distinction was made by Rabbi Elchanon Ben-Nun in his charac-terization of the overall shape of the discussion at a preelection Gush Emunim symposium in 1981. See "To Influence the Results of the Election," *Nekuda*, no. 26, March 3, 1981, p. 15. A more systematic discussion of essentially the same two perspectives is presented in Eliezer Schweid, "The Underground and the Ideology of Gush Emunim," *Nekuda*, no. 75, July 6, 1984, pp. 18–22.

57. Eliyakim Haetzni, *The Shock of Withdrawal from the Land of Israel* (in Hebrew) (Jerusalem: Elisha, 1986) p. 19.

58. Yisrael Ariel, "Was There Indeed a Revolt," p. 16.

59. Dan Tor, "To Continue to Push," p. 13. This article is dedicated to Yair (Abraham Stern, leader of the prestate Jewish terrorist organization known as Lehi, or the Stern Gang), whom Tor calls "the greatest pusher of the end of the generation of the Redemption."

60. Moshe Tzuriel, "In Defense of Redemption Initiatives," *Nekuda*, no. 105, December 9, 1986, p. 15. See also Dan Tor, "To Continue to Push," pp. 12–13.

61. Beni Katzover, remarks at a Gush Emunim symposium on political strategy held in March 1981. *Nekuda*, no. 26, April 3, 1981, p. 6.

62. Eleazar Waldman, "Do Not Aspire to Little by Little ," *Nekuda*, no. 59, June 10, 1983, p. 20.

63. *Ibid.,* p. 20 (emphasis in original).

64. Beni Katzover, "Plan to Return to the System of Struggle of Sebastia," *Nekuda*, no. 83, February 1, 1985, p. 13; and "The People Is with Us: We Must Break from the System," *Nekuda*, no. 93, November 22, 1985, p. 14.

65. Quoted from *Nekuda* in Yehuda Litani, "The Mass of Judea, Samaria, and Gaza," *Haaretz*, December 26, 1980.

66. Eliyakim Haetzni, *Shock of Withdrawal*. For a similar argument, see Baruch Lior, "To Prepare the Generations for Prayer and War," *Nekuda*, no. 85, April 5, 1985, pp. 11–12.

67. Resolutions quoted in Moshe Shapira, "The State of Israel vs. the State of Yesha," *Nekuda*, no. 93, November 22, 1985, p. 11. When another settler publication, *Aleph Yud*, published an article in October 1985 calling openly for armed struggle against the Peres government, it was suspended by government order.

68. The term used, *shtadlan,* has a particularly distasteful meaning in Zionist parlance, referring to the kowtowing "court Jews" of the Diaspora, who tradi-tionally protected Jewish communities by serving at the beck and call of the gentile ruler.

69. Dan Tor, "All the Flags Have Been Folded," *Nekuda*, no. 79, September 1984, p. 11.

70. Baruch Lior, "To Prepare the Generations," pp. 12–13.

71. *Ibid.,* p. 12. For an extended version of this argument, see Haetzni, *Shock of Withdrawal*, pp. 20–29.

72. Tzuriel, "In Defense of Redemption Initiatives," p. 14.

73. See, for example, Haetzni, *Shock of Withdrawal*, p. 10.

74. Shlomo Aviner, "Our Attachment to the Land of Israel," *Artzi*, vol. 1 (1982) p. 14.

75. Yitzhak Shilat, "To Return to the Way of the King," *Nekuda*, no. 89, July 26, 1985, p. 15. For a similar but secular use of long periods of biblical history to characterize the future course of the redemption process and justify a consensus-

building approach, see Israel Eldad, "I Have Not Fallen from the Ladder," *Nekuda*, no. 65, April 11, 1983, pp. 11–12. Characterizing the view that the redemption process is lengthy, intricate, and only partially dependent on human action as the majority view is consistent with the results of a 1984 opinion survey of 100 settlers of American background. See Chaim Waxman, "American Settlers in the Territories," in Newman, *Impact*, p. 219.

76. "Strength in a Time of Crisis," *Nekuda*, no. 73, May 5, 1984, p. 6.

77. Moshe Levinger, "Don't Throw Away the Old Banners," *Nekuda*, no. 97, March 25, 1986, p. 7. For similar arguments, opposing any sort of intra-Jewish or antistate violence and for maintaining the utmost tolerance toward Jewish critics, see Yaakov Ariel, "The Authority of the Halacha," *Nekuda*, no. 74, June 21, 1984, pp. 20–21; Eliezer Schweid, "Democracy Challenged," *Nekuda*, no. 78, September 21, 1984, pp. 15–19; the interview with Yehoshua Zuckerman in *Nekuda*, no. 54, February 4, 1983, p. 4; and Yitzhak Shilat, "Without Hysteria," *Nekuda*, no. 93, November 22, 1985, p. 10.

78. Interview with Rabbi Yehoshua Zuckerman, by Bembi Erlich, *Nekuda*, no. 73, May 25, 1984, p. 9.

79. Remarks by Yaakov Ariel, rabbi of the Neve Dekalim settlement, where the symposium was held. *Nekuda*, no. 59, June 10, 1983, p. 17.

80. Yosef Ben-Sholomo, "Ideological Struggle with the Right and Left," *Nekuda*, no. 85, April 5, 1985, pp. 20–22. The dissimulation involved in the consensus-building approach, which itself is derived from Abraham Isaac Kook's formula for secular-religious relations, helps explain the difference between the policies and outlooks articulated by Ben-Shlomo in *Nekuda* and those he shares with nonfundamentalist Jewish audiences. See his interview in *Tikkun*, vol. 2, no. 2 (1987) pp. 72–77.

81. Interview with Moshe Levinger, *Nekuda*, no. 83, February 1, 1985, p. 7.

82. Moshe Levinger, "With Alertness and Security," *Nekuda*, no. 93, November 22, 1985, p. 8. For the same argument, see also Yoel Ben-Nun, "Not to Be Nervous and Not to Be Made Nervous," *Nekuda*, no. 68, January 13, 1984, pp. 4–7.

83. See appendix 3 for a biographical sketch of Uri Elitzur.

84. Uri Elitzur, "I Am No More Zionist and You are No More Sane," *Nekuda*, no. 53, January 14, 1983, p. 19.

85. He has been a regular contributor, for example, to the left-of-center news magazine *Koteret Rashit*.

86. Yoel Ben-Nun, "For Security and Faith; Against Screams of Crisis," *Nekuda*, no. 85, April 5, 1985, p. 11.

87. Ben-Nun, "Way of Lights," pp. 8–11.

88. Ben-Nun, "State of Israel," p. 29. See also Ben-Nun, "Not to Be Nervous," pp. 4–7.

89. Ben-Nun, "For Security and Faith," p. 11.

90. *Ibid.*, pp. 10–11.

91. Yoel Ben-Nun, "Authority Now," *Nekuda*, no. 88, June 24, 1985, pp. 18–19.

92. Eleazar Waldman, "Yes, Conquer the Mount," *Nekuda*, no. 55, February 27, 1983, p. 21.

93. See, especially, Eleazar Waldman's defense of the Lebanon War, "Struggle," p. 21. For the secular fundamentalist equivalent of this message, involving Israel's future role as a technological savior for much of mankind, see Yuval Neeman, "National Goals," p. 268.

94. Quoted in Miriam Shiloh, "Do Not Hate!" *Nekuda*, no. 34, September 28, 1981, p. 17.
95. Kook, "Between the People," p. 19; Ariel, "Our Relations with Arabs," p. 13; and Dov Lior, "The Arabs and Us," *Artzi*, vol. 4 (Spring 1986) p. 21. See also the advice of Moshe Ben-Yosef (Hagar) not to burn copies of the New Testament, but only because, indirectly, Christian beliefs affirm the Jewish people's connection to the Land of Israel. *Nekuda*, no. 93, November 22, 1985, p. 26.
96. Kook, "Between the People," p. 20. The reference here is to George Eliot's proto-Zionist novel *Daniel Deronda*.
97. Yonatan Aharoni, "Every Jew and Mt. Ephraim," in Ben-Ami, *Book of the Whole Land*, p. 40. For elaboration of the same argument, see also the essay in that volume by Benjamin Oppenheimer, "Israel and Its Land: Principles of Jewish Nationalism," pp. 45–61.
98. Esther Azolai, "Conquest of the Land: The Moral Dimension," *Nekuda*, no. 77, August 31, 1984, pp. 18, 31. For the same argument put forward even more graphically, see Etzion, "From the Laws of Existence," pp. 22–24.
99. Moshe Levinger, "We and the Arabs," *Nekuda*, no. 36, November 27, 1981, p. 15. For a clear statement of the notion of the distinctive "mission" of the Jews, which overrides all other considerations and makes them unique as a people, see Moshe Simon, "The People Denies Its Destiny," *Nekuda*, no. 91, September 15, 1985, pp. 6–7, 36.
100. Moshe Ben-Yosef, "A Good Jerusalem Boy No Longer," *Nekuda*, no. 88, June 24, 1985, p. 9.
101. Moshe Ben-Yosef, "The Emancipation Has already Destroyed the Third Commonwealth," *Nekuda*, no. 94, December 20, 1985, p. 14. Concerning the "Christianized" and "anemic travesty of our creed that was evolved during the Emancipation," see Eldad, *Jewish Revolution*, p. 173. See also Yaakov Ariel's characterization of the "desolation" brought upon the Jewish people by the Emancipation in "Our Relations with the Arabs," p. 19.
102. *Ibid.*, p. 31.
103. Moshe Ben-Yosef, "Secular Zionism by Religious Means," *Nekuda*, no. 78, September 21, 1984, pp. 28–31.
104. Interview with Moshe Ben-Yosef by Ofra Amitai, *Nekuda*, no. 100, July 11, 1986, p. 28. For the detailed argument, see Ben-Yosef, "The Struggle for Survival against the Liberal Holocaust," *Nekuda*, no. 80, November 23, 1984, pp. 20–22.
105. Amitai interview with Ben-Yosef, p. 28.
106. Moshe Ben-Yosef, "Emancipation," p. 15.
107. Moshe Ben-Yosef, "From the Vision to Nihilism," *Nekuda*, no. 91, September 15, 1985, p. 24.
108. Moshe Ben-Yosef, "Where Is the Border?" *Nekuda*, no. 95, January 21, 1986, p. 23.
109. Ben-Yosef, "Struggle for Survival," p. 22.
110. For Tzvi Shiloach's views, see Gideon Levy, *Haaretz*, March 23, 1984; Amiel Unger "The Broken Dream of the National Unity Government," *Nekuda*, no. 98, April 23, 1986, pp. 16–17; and Israel Eldad (Interview, *Bamachane*, July 10, 1985, in JPRS 85-110, August 25, 1985) p. 42. See also Dan Nimrod, *Peace Now: Blueprint for National Suicide* (Montreal: Dawn Publishing, 1984).

111. Yosef Nedva, "Sane Zionism—or Believing Zionism?" *Artzi*, vol. 2 (1982) p. 45.

112. Haetzni, *Shock of Withdrawal* p. 35.

113. Eliyakim Haetzni, "Even Now a Civil War is Liable to Erupt," *Nekuda*, no. 82, January 4, 1985, p. 18 (emphasis in original).

114. Haetzni, *Shock of Withdrawal*, p. 33. For excellent analyses of the potential for this kind of civil revolt, see Ze'ev Schiff, *Haaretz*, November 21, 1985; Lea Anbel, "The Hussein Initiative: What Will the Settlers in the Territories Do," *Koteret Rashit*, no. 131, June 5, 1986, p. 7; and Mark Gefen, "The Revolt in Judea and Samaria is Coming Out of Hiding," *Al-Hamishmar*, November 8, 1985 (translated in FBIS, November 15, 1985, pp. I9–I11).

115. In a poll of 539 Gush Emunim settlers in 1981–82, two-thirds responded that they either agreed or strongly agreed that according to Jewish law, death must be chosen before acceptance of withdrawal from the West Bank. Support for this principle was evenly divided between religious and nonreligious settlers. See Weisburd, "Deviance as Social Reaction," pp. 222, 224.

116. See, for example, "Zionists for Palestine," *Nekuda*, no. 81, December 14, 1984, p. 5. For similar sentiments, see Yehuda Zoldan, "Fewer Conflicts, More Meetings," *Nekuda*, no. 99, May 30, 1986, pp. 8–9; Unger, "Broken Dream," pp. 16–17; and Eliyakim Haetzni, "Abandoning Parts of the Land of Israel to Foreign Sovereignty Is Not Zionism," *Nekuda*, no. 100, July 11, 1986, p.22.

117. Eliezer Schweid, "The Underground and the Ideology of Gush Emunim," *Nekuda*, no. 75, July 6, 1984, p. 20.

118. Yehuda Hankin, "Judaism or Democracy," *Nekuda*, no. 109, April 14, 1987, p. 18.

119. Tzuriel, "Defense," p. 15.

120. Haetzni, *Shock of Withdrawal*, pp. 28–29.

121. Zoldan, "Fewer Conflicts," pp. 8–9.

122. "Celebration of a Decade," *Nekuda*, no. 69, February 3, 1984, p. 3.

123. "Beware of Leftism," *Nekuda*, no. 98, April 23, 1986, p. 7.

124. Menachem Froumin, "To Conquer the Source of Scorn," *Nekuda*, no. 108, March 13, 1987, p. 23.

125. Avraham Mintz, "The Left Is Serious, the Left Is Dangerous," *Nekuda*, no. 109, April 14, 1987, p. 32.

126. *Nekuda*, no. 95, January 21, 1986, p. 3. For rabbinical opinions similar to Ben-Nun's, see Shilat, "Without Hysteria," p. 10; and Shapira, "State of Israel," p. 11.

127. Yehuda Amital, address delivered to students at the Kfar Etzion Yeshiva, *Nekuda*, no. 52, December 24, 1982, p.10.

128. *Nekuda*, no. 86, April 26, 1985, pp. 27–28; and *Nekuda*, no. 96, February 21, 1986, p. 19.

129. Eliyakim Haetzni, "Mysticism Goes Well with Communism," *Nekuda*, no. 49, October 22, 1982, pp. 14–15; Yoel Ben-Nun, "Independence Is Not a Gift," *Nekuda*, no. 73, May 25, 1984, pp. 20–21.

130. Eleazar Waldman, "Questions and Answers," *Artzi*, vol. 3 (1983) p. 22.

131. See, in Ben-Ami, *Book of the Whole Land*, Shmuel Katz, "Toward a Sane National Policy: Background and Plan," pp. 271–281, and Dov Yosephi, "Israel Between the Two Superpowers," pp. 282–286. More recent versions of this argument appear regularly in the many publications of a prominent Gush Emunim

support group in Canada, Dawn Publishing. See, for example, Dan Nimrod, ed., *Views of the Middle East Conflict Rarely Seen in the Media,* (Montreal: Dawn Publishing, 1985).

132. Mordechai Nisan, *American Middle East Foreign Policy: A Political Reevaluation* (Montreal: Dawn Publishing, 1982) pp. 170, 185.

133. "A Strategy for Israel: Confrontation or Conciliation?" *American Zionist* (May–June 1976) pp. 19–21.

134. *Nekuda,* no. 54, February 4, 1983, p. 2. For a comparison of Israel to North Vietnam, willing and able to fight either superpower to the death, see Ora Shem-Ur, *The Challenges of Israel* (New York: Shengold Publishers, 1980) p. 62.

135. See references to and quotes from Menachem Kasher, Shlomo Aviner, and, especially, Israel Hess in Amnon Rubinstein, *The Zionist Dream Revisited: From Herzl to Gush Emunim and Back* (New York: Schocker Books, 1984) p. 116 and Uriel Tal, "Foundations of a Political Messianic Trend in Israel," *Jerusalem Quarterly,* no. 35 (Spring 1985) pp. 42–44; and Ehud Sprinzak, *Gush Emunim: The Politics of Zionist Fundamentalism in Israel* (New York: American Jewish Committee, 1986) p. 12. The most explicit version of this argument appears in an article by Israel Hess entitled "The Torah's Commandment of Genocide," published in *Bat Kol,* the student journal of Bar-Ilan University, February 26, 1980. See also Amoz Oz, *In the Land of Israel,* (New York: Harcourt Brace Jovanovich, 1983) pp. 87–100.

136. Haim Tsuria, "The Right to Hate," *Nekuda,* no. 15, August 28, 1980, p. 12.

137. In 1985, for example, an extended debate was published in the pages of *Nekuda* on the proper lessons to be drawn from the biblical incident in which Shimon and Levy organized a slaughter of the inhabitants of Shechem.

138. Dov Lior, remarks at "The Arabs and Us," a symposium held at the Yehsiva Hesder Yamit, reported in *Artzi,* vol. 4 (Spring 1986) p. 21.

139. Dov Yosephi, "A Humane Solution to the Demographic Problem," in Ben-Ami *Book of the Whole Land,* pp. 345, 349 (emphasis in original).

140. Yedidya Segal, "Neither Arabic nor Arabs," *Nekuda,* no. 9, May 16, 1980, pp. 12–13.

141. Eilan Tor, "The Remedy for National Mental Illness," *Nekuda,* no. 39, May 2, 1982, p. 9.

142. Eli Susser, remarks at a Gush Emunim symposium, reported in *Nekuda,* no. 63, September 7, 1983, p. 21, (emphasis in original).

143. David Rosensweig, "Peace for the Galilee War: The Wrong Address," *Nekuda,* no. 63, December 23, 1983, p. 23. This article sparked a wide debate in Israel proper and among the settlers. Letters to the editor in *Nekuda* on the issue were mostly supportive of Rosensweig. See, in particular, *Nekuda,* no. 69, February 3, 1984, pp. 28–29.

144. Jerusalem Domestic Service, April 14, 1986 (transcribed in FBIS April 16, 1986, p. 15).

145. Moshe Ben-Yosef, "In Defense of the Transfer," *Nekuda,* no. 109, April 14, 1987, pp. 16–17.

146. See chapter 7, page 179, for information on a 1987 poll of rabbis in the West Bank and Gaza Strip that suggests that support for some sort of transfer option may be stronger than I indicate here.

147. David Weisburd and Vered Vinitzky, "Vigilantism as Rational Social Control: The Case of the Gush Emunim Settlers," in Myron Aronoff, ed., *Cross-Currents*

in Israeli Culture and Politics Political Anthropology, vol. 4, (New Brunswick, New Jersey: Transaction Books, 1984) p. 74. Concerning Rafael Eitan's solution for the problem of local Arab unrest (sticks and beatings are preferable to the use of lethal force), see an interview broadcast on April 17, 1983, by Jerusalem Domestic Television Service (transcribed in FBIS, April 18, 1983, pp. I5–7).

148. "We Must Block Terror," *Nekuda,* no. 90, August 23, 1985, p. 5.

149. Jerusalem Domestic Service, May 6, 1987 (transcribed in FBIS, May 7, 1987, p. 6).

150. Michal Capra, "Beer and Olive Oil," *Sof Shavua* (Weekly supplement of *Maariv*), November 27, 1987, pp. 10, 50.

151. Translated from *Hatzofe,* April 17, 1987, in Harry Milkman, ed., *Israeli Press Highlights,* American Jewish Committee, (Press Summary—April 23, 1987) p. 3. See also Tzvi Slonim's description of settler reaction to these events in the *Bama'ale Newsletter,* issued by the aliyah department of Gush Emunim in New York (Spring 1987) p. 1.

152. "The Rabbis of Judea, Samaria, and Gaza: Encourage the Emigration of the Arabs," *Nekuda,* no. 115, November 1987, p. 37. For details concerning this poll, see chapter 7, note 2.

153. Ariel, "Our Relations with the Arabs," p. 16.

154. See Hanan Porat, "Policies toward the Arabs of the Land of Israel," *Artzi,* vol. 4 (Spring 1986) p. 8.

155. Kook, "Between the People," p. 20.

156. In the next issue of *Nekuda* one settler wrote on behalf of several who had joked among themselves at the embarrassing truth contained in this photograph. See *Nekuda,* no. 69, February 3, 1984, p. 29.

157. For various positions on these issues, see Shlomo Aviner, "The Wholeness of the Land of Israel," *Artzi,* vol. 1 (1982) pp. 26–27; Ariel, "Our Relations with the Arabs," pp. 13–18; Lior, "The Arabs and Us," p. 21–22; Bezalel Zolty, "Lo Tehonnem: Halakhic Limitations on Gentile Property in Eretz Israel," in Tomaschoff, *Whose Homeland,* pp. 156–159; and Mordechai Nisan, "A New Perspective on Israeli-Arab Peace: Minority Rights in the Middle East," *Plural Societies* vol. 15 (1984) pp. 6–8. For an excellent summary of the classic sources involved in this debate, see J. David Bleich, "Judea and Samaria: Settlement and Return," *Tradition,* vol. 18, no. 1 (Summer 1979) pp. 60–65, 73–76.

158. For one of the only systematic presentations of this position, see Dan Be'eri, "Autonomy for the Arabs of the Land of Israel," *Nekuda,* no. 87, May 24, 1985, pp. 10–11, 25.

159. Ariel, "Our Relations with the Arabs," p. 19. Ariel implies that the citizenship option would be available only to Arabs who convert to Judaism. For application of the dhimmi model, see Nisan, "A New Perspective," pp. 9–12.

160. When 539 Gush Emunim settlers were polled in 1981–1982, 64 percent disagreed or strongly disagreed with the statement "If Judea and Samaria are officially annexed, the local Arabs should be granted Israeli citizenship and given the right to vote." Only 13 percent agreed or strongly agreed. See Weisburd and Vinitzky, "Vigilantism," p. 81. For Tehiya's outlook, see Yuval Neeman's discussion of the future of the Arab population (emigration, refugee resettlement outside the Land of Israel, and resident status for most of those that remain) in "National Goals," pp. 264–266.

161. See Yosef Nedva, "Co-existence: The Danger and the Opportunity," *Nekuda,* no. 56, March 28, 1983, pp. 13–14.

162. For these opposing perspectives, see, for example, Yakki Fried, "Diary of a Terrorist," *Nekuda,* no. 33, August 28, 1981, p. 9; Amiel Unger, "Yesha after the Subsidies," *Nekuda,* no. 58, May 17, 1983, pp. 22–23; Aharon Baruchin, "Who Will Build?" *Nekuda,* no. 91, September 15, 1985, p. 2; and Simcha Stettner, remarks at the symposium "The Arabs and Us," p. 22.

163. Yaakov Ariel, "Rosenzweig Recognizes a Palestinian Entity," *Nekuda,* no. 69, February 3, 1984, p. 28; Nisan, "A New Perspective," p. 10; and Porat, "Policies toward the Arabs," p. 8.

164. Personal interview with Yonathan Blass, Ofra, April 1984.

165. Porat, "Policies toward the Arabs," p. 5.

166. In the previously cited 1984 survey of opinions of settlers of American background, the following responses were given to a general question about policy toward local Arabs: *Leave as is except for troublemakers,* 30 percent; *offer citizenship, and require that those who refuse leave or remain second-class,* 30 percent; *must find way for peaceful coexistence somehow,* 17 percent; *provide economic incentives for them to leave,* 10 percent; *force them out,* 4 percent; *divide the territories,* 3 percent; *don't know,* 6 percent. See Chaim I. Waxman, "Political and Social Attitudes of Americans among the Settlers in the Territories," in Newman, (ed.) *Impact,* p. 215.

167. Shiloh, "Do Not Hate!" pp. 16–17. For similar sentiments, see Chagi Huberman, "Objectivity with Limited Liability," *Nekuda,* no. 64, October 14, 1983, pp. 14–15; Shlomo Kaniel, "Between Good and Evil," *Nekuda,* no. 77, August 31, 1984, pp. 14–15; Hagai Ben-Artzi, "The Moral Attitude toward the Arabs," *Nekuda,* no. 84, January 3, 1985, pp. 12–13; and Zev Ben-Shachar, "Love Your Neighbor as Yourself," *Nekuda,* no. 78, September 21, 1984, pp. 32–33.

168. Hanoch Alon, "Preventive Knowledge," *Nekuda,* no. 7, March 21, 1980, pp. 6–7; and Liora Karet, remarks at "Yesha and Israeli Society," a Gush Emunim symposium, reported in *Nekuda,* no. 63, September 7, 1983, p. 36.

169. "A Good Neighbor Is Good," *Nekuda,* no. 77, August 31, 1984, p. 5.

170. Yehuda Shabib, "The Lost Honor of Dinah Daughter of Leah," *Nekuda,* no. 81, December 14, 1984, p. 22.

171. Ben-Artzi, "Moral Attitude," p. 13.

172. See Waldman, "Struggle," pp. 27–28.

173. "Gush Emunim Extends hand for peace to Jericho," *Jerusalem Post International Edition,* week ending May 9, 1987, p. 3.

174. See Gideon Erlich, "Truth and Faith," *Nekuda,* no. 47, September 3, 1982, pp. 6–7; and Yehezkel Levi, "Arguments without Foundation," *Nekuda,* no. 86, April 26, 1986, pp. 25–26.

175. Yoel Ben-Nun, "Equality and Participation—Man-made Values," *Koteret Rashit,* no. 151, October 23, 1985, pp. 44–45.

176. Eliyakim Haetzni, "The Chasm is Bridged," *Nekuda,* no. 66, November 25, 1983, pp. 12–13.

177. Personal interview with Yisrael Harel, Ofra, April 1984.

178. Ben-Nun, "Not to Be Nervous," p. 7 (emphasis in original). For similar arguments, see the editorial in this same issue, p. 3; Orna Dann, "On Yaakov

Feitelson: Jacob's Ladder," *Nekuda*, no. 67, December 23, 1983, pp. 8–9; and Kaniel, "Between Good and Evil," pp. 14–15.

179. Waldman, "Struggle," p. 27.

180. Hanan Porat, "Controversy with Rav Amital," p. 28.

181. *Ibid.* (emphasis in original). "Repair of the world," is a concept in Jewish mysticism referring to the Jewish task of completing and uniting a fractured cosmos in order to help bring about the final redemption.

182. Aran, *Land of Israel,* p. 14.

183. Waldman, "Struggle," p. 20.

184. *Ibid.,* p. 14. See also the conclusion in Michael Hershkowitz, "On Values and Morality," *Artzi,* vol. 4 (Spring 1986) pp. 80–91. For a nonreligious formulation of the same point, see Yoram Ben-Meir, "On the Internal Point," *Artzi,* vol. 1 (1982) p. 19.

185. Michael Schwartz, "War, Peace, and Territories in the Eyes of Islam," *Artzi,* vol. 4 (Spring 1986) p. 37.

186. Arnold M. Soloway, *The Role of Arab Political Culture and History in the Conflict with Israel* (Montreal: Dawn Publishing, 1985) pp. 6–7. Concerning the "implacable" nature of the Arab-Israeli conflict, see also Paul Eidelberg, *The Case of Israel's Jewish Underground,* (Montreal: Dawn Publishing, 1985) pp. 6–7; and Shem-Ur, *Challenges,* pp. 21, 48–52.

187. Shmuel Katz, *No Solution to the Arab-Palestinian Problem,* (Montreal: Dawn Publishing, 1985) pp. 35–36. See also Moshe Sharon "Interim Arrangements in Light of the Pax Islamica," in Ben-Ami, *Book of the Whole Land,* pp. 263–268.

188. Interview with Rafael Eitan, in *Yediot Acharonot,* January 21, 1983 (translated in FBIS, January 27, 1983, p. 13); and *Maariv,* February 27, 1983 (translated in FBIS, March 1, 1983, p. 19).

189. "Tzomet Expects a Green Light from the Settlements," *Nekuda,* no. 67, December 23, 1983, pp. 26–27.

190. Interview with Abraham Yoffe, in Ben-Ami, *Book of the Whole Land,* p. 192. See also the interview in this volume with General Aharon Davidi, "The War Aims of the People of Israel," pp. 199–203.

191. *Ibid.,* p. 188. Concerning the likely use of Israeli military force during the next 60–70 years to block the Strait of Hormuz and blockade Arab ports against receipt of arms shipments, see Shem-Ur, *Challenges,* pp. 58–79.

192. Ari Jabotinsky, "The Administered Areas under Arab Imperialism," in Ben-Ami, *Book of the Whole Land,* pp. 207–209 (emphasis in original).

193. Tzvi Shiloach, "The Destiny of Greater Israel in Its Ancient Land," in Ben-Ami, *Book of the Whole Land,* pp. 213–240.

194. Ezra Zohar, "Israel and the Periphery Facing Pan-Arabism," in Ben-Ami, *Book of the Whole Land,* pp. 227–240.

195. Neeman, "National Goals," p. 113.

196. *Ibid.,* p. 114.

197. Yoel Ben-Nun, "The Arab-Israeli Conflict as a Cultural-Religious Problem," *Artzi,* vol. 4 (Spring 1986) p. 46.

198. Yaakov Ariel, "Return of the Regained Territories," pp. 154–155.

199. *Zot Haaretz,* editorial, November 6, 1976, reprinted in Ben-Ami, *Book of the Whole Land,* p. 33.

200. Eliyakim Haetzni, "Peace without a Treaty," *Nekuda,* no. 51, December 3, 1982, pp. 10–11.

201. Eliyakim Haetzni, "The People is Retreating from Its Last Line of Defense," *Nekuda,* no. 83, February 1, 1985, pp. 8–9, 26.

202. Eliyakim Haetzni, "After the Next War," *Nekuda,* no. 98, April 23, 1986, p. 35.

203. Yoel Ben-Nun, "Syria is the Partner," *Nekuda,* no. 58, May 17, 1983, p. 5; interview with Moshe Levinger, *Nekuda,* no. 83, February 1, 1985, p. 6.

204. Meir Har-Noi, "To Shift into Reverse," *Nekuda,* no. 97, March 25, 1986, p. 19.

205. Eliyakim Haetzni, "Shivers," *Nekuda,* no. 85, April 5, 1985, p. 16.

206. Eliyakim Haetzni, "The Negro Doesn't Change His Skin," *Nekuda,* no. 92, October 23, 1985, p. 29.

207. Amiel Unger, "Return to the Days of Sebastia," *Nekuda,* no. 85, April 5, 1985, pp. 13–14.

Notes to Chapter 6

1. Charles Liebman and Eliezer Don-Yehiya, *Religion and Politics in Israel* (Bloomington, Indiana: University of Indiana Press, 1984) p. 78.

2. In 1979 the chief rabbi issued a formal ruling that "according to our holy Torah and the clear and authoritative law, there is a strict ban on transferring ownership to the gentiles of any part of the Land of Israel, because it is sanctified by the sacredness of the biblical Covenant between the pieces." The reference is to Genesis 15: 9–17, in which Abraham receives God's promise of future greatness while a smoking furnace is seen to pass between the divided carcasses of three animals. See Uriel Tal, "Foundations of a Political Messianic Trend in Israel," *Jerusalem Quarterly,* no. 35 (Spring 1985) p. 41.

3. See, for example, polls by Modi'in Ezrahi, in *Maariv,* January 27, 1987, and April 21, 1987; and by Dahaf, in *Yediot Acharonot,* June 19, 1987.

4. In this regard, see David Grossman's confident prediction that the education and upbringing of the thousands of children now in Gush Emunim settlements guarantees the emergence of several more Jewish terrorist undergrounds in the future. David Grossman, "Don't Have So Much Mercy on Them," *Koteret Rashit,* no. 230, April 29, 1987, p. 26. See also an editorial in *Nekuda,* no. 112, July 31, 1987, p. 6, on the subject of the children of Judea, Samaria, and Gaza as a "settler reserve."

5. Yehuda Hazani, "A 'Lobby' for the Glory of God," *Nekuda,* no. 84, March 1, 1985, p. 24; "Blessings for the Lobby," *Nekuda,* no. 85, May 4, 1985, p. 7; interview with Member of Knesset Uzi Landau, *Nekuda,* no. 85, May 4, 1985, pp. 8–9; Menachem Friedman, "Yesha for Our Guys," *Nekuda,* no. 88, June 24, 1985, pp. 19–20; and Eliezer Schweid, "From National Movement to Pressure Group," *Nekuda,* no. 89, July 26, 1985, pp. 16–17.

6. Charles S. Liebman, "The Religious Component in Israeli Ultra-Nationalism," *Jerusalem Quarterly,* no. 41 (Winter 1987) p. 136.

7. Meron Benvenisti, *1986 Report: Demographic, Economic, Legal, Social, and Political Developments in the West Bank* (Jerusalem: West Bank Data Base Project, 1986) p. 60.

8. For the success story of Kfar Adumim, see Ofra Amitai, "Bridge over Wadi Kelt," *Nekuda,* no. 106, January 9, 1987, by pp. 8–9, 13; and "A Holiday for Kfar Adumim," *Nekuda,* no. 107, February 13, 1987, p. 6. For discussions of failure in this sphere, see Bembi Erlich, "Mixed Samaria," *Nekuda,* no. 108, March 13, 1987, p. 18; letters to the editor, *Nekuda,* no. 109, April 14, 1987, p. 1; and

Yehoshua Zohar, "The Hidden Future of Secular Settlement," *Nekuda*, no. 109, April 14, 1987, p. 4.

9. See, for example, "The Collectivized System," *Nekuda*, no. 76, August 10, 1984, p. 5; Rafi Vaknin, "With Our Own Hands We Prevent Massive Settlement of Judea, Samaria, and Gaza," *Nekuda*, no. 89, October 23, 1985, pp. 26–27; and Moshe Amir, "The Mistakes of Rafi Vaknin," *Nekuda*, no. 92, October 23, 1985, pp. 27, 29.

10. Yair Sheleg, "Yeshivot Hesder: Between Vision and Reality," *Nekuda*, no. 86, April 26, 1985, pp. 12–13; and Yair Sheleg, "Wanted: Settlers and Educators," *Nekuda*, no. 87, May 24, 1985, pp. 12–14.

11. Meron Benvenisti, *The West Bank Data Project: A Survey of Israel's Policies* (Washington, D.C.: American Enterprise Institute, 1984) pp. 54–55. Not surprisingly, Gush Emunim spokesmen disagree with the judgment that the reservoir of ideologically motivated settlers has been exhausted. See Yisrael Harel's remarks in this regard, quoted in Hagai Segel, "What Happened to the Hundred Plan?" *Nekuda*, no. 105, December 9, 1986, p. 38.

12. Benvenisti, *1986 Report*, p. 50. See also Benvenisti, *West Bank Data Project*, p. 59.

13. Benvenisti, *West Bank Data Project*, p. 62. For a detailed discussion of the relationship between large-scale subsidized settlement and changes in Israelis' concepts of the relationship of the West Bank and Gaza to their state, see Ian Lustick, "Israeli State-Building in the West Bank and Gaza Strip: Theory and Practice," *International Organization*, vol. 41, no. 1 (Winter 1987) pp. 151–171.

14. "Good Luck to Project Absorption," *Nekuda*, no. 58, May 5, 1983, p. 3.

15. Lustick, "Israeli State-Building."

16. Benvenisti, *1986 Report*, p. 47.

17. See Yitzhak Shilat (head of the Maale Adumim Yeshiva), "Without Hysteria," *Nekuda*, no. 93, November 22, 1985, pp. 10–11; Chava Pinchas-Cohen, "The Eli Story: Today They Are the Majority," *Nekuda*, no. 96, February 21, 1986, pp. 20–21, 28.

18. Findings of a study conducted by Chaim Waxman, reported in Yaakov Warren, *Counterpoint*, vol. 2, no. 13 (July 1985) p. 2.

19. "Citizens Won't Leave," *Counterpoint*, vol. 4, no. 1 (October–November 1986) p. 10.

20. Giora Goldberg and Efraim Ben-Zadok, "Gush Emunim in the West Bank," *Middle Eastern Studies*, vol. 22, no. 1 (January 1986) p. 67. Data available for votes by Jewish (mainly Gush Emunim—oriented) residents of the Gaza Strip in that election are pooled with those cast by the many more residents of Yamit, of whom relatively few identified with the fundamentalist movement. Of votes cast in the Gaza Strip and Sinai, 64.5 percent went to those same parties.

21. Benvenisti, *1986 Report*, p. 50; and Peter Grose, *A Changing Israel* (New York: Vintage, 1985) pp. 14–15.

22. Benvenisti, *1986 Report*, p. 50.

23. Ron Nahman, remarks at "To Influence the Results of the Elections," Gush Emunim symposium, reported in *Nekuda*, no. 26, April 3, 1981, p. 5; and Ron Nahman, lecture and audiovisual presentation, Tufts University, Medford, Massachusetts, March 1, 1987.

24. Benvenisti, *1986 Report*, pp. 50–51.

25. *Haaretz*, November 6, 1982.

26. *Maariv*, August 4, 1987 (translated in FBIS, August 5, 1987, p. L4).

27. *Davar,* June 10, 1986. See also Levy's militant speech to 3,000 settlers gathered in Ariel, reported in *Jerusalem Post,* May 5, 1987.

28. Though clearly exaggerating, in the last months of the second Likud government, Yisrael Harel characterized Gush Emunim settler opinion on matters pertaining to the West Bank as "almost a diktat" in the view of responsible ministers. Personal interview, Ofra, April 15, 1984.

29. Yigal Cohen-Orgad, "1984," *Nekuda,* no. 115, November 1987, pp. 32–35.

30. *Jerusalem Post,* September 26, 1986.

31. See *Jerusalem Post,* July 21, 22, and 25; and *Hatzofe,* July 17, 1987 (translated in FBIS, July 20, 1987, p. L6). See also the biography of Uri Elitzur in appendix 3.

32. As the 1986 and 1987 polls reported in appendix 2 indicate, the deep division between the two political blocs mirrors an equally deep and wide division on the issue within the Jewish public. Not only are Israeli Jews virtually equally split on a clear choice regarding a momentous issue—nearly half favor territorial compromise and half refuse to countenance withdrawal from any part of the areas—but only a negligible proportion report themselves as undecided or indifferent.

33. Concerning Tehiya's extraction of a commitment from Prime Minister Shamir to reach the target of 100,000 Jews on the West Bank by the end of 1988, in return for its abandoning efforts to bring down the government, see *Jerusalem Post,* July 20, 1987.

34. David Grossman, "At Night There Was a Burning Here," *Koteret Rashit,* no. 230, April 29, 1987, p. 69. Each village named was the scene of a massacre, by Jews, of Arab civilians. Unit 101 was a secret group of commandos used in the 1950s for retaliation raids against villages in the West Bank; the Israeli government at the time blamed these raids on civilian vigilantes. Ariel Sharon is one of Unit 101's best-known veterans.

35. Orit Shohat, "Blackening the Skull Cap," *Haaretz,* June 28, 1985 (translated in JPRS, no. NEA-85-127, October 4, 1985, pp. 42–48); Yaakov Rodan and Rachel Katsman, "Israel's Religious Revival: A Return to Which Orthodoxy?" *Counterpoint,* vol. 3, no. 3 (January 1986) pp. 6–10; Daniel Ben-Simon, "Merkaz Harav: Here Gush Emunim Was Born," *Haaretz,* April 4, 1986; Dan Beeri, "Zionism, More than Ever," *Nekuda,* no. 95, January 21, 1986, pp. 8–9; Israel Rosenson, "Who Will Rein In the Fighters of Extremism," *Nekuda,* no. 104, November 7, 1986, pp. 19, 27; and Avraham Neuriel, "The Hareidization of Religious Zionism," *Nekuda,* no. 105, December 9, 1986, pp. 18–19. For a general treatment of this topic, see Janet Aviad, *Return to Judaism: Religious Renewal in Israel* (Chicago: University of Chicago Press, 1983) especially pp. 63–70, 112–114.

36. Yair Sheleg, "From Burg to Gush Emunim and Back Again," *Bamachane,* September 18, 1985 (translated in JPRS, no. NEA-85-150, December 23, 1985, pp. 37–41); and Uri Orbach, "Bnei Akiva: To Benefit from All the Worlds," *Nekuda,* no. 99, May 30, 1986, pp. 20–23.

37. For the potential overlap of Haredi and ultranationalist political objectives, see Charles S. Liebman, "The Religious Component in Israeli Ultra-Nationalism," *Jerusalem Quarterly,* no. 41 (Winter 1987) p. 131. Concerning the common antidemocratic basis of Agudat Yisrael and Gush Emunim, see Liebman and Don-Yehiya, *Religion and Politics,* pp. 135–136. Regarding the ultranationalist and annexationist positions advocated by the Lubavitch Hasidim, see Allan L.

Nadler, "Piety and Politics: The Case of the Satmar Rebbe," *Judaism*, vol. 31, no. 2 (Spring 1982) pp. 150–151.

38. Janet Aviad, *Return to Judaism*, pp. 131–132. Concerning beliefs within the Haredi community that the Messiah's arrival may be imminent, see Yaakov Rodan, "Struggle Behind the Walls," *Counterpoint*, vol. 3, no. 6 (August 1986) p. 9.

39. See E. Offenbacher, "Prayer on the Temple Mount," *Jerusalem Quarterly*, no. 36 (Summer 1985) pp. 133–134; and Robert J. Rosenthal, "God, Terror and the Rock," *Philadelphia Inquirer*, April 8, 1984, pp. 19, 31.

40. In March 1986 Immanuel was reported to have 4,000 residents. See *Counterpoint*, vol. 4, no. 1 (October–November 1986) p. 12.

41. Erez Yisrael, "They Are Killing Themselves in the Tent of the Torah," *Hashavua* (weekly supplement to *Davar*), no. 51, December 18, 1987, p. 8.

42. Yehuda Etzion, "From the Banner of Jerusalem to the Movement of Redemption," *Nekuda*, no. 94, December 20, 1985, pp. 9, 28.

43. For background on the issue and information on the specific halachic positions of these rabbis, see "Target: Temple Mount," *Jerusalem Post International Edition*, week ending October 15, 1983; "Dispute over Chief Rabbi's comment on Mount," *Jerusalem Post International Edition*, week ending February 8, 1986; and a number of articles in *Counterpoint*, vol. 3, no. 3 (February 1986), especially Yisrael Medad, "Battle on the Temple Mount," pp. 8–9. Rabbi Goren's most recent action has been the construction of a sculpture overlooking the Temple Mount consisting of six Jewish stars atop flames burning in fountains. Though officially the monument was built as a Holocaust memorial, he acknowledges that the fire and water do recall the libations and offerings on the altar of the Temple. See *Koteret Rashit*, no. 230, April 29, 1987, p. 7.

44. See appendix 5 for the picture that accompanied a 1984 article on the Temple Mount by Yehuda Etzion, "From the Laws of Existence to the Laws of Destiny," *Nekuda*, no. 75, July 6, 1984, p. 26. The picture shows the Old City of Jerusalem with a rebuilt Temple in the place of the the Dome of the Rock and the el-Aksa Mosque. The same photomontage or similar ones reportedly have been prominently displayed in public rooms and in private homes in Gush Emunim settlements, including the home of Yoel Ben-Nun. See David Grossman, "Don't Have So Much Mercy On Them," *Koteret Rashit*, no. 230, April 24, 1987, p. 26.

45. See the official Gush Emunim advertisement for the rally, signed by the four most important organizations whose activities are related to the Temple Mount, *Nekuda*, no. 99, May 30, 1986, back cover; and Israel Domestic Service, in FBIS, June 6, 1986, P. 11.

46. Baruch Lior, "To Prepare the Generations for Prayer and War," *Nekuda*, no. 85, April 5, 1985, pp. 12–13. For similar arguments, see Motti Nachmani, "What Is Going On with the Temple Mount," *Nekuda*, no. 47, September 3, 1982, p. 7; Yigal Ariel, "The Temple Mount as Waqf Property," *Nekuda*, no. 58, May 17, 1983, pp. 18–19; Shabatai Ben Dov, "Fasts of the Temple Destruction," *Nekuda*, no. 61, July 18, 1983, pp. 8–9; interview with David Rotem, lawyer for the Gush Emunim underground, *Nekuda*, no. 75, July 6, 1984, pp. 10–11; Moshe Ben-Yosef, "Prelude to the Mount," *Nekuda*, no. 96, February 21, 1986, p. 19. For the most sophisticated discussion of how best to conduct the struggle for the Temple Mount, see Israel Medad, "The Mountain before the Temple," *Nekuda*, no. 89,

July 26, 1985, pp. 10–11 (translated in JPRS, no. NEA-85-148, December 18, 1985, pp. 56–59).

47. Israel Eldad, "In the Den of the Numerologists," *Nekuda,* no. 78, September 21, 1984, p. 14; Moshe Levinger, "We Must Not Discard the Old Banners," *Nekuda,* no. 97, March 25, 1986, p. 8; and Shlomo Aviner, *Let Us Not Go Up to the Mount* (in Hebrew) (Jerusalem: Aturei Kahanim, no. 3, n.d.).

48. "The Temple Mount Is Not in Our Hands," *Nekuda,* no. 87, May 24, 1985, p. 4.

49. "The Fuse," *Nekuda,* no. 95, January 21, 1986, p. 4.

50. "Messiah Now," *Nekuda,* no. 105, September 5, 1986, p. 5.

51. *New York Times,* October 12 and 13, 1987; and Jerusalem Domestic Service, December 18, 1987 (translated in FBIS, December 18, 1987, p. 31). For a recent discussion of the status of the Temple Mount issue for fundamentalist activists who focus on this question, see Yisrael Medad, "Court of the Lord in Court of the Law," *Counterpoint,* vol. 5, no. 1 (November 1987) pp. 4–5.

52. Doron Rosenblum, "The Temple Mount Will Be Blown Up," *Koteret Rashit,* no. 131, June 5, 1985, pp. 20–21.

53. Yoel Ben-Porat, "The Messiah Brigades Must Be Stopped," *Maariv,* May 10, 1987 (translated in *Israel Press Briefs,* no. 53, May–June 1987 p. 14).

54. Shlomo Aviner, *Let Us Not Go Up,* pp. 1–2, 4.

55. Concerning the furor within Gush Emunim over Weiss's leadership and its relationship to the deeper division between vanguardists and consensus builders, see the following: In *Nekuda,* no. 104 Menachem Froumin, "I Am Splitting," (November 7, 1986) pp. 10–11, 31; and Daniella Weiss, "The Wicked Ones," pp. 10–11, 31. In *Nekuda,* no. 105, December 9, 1987, Amiel Unger, "The 'Machteret' as a Stage Set," pp. 24–25; Meir Harnoi, "No Reason for a Split," pp. 25–26; Yonah Sieff, "Demanding a Framework for New Ideas," pp. 26–27; and Dan Tor, "A Grain of Fakery," pp. 28–30. In *Nekuda,* no. 106, January 9, 1987, Beni Katzover, "There Will Be No Hope in Political Parties," pp. 10–12. In *Nekuda,* no. 107, February 13, 1987, "Coordination Is Needed," p. 7. In *Nekuda,* no. 108, March 13, 1987, Hannah Gopher, "All Must Remain Inside the Family," p. 4; Bembi Erlich, "To Draw Conclusions," p. 4; Tzvi Maoz, "And Now for a Professional, Institutionalized Leadership," pp. 20–21; Menachem Froumin, "To Conquer the Source of Disrespect," pp. 22–23; Yitzhak Armoni, "Return to the Source: The Way of Faith," pp. 24–25; and Daniella Weiss, "I Never Said the Kibbutzim Were Failures," pp. 26–27, 33. In *Nekuda,* no. 109, April 14, 1987, Eyal Kafkafi, "The Parting of the Ways," pp. 24–25, 36; and Yossi Tzuriel, "A Movement in Place of Gush," pp. 26–27. This debate, alloted considerable space by *Nekuda,* became so intense that vanguardists raised an unprecedented number of questions about the editorial direction and value of *Nekuda* itself. See in *Nekuda,* no. 109, April 14, 1987, Alexander Azariah, "Is There Not One Righteous Man in Sodom?" p. 3; "The Lies and Grievances Cry Out to Heaven," open letter on behalf of Daniella Weiss from forty-four settlers in Kedumim, pp. 34–35; and Eliyakim Haetzni, "*Nekuda:* Come Down off the Roof," pp. 35, 50.

56. Aviva Shabi, "Splits in Gush," *Yediot Acharonot,* May 15, 1987; and Jerusalem Domestic Service, May 15, 1987 (translated in FBIS, May 15, 1987, p. 16).

57. For self-perceptions of malaise within Gush circles, see "The March Was No Party," *Nekuda,* no. 99, May 30, 1986, p. 7.

Notes to Chapter 7

1. For an argument that it was precisely the vested interests and intransigence of settlers that prevented the permanent incorporation of Ireland by Great Britain, and of Algeria by France, see Ian S. Lustick, *State-Building Failure in British Ireland and French Algeria* (Berkeley, California: University of California Institute of International Studies, 1985).

2. The poll was conducted by the Tzomet Institute. Of the 120 questionnaires distributed, fifty-two (43 %) were returned . For the full results of the poll, see "The Rabbis of Judea, Samaria, and Gaza: Encourage the Emigration of the Arabs," in *Nekuda,* no. 115, November 1987, p. 37.

3. For a useful summary of this debate, see Avishai Ehrlich, "Is Transfer an Option?" *Israeli Democracy,* vol. 1, no. 4 (Winter 1987) pp. 36–38. See also Yohanan Ramati, "The Transfer of Refugees—Without Demagoguery," *Davar,* October 4, 1987.

4. This projection is based on the age-specific proportions of Arabs and Jews living in Israel and the territories, as listed in the *Statistical Abstract of Israel* (Central Bureau of Statistics, Jerusalem, Israel) 1986 and 1987. Estimates published widely in the Israeli press at the end of 1987 concluded that there were 750,000 Arabs within Israel (including expanded East Jerusalem), 830,000 in the West Bank, and 650,000 in the Gaza Strip.

5. Doron Rosenblum, "The Temple Mount Will Be Blown Up," *Koteret Rashit,* no. 131, June 5, 1985, pp. 20–21.

6. On the ultimately successful effort of Gush Emunim veterans to oust the Likud-supported general secretary of the Yesha Council, see Uriel Ben-Ami, "Threats and Blackmail in Yesha," *Davar,* November 13, 1987.

7. *Jewish Week,* June 12, 1987, p. 5. See also Jerusalem Domestic Service broadcast, June 9, 1987 (transcribed in FBIS, June 9, 1987, p. L1).

8. Warnings that civil war could break out are not uncommonly offered by leading and responsible personalities within the fundamentalist movement. See, for example, an interview with Hanan Porat, *Counterpoint* (October–November 1985) p. 10; and Otheniel Shindler in *Koteret Rashit,* no. 131, June 5, 1986, p. 7. Since the early 1980s, one former head of Israel's secret service, Avraham Achitov, and many Israeli intellectuals and journalists—including Yaakov Talmon, A. B. Yehoshua, Shaul Friedlander, and Eliyahu Saltpeter—have warned of the possibility of civil war, often drawing for parallels on Weimar Germany. See Ian S. Lustick, "The West Bank and Gaza in Israeli Politics," in Steven Heydemann, ed., *The Begin Era* (Boulder, Colorado: Westview Press, 1984) pp. 86–88. For a more recent discussion of fundamentalists' willingness to confront the army, see Dan Margalit in *Haaretz,* June 11, 1987 (translated in FBIS, June 12, 1987, pp. L3–4). Yisrael Medad, a religious activist within Tehiya and a leader of two groups with activities related to the Temple Mount, published an article in *Nekuda,* prior to the Yamit evacuation, arguing that the evacuation could and would be halted only if a Jewish takeover of the Temple Mount was effected immediately. See Yisrael Medad, "The Temple Mount Is in Our Hands—The Time Has Come," *Nekuda,* no. 39, February 5, 1982, pp. 4–5.

9. Poll conducted by Modi'in Ezrahi, reported in Yochanan Peres, "Most Israelis Are Committed to Democracy," *Israeli Democracy* (February 1987) p. 16.

10. For discussions of this possibility, emphasizing Sharon as a possible leader of such a coup or Oriental Jews as the likely mass base, see Saadia Rachamim, "Sharon and the 'Original Sin,' " *Koteret Rashit,* no. 102, November 14, 1984, p. 5; "To Destroy the Temple Mount Mosques," *Koteret Rashit,* no. 112, January 23, 1985, pp. 26–28; "The Danger Within," *Jerusalem Post,* June 19, 1984; and Yossi Melman, "And Tomorrow—the Whole Country," *Davar,* July 19, 1985. See also Yoram Peri, *Between Battles and Ballots* (Cambridge, England: Cambridge University Press, 1982) pp. 284–287. For an evocative fictional account of the overthrow of Israeli democracy, see Amos Kenan, *The Road to Ein Harod* (London: El-Saqi Books, 1986). The Hebrew edition was first published in 1984.
11. For specific suggestions regarding American policy in this area, see Ian S. Lustick, "Israeli Politics and American Foreign Policy," *Foreign Affairs,* vol. 61, no. 2 (Winter 1982/83) pp. 557–577; and Ian S. Lustick, "Israel's Dangerous Fundamentalists," *Foreign Policy,* no. 68 (Fall 1987) especially pp. 134–139.
12. Gershom Scholem, "Toward an Understanding of the Messianic Idea in Judaism," in *The Messianic Idea in Judaism and Other Essays on Jewish Spirituality* (New York: Schocken Books, 1971) pp. 35–36.

Index

About the Author

Ian S. Lustick, Associate Professor of Government at Dartmouth College, is a specialist on Middle Eastern politics, with particular reference to Israel and Arab–Israeli relations. While on leave from Dartmouth College in 1979 and 1980 he worked at the State Department's Bureau of Intelligence and Research as a Council on Foreign Relations fellow responsible for analysis of Israel–West Bank affairs.

Dr. Lustick has written numerous books and articles on Israeli politics, the Arab–Israeli conflict, American foreign policy, and various topics in comparative and international politics. His books include *For the Land and the Lord: Jewish Fundamentalism in Israel* (Council on Foreign Relations, 1988), *Books on Israel* (ed., SUNY, 1988), *State-Building Failure in British Ireland and French Algeria* (University of California, Institute of International Studies, 1985), and *Arabs in the Jewish State: Israel's Control of a National Minority* (Texas University, 1980). His articles have appeared in such publications as *Foreign Affairs, Foreign Policy, American Political Science Review, International Organization, Middle Eastern Studies, The Middle East Journal, Megamot,* and *World Politics.*

Dr. Lustick is one of the founders of the Association for Israel Studies and serves on its Board of Directors. He is a member of the Middle East Studies Association, the American Political Science Association, and the Council on Foreign Relations. Active as a consultant in both the public and private sectors, Dr. Lustick has also been the recipient of several research fellowships. His work has been highly praised for its originality and depth of analysis. He is currently writing a book which uses comparison of the Irish and Algerian problems in British and French political history as a vehicle for exploring the dynamics of the Israel–West Bank and Gaza relationship.

Dr. Lustick was born in 1949 in Syracuse, New York. He received a Bachelor's Degree in Politics from Brandeis University in 1971. In 1972 and 1976, respectively, he was awarded M.A. and Ph.D. degrees in Political Science from the University of California, Berkeley.